FANTASY

Fantasy provides an invaluable and accessible guide to the study of this fascinating field. Covering literature, film, television, ballet, light opera and visual art, and featuring a historical overview from Ovid to the *Toy Story* franchise, it takes the reader through the key landmark moments in the development of fantasy and its criticism. This comprehensive guide examines fantasy and politics, fantasy and the erotic, quest narratives and animal fantasy for children. The versatility and cultural significance of fantasy is explored, alongside the important role fantasy plays in our understanding of reality from childhood onwards.

Written in a clear, engaging style and featuring an extensive glossary of terms, this is the essential introduction to fantasy.

Lucie Armitt is Professor of Contemporary English Literature at the University of Lincoln, UK. She has been researching and publishing in the field of fantasy since 1991 and is the author of several books, articles and book chapters on the subject. She is especially interested in the influence fantasy has upon culture in general and the important role it plays in our understanding of the real.

THE NEW CRITICAL IDIOM

SERIES EDITOR: JOHN DRAKAKIS, UNIVERSITY OF STIRLING

The New Critical Idiom is an invaluable series of introductory guides to today's critical terminology. Each book:

- provides a handy, explanatory guide to the use (and abuse) of the term;
- offers an original and distinctive overview by a leading literary and cultural critic;
- relates the term to the larger field of cultural representation.

With a strong emphasis on clarity, lively debate and the widest possible breadth of examples, The New Critical Idiom is an indispensable approach to key topics in literary studies.

Reception
Ika Willis

The Sublime
Second edition
Philip Shaw

Satire
John T. Gilmore

Race
Martin Orkin with Alexa Alice Joubin

Trauma
Stef Craps and Lucy Bond

Children's Literature
Carrie Hintz

Pastoral
Second edition
Terry Gifford

Fantasy
Lucie Armitt

For more information about this series, please visit: www.routledge.com/literature/series/SE0155.

FANTASY

Lucie Armitt

LONDON AND NEW YORK

First published 2020
by Routledge
2 Park Square, Milton Park, Abingdon, Oxon OX14 4RN

and by Routledge
52 Vanderbilt Avenue, New York, NY 10017

Routledge is an imprint of the Taylor & Francis Group, an informa business

British Library Cataloguing in Publication Data
A catalogue record for this book is available from the British Library

Library of Congress Cataloging-in-Publication Data
A catalog record has been requested for this book

ISBN: 978-1-138-67691-6 (hbk)
ISBN: 978-1-138-67702-9 (pbk)
ISBN: 978-1-315-55982-7 (ebk)

Typeset in Times New Roman
by Taylor & Francis Books

For Bethany and Rowan

Contents

Figures

ACKNOWLEDGEMENTS

I have been in awe and admiration of John Drakakis since I first met him in December 1992 and was extremely flattered to be invited by him to submit a proposal for this volume on *Fantasy*. His encouragement, generosity of feedback and belief in me have meant a great deal. Similarly, I must thank Zoe Meyer, Polly Dodson and Ruth Hildson at Routledge for their patience, support and editorial guidance throughout the writing process. I am grateful to the College of Arts Research Leave Scheme at the University of Lincoln for granting a semester's leave early on in the research stages of this volume. During the course of writing this book I had the great fortune to make the professional acquaintance of three colleagues from the University of Liverpool whose own work has helped to expand the range of my own expertise in the subject: Julian Ferraro, to whom I am especially grateful for bringing Scott McCloud's ground-breaking work on comics and animation to my attention; and David Hering and Will Slocombe, both of whom helped expand my own knowledge of contemporary writers of fantasy, especially George Saunders's story 'Escape from Spiderhead', discussed in detail in Chapter 5.

Sometimes it takes decades for ideas to percolate properly in one's mind. From 1989 to 1994, I worked alongside David Rudd at the University of Bolton and we shared many wonderful conversations about our respective early career research plans and projects. In researching this book I finally found the excuse I needed to read his impressive work on Enid Blyton. His ethnographic methodology, combined with a refusal to be bamboozled by popular or media opinion, made his ideas invaluable to my own argument and I am grateful to him here. Equally, one's own students often prove invaluable guides to the next 'new thing' in popular literary culture, and I have Anna Infante to thank for introducing me to Charlotte Roche's novel *Wetlands*. I owe an especial debt of gratitude to Duncan Foster, whose encyclopaedic mind, ready wit, endless source of anecdotes and allusions have prompted many splendid conversations on a range of materials finding their way into this book, among which I single out for mention here Diaphanous Doorscrapers, Dynamation and *A Midsummer Night's Dream*.

From the age of three to thirteen, Rowan Armitt-Brewster watched Peter Jackson's *Lord of the Rings* film trilogy on what seemed to me to be an endless loop, dedicating painstakingly detailed attention to every nuance of character, battle formation and dialogue. By proxy, I acquired a close and familiar knowledge of the films, which has proved invaluable in preparing several sections of this book. *Game of Thrones*, on the other hand, is a television series with which I had not engaged before and I am supremely grateful to Bethany Armitt-Brewster for her extensive knowledge of and guidance through the series, especially in directing me towards particular episodes of significance. Scott Brewster has, as always, been tirelessly supportive of my research and the colossal amount of time I spend in my study. According to him, my main role model is the fantasy sweet entrepreneur Willy Wonka, not, it seems, because of his fabulous ingenuity, but his words to Charlie Bucket's grandpa towards the end of Mel Stuart's 1971 film starring Gene Wilder: 'I am extraordinarily busy, sir … Good day!'.

1

DEFINING FANTASY

Fantasy is the ultimate guilty pleasure, something in which we all indulge privately and often deliciously, be our daydreams of a romantic, opportunistic, consolationist or sexual nature, but in relation to which we are never encouraged to over-indulge. Often seen as the enemy of hard-headed, capitalist go-getting achievement, fantasy is something we rarely feel comfortable about sharing, even or perhaps especially with those to whom we are closest. It may be its secretive place in our thoughts that explains the typically polarized response aesthetic fantasy provokes in readers and audiences, who are either drawn enthusiastically, even fanatically towards, or repulsed utterly by it. From an academic point of view, fantasy criticism has traditionally carried an element of stigma, seemingly based on the assumption that the business of fantasy cannot ever be sufficiently 'serious' to merit proper scholarship. In her 1984 book, *Fantasy and Mimesis*, Kathryn Hume makes two related observations about fantasy's place (or lack of it) in the canon of English Literature:

> To many academics ... 'fantasy' is a subliterature in lurid covers sold in drugstores; or it is a morbid manifestation of the romantic spirit

> found in the works of Hoffmann, Poe, and less reputable gothic writers. Or fantasy means Tolkien and his ilk – nineteenth- and twentieth-century authors whose *oeuvres* are not part of traditional literature courses.
>
> (Hume 1984: 3)

Though Hume's starting-point in this passage remains largely true, there has been a degree of shift over the last 35 years and certainly the Gothic is now taken far more seriously than Hume implies. Her list of disparaged writers is equally outdated: E.T.A. Hoffmann, Edgar Allan Poe and J.R.R. Tolkien are now not only deemed 'reputable' but perhaps even 'canonical'. For example, while Brian W. Aldiss reminds us that Tolkien's *The Lord of the Rings* trilogy was 'the *cult* book of the sixties' (Aldiss 1995: 24–25, my emphasis), by 2000 Tolkien had been voted 'Author of the [twentieth] century' in a series of mainstream newspaper polls (Coren 2001). While I would hesitate to concur with Tom Shippey's claim that 'The dominant mode of the twentieth century has been the fantastic' (Shippey 2001: vii), it is worth remembering that Tolkien's award was based solely on readers' views of his literary output; his position can only have been consolidated by the subsequent colossal success of Peter Jackson's cinematic adaptations of the *Lord of the Rings* trilogy (2001–2003), augmented by *The Hobbit* films (2012–2014). This popular appetite for epic fantasy bleeds increasingly into television drama, with series such as *Merlin* (2008–2012), *Once Upon a Time* (2011–2018), *Game of Thrones* (2011–) and *Outlander* (2014–) proving hugely successful. As Michael Coren observes, however, the decision to raise Tolkien above all other writers was controversial, hence the response of an unnamed 'English novelist … [who] said it showed why teaching people to read was not such a good idea, and why all the libraries should be closed down.' Coren adds, 'He was joking, but only just' (Coren 2001: 2).

What we must not miss is the versatility of fantasy and the fact that, at its most sophisticated it is the driver not only for epic fantasy narratives, but opera (Mozart's *The Magic Flute*), painting (Marc Chagall's *The Betrothed* or *The Concert*), ballet (Tchaikovsky's *The Nutcracker Suite*), or classical music (Elgar's

The Dream of Gerontius). All these texts and narratives deal in the juxtaposition of competing worlds, wherein one world, purportedly representing 'reality', is left behind in preference for another which is unknown and 'foreign' in the sense of being strange, fabulous or grotesque. The laws of physics, logic, time, physiognomy, life and death and/or geography are usually subverted in preference for a narrative vision which is improbable, impossible, or beyond belief. As David Butler argues, the urge for fantasy is at the heart of all speculation as well as 'every time we ask the question "what if?", irrespective of whether the question is followed by the statement "dragons roamed the air", "we could land on the moon", "poverty was eliminated", or "a cure for cancer was found"' (Butler 2009: 4). James Walters makes a similar point when he argues that 'fantasy is just as likely to emerge in a crime thriller about an escaped convict as it is in a story about a mythical kingdom in which the destinies of all creatures are decided by the fate of a magical ring.' Again, Walters observes, 'To take *The Wizard of Oz* … as an example, we might want to question whether it is a children's film, fantasy film or musical, but we must also anticipate that a reasonable answer to such an enquiry would be "yes"' (Walters 2011: 2, 74).

To move from scope to type, several sub-genres always coalesce around fantasy and examples of all the following will be found in this volume: the fairy story, quest myth, fable, epic fantasy, nonsense narrative, sword and sorcery, talking animal fantasy, political fantasy including the utopia and dystopia, and erotic fantasy, upon which Chapter 6 is based. I have commented elsewhere on the difficulties that arise from overly prescriptive attitudes towards genre identity.[1] As Andrew Rayment puts it, 'Armitt could, perhaps, be considered a kind of spokesperson' for those critics for whom the 'attempt to shoehorn a text into a binding yet artificial category is a "travesty" of compartmentalization, a "death wish" of division and sub-division' (Rayment 2014: 10). Nevertheless, close neighbours of fantasy such as science fiction, the ghost story, the horror story and the Gothic are not discussed in detail in this book, except insofar as they help to cast clearer light on what fantasy is not. Readers interested in these undoubtedly adjacent and often overlapping genres are recommended to read companion volumes in the Routledge New Critical Idiom series such as Fred Botting's *Gothic*, Maggie Ann Bowers's *Magical Realism* and Adam Roberts's *Science Fiction*.

WHAT IS FANTASY?

At their most conventional, at least in structural terms, fantasy narratives such as *Alice in Wonderland* (1865) immerse the reader into an alternative world with its own logic, landscape and temporality and subsequently return that reader intact to the frame world of realism, in this case the river-bank where Alice has been sitting with her sister. The fantasy world is not usually assumed to have collapsed when left, although Alice's departure is certainly accompanied by chaos as the pack of courtier cards (court guards) explodes into the air 'and came flying down upon her: she gave a little scream … and tried to beat them off, and found herself lying on the bank, with her head in the lap of her sister' (Carroll 1929: 102). It is in this type of narrative that one experiences, most clearly, the type of 'joyous turn' or '*eucatastrophe'* which, according to Tolkien, characterizes 'the true form of fairy-tale, and its highest function' (Tolkien 2001: 68). It is clear to see here that, for Tolkien, the term fairy tale is broadly synonymous with fantasy, and that might surprise us. In fact, multiple definitions of fantasy abound, often mutually contradictory and occasionally pointlessly pedantic. Easily the best I have encountered, not least for its succinct clarity, is articulated by H. Bruce Franklin: 'On one side lies fantasy, the realm of the impossible. On the other side lie all forms of fiction that purport to represent the actual, whether present or past …' (Franklin 2009: 23).

Nevertheless, many critics on fantasy have expended serious time and effort refining their own definitions and some of the more influential are discussed here. For Ann Swinfen,

> The essential ingredient of all fantasy is 'the marvelous', which will be regarded as anything outside the normal space-time continuum of the everyday world. Pure science fiction is excluded, since it treats essentially of what does not exist now, but might perhaps exist in the

> future. The marvelous element which lies at the heart of all fantasy is composed of what can never exist in the world of empirical experience.
>
> (Swinfen 1984: 5)

Swinfen's definition broadly accords with Franklin's, but narrows his focus to something called 'the marvellous'. The marvellous, in this sense, is borrowed from Tzvetan Todorov, the most influential critic of fantasy since Tolkien himself. Tolkien interests himself in what he calls the Secondary World of fantasy, within the terms of which a 'green sun will be credible' (Tolkien 2001: 49). Todorov's remit is wider than Tolkien's because he is tackling a broader umbrella term than genre fantasy: he evaluates what he calls 'the literary fantastic', writing which cannot be constrained by the artificial enclosures of genre and which requires 'a breach in the acknowledged order, an irruption of the inadmissible within the changeless everyday legality' (Todorov 1975: 41). It is the same impulse that admits magic realism; it is also the impulse that enables the intrusion of that particular *frisson* we associate with the uncanny, the ghost story or the horror narrative, when one world *bleeds* into the everyday world of realism and ruptures the membrane between the two. For Todorov, the fantastic is to be found at every point of the literary spectrum, but depends upon a balancing act between the uncanny and the marvellous. The marvellous, he explains, is a fictional world requiring 'new laws of nature ... to account for the phenomena', in other words, what we will call fantasy (Todorov 1975: 41). For Todorov, the fantas-*tic* is a readerly concept, requiring ongoing hesitancy between these two options, such that we are unclear whether supernatural or psychological (hallucinatory or deluded) causes are at work.

That emphasis on the reader is shared by critics interested in what fantasy does. In an essay titled 'One Hump of Two', Aldiss argues 'I regard fantasy, as distinct from SF, as having a spiritual, or perhaps I mean a religious, or perhaps I mean a metaphysical side' (Aldiss 1995: 133). The problem here is that, precisely because of its freedom to imagine, fantasy can actually do anything. For instance, one can see clearly how Aldiss's definition applies to C.S. Lewis's *The Chronicles of Narnia*, but it seems less true of William Thackeray's *The Rose and the Ring,* discussed below or, come to that, *Alice in Wonderland.* William Gray seems to accord with Aldiss when he argues that 'one of the great contributions ... [made by] writers of children's fantasy literature is to trust in the capacity of younger readers to engage with big philosophical questions' (Gray 2008: 7). However, any number of literary works enable children to engage with 'big philosophical questions', so this is also unsatisfactory as the determining feature of fantasy.

Rosemary Jackson subtitles her book on fantasy 'the literature of subversion', a position which leads her to emphasize the ways in which fantasy narratives challenge the status quo, whether through a focus on sexual taboo and other bodily transgressions, readerly disturbance through 'dislocated narrative form' (Jackson 1988: 23), or 'attempt[s] to articulate "the unnameable" ... visualize the unseen, or ... play upon "thingless names"' (Jackson 1988: 41). Jackson's work on fantasy is darker than that of most critics, partly because of her prioritization of psychoanalytically informed readings, an approach that frequently moves towards the Gothic or the surreal and that emphasizes both the importance of Sigmund Freud's work on desire, taboo and the uncanny and a more poststructuralist approach to the play of language, 'opposing the novel's closed, monological form with open, dialogical structures' (Jackson 1988: 25). One of Jackson's most interesting observations is to identify the frequency with which fantasy focuses upon mirrors and reflection, opening up 'spaces behind the visible, behind the image, introducing dark areas from which anything can emerge' (Jackson 1988: 43). Thereby the *frisson* of competing worlds imposes itself upon the reader's psyche.

Hume's *Fantasy and Mimesis* is also motivated by an interest in what fantasy texts achieve for the reader. She refuses to segregate fantasy literature wholly from realism, identifying mimesis (the drive towards realism) and fantasy as twin urges in all texts. Thus verisimilitude, or life-likeness, becomes as much the aim of fantasy as realism, but manifests itself differently. That approach enables Hume to include, within the category 'escapism, the literature of illusion', not only L. Frank Baum's *The Wonderful Wizard of Oz* (1900), but a realist traveller's tale such as Daniel Defoe's

Robinson Crusoe (1719), a reach I would consider too inclusive to be helpful. As Tolkien observes, 'Such tales [as Defoe's] report many marvels, but they are marvels to be seen in this mortal world ... distance alone conceals them' (Tolkien 2001: 12). Certainly there is a place for travel in fantasy, but it is travel to an impossible world. As I have observed elsewhere: 'A reader of Doris Lessing's realist first novel, *The Grass is Singing* (1950), may find she can relive at least an element of that literary experience by reading up on or even visiting present-day Zimbabwe, but none of us can holiday in the Garden of Eden' (Armitt 2005: 8).

Historically, some of the most interesting theoretically engaged critics have found metaphors of fantasy foundational to their ideas. Much of Freud's literary-based work oscillates around questions of fantasy, not least his often overlooked essay 'Creative Writers and Daydreaming' (1907), in which he roots all imaginative writing in play, a concept we will come to regard as central to fantasy:

> Might we not say that every child at play behaves like a creative writer, in that he creates a world of his own, or, rather, re-arranges the things of his world in a new way which pleases him? It would be wrong to think he does not take that world seriously; on the contrary, he takes his play very seriously and he expends large amounts of his emotion on it. The opposite of play is not what is serious but what is real.
>
> (Freud 1990: 131–132)

In his essay 'Fantasy as a Political Category', Slavoj Žižek also explores the ideological foundations of fantasy. The reading of Žižek's essay offered by Elizabeth Wright and Edmond Wright situates it analogously with my competing-worlds approach to fantasy, arguing that 'for fantasy to work, the everyday world has to be kept separate from the fantasy that upholds it' (Wright and Wright 1999: 88). This is absolutely not to suggest that fantasy is disengaged from reality, for the two are mutually dependent. Instead, an interpretative space opens up between the narrative boundaries containing the respective worlds of fantasy and 'the real', within which ideological play makes merry. Žižek's most resonant example of this dynamic coheres around the on-board evacuation drill performed for air passengers. As he observes, the effectiveness of that performance relies on a shared sense of fantasy between crew and passengers: 'After a gentle landing on water … as on a beach toboggan, [each passenger] slides into the water … like a nice collective lagoon holiday experience' (Wright and Wright 1999: 91). Žižek continues, not dissimilarly to Jackson, by suggesting that the underside of that world of inverted logic manifests itself, most frequently, in repressed fantasy tropes: 'Are not the images of the ultimate horrible Thing, from the deep-sea gigantic squid to the ravaging twister, fantasmatic creations *par excellence*?' (Wright and Wright 1999: 92).

Donna J. Haraway, in her essay 'A Cyborg Manifesto' (1985), writes another politicized monster narrative. Adopting the metaphor of the cyborg as 'a hybrid of machine and organism, a creature of social reality as well as a creature of fiction', she goes on to re-think women's relationship to gender, technology and mythology (Haraway 1991: 149). In tracing how women have come to acquire that hybridized identity, she returns to the question of origins and interrogates our cultural assumptions about how 'shared' such originary mythologies actually are, especially when they subordinate women to men. So, in answer to the Biblical Genesis myth in which 'the Lord God formed man of the dust of the ground' (Genesis 2:7) and later 'caused a deep sleep to fall upon Adam … and he took one of his ribs … And the rib, which the Lord God had taken from man, made he a woman' (Genesis 2:21–22), Haraway simply observes: 'The cyborg would not recognize the Garden of Eden; it is not made of mud and cannot dream of returning to dust' (Haraway 1991: 151). Mythology, as we will see throughout this book, plays a key role in driving fantasy quest narratives, not least the gender politics within them. Myths also question the boundaries between possibilities and impossibilities. For Haraway, 'The cyborg appears in myth precisely where the boundary between human and animal is transgressed' (Haraway 1991: 152). Such boundary negotiations are intrinsic to all fantasy, as are the means by which we move between competing worlds.

PORTALS AND ENTRY-POINTS

Arguably the key aspect of any fantasy narrative is the mechanism whereby the reader is permitted entry into another world. In a conventional fairy story, this entry occurs linguistically: as soon as we read 'Once upon a time' we know we are entering the world of the fairy story which, as we shall see, is wholly different from entering the world of traditional fairy-lore. In other narratives, a journey needs to be undertaken, away from the world of realism and into the unfathomable. Ancient sea charts played wholly upon the perceived relationship between the unknown and the unknowable when, in the centuries before Western colonial expansion, areas of the world not reached by European sailors were marked on the map 'Here be dragons'. Sometimes, however, a world of magic can be conjured up before one's own fireside, such as in *The Rose and the Ring* (1855), a fairy story written by Thackeray under the pseudonym M.A. Titmarsh, originally for his own children. The narrative opens: 'My friend, Miss Bunch, who was governess of a large family, that lived in the *Piano Nobile* of the house inhabited by myself and my young charges … begged me to draw a set of Twelfth-Night characters for the amusement of our young people' (Titmarsh 1855: iii). Thackeray supplements his tale with illustrations, showing the children in question gathering around a blazing hearth. In naming their governess Miss Bunch, Thackeray evokes echoes of 'Mother Bunch', another name for Mother Goose, one putative originator of fairy tales. As readers, this combination of domestic cosiness and a shared cultural storyteller allows us to feel entitled to draw up our own seats: we all become part of Miss Bunch's 'large family'.

At the other end of the spatial scale, when the fantasy realm covers complex or panoramic terrain, cartography is often used to familiarize the reader with this imagined realm. The best-known example of cartographic fantasy is Tolkien's *The Lord of the Rings* trilogy, discussed in detail later, but even a comparatively circumscribed world such as J.M. Barrie's *Peter Pan in Kensington Gardens* (1906; hereafter *Kensington Gardens*), opens with a map, accompanied by the cautionary note to the reader that 'You must see for yourselves that it will be difficult to follow Peter Pan's adventures unless you are familiar with the Kensington Gardens' (Barrie 1999: 3). Thence are we escorted along the 'Broad Walk', beside the 'Round Pond', 'the Hump, which is the part of the Broad Walk where all the big races are run' and on towards 'the gate that is called after Miss Mabel Grey' (Barrie 1999: 4–5). On one level, the Gardens are established as a single, manageable site, as indicated by the map and its mimetic relationship to the actual Kensington Gardens in London. Experientially, however, the narrator reminds us that a small child is unlikely to be able to travel right across it in one visit:

> No child has ever been in the whole of the Gardens, because it is so soon time to turn back ... if you are [a small child], you sleep from twelve to one. If your mother was not so sure that you sleep from twelve to one, you could most likely see the whole of them.
>
> (Barrie 1999: 3)

Throughout Barrie's narrative, the language used belongs to a small child's sense of pretend play. As Roger Abrahams argues, 'In all kinds of play, we are engaged with those special set-aside worlds in which rules and systems operate energetically yet effortlessly', a point that makes play almost analogous with fantasy (Abrahams 1980: 119). W.R. Irwin also emphasizes the fact that play constructs 'worlds ordered by internal logic … [which] maintain temporarily an identity that is sufficient and plausible … but … even when the activities of the play … absorb the player, he still knows that he is playing by choice, that his game is factitious, and that he cannot avoid returning to the ordinary' (Irwin 1976: 23). Thus is the connection between child's play and the circumscribed world of fantasy secured. *Kensington Gardens* is a novel in which fairies feature centrally as characters, although they shun contact with the children who play in the park and Peter has to go to some lengths to prove to the fairies that 'he was not an ordinary human and had no desire to do them displeasure' (Barrie 1999: 27). In that sense this novel forms a much more effective bridge between the sanitized nursery-world of post-Victorian fairy stories and the much more brutal tales of traditional fairy-lore. Fairies are, in rural fairy-lore, associated with the dead, with those who live underground, with impish beings who steal children and replace them with 'changelings', who blind humans who spy them out, who wreak death and tyranny upon (usually) rural communities. As Edwin Sidney Hartland observed in 1891: 'supernatural personages, without distinction, dislike not merely being recognized and addressed, but even being seen, or at all events being watched, and are only willing to be manifested to humanity at their own pleasure and for their own purposes' (Hartland 1891: 69).

In Kate Greenaway's watercolour painting *The Elf Ring* (1905; Figure 1.1), we see a child entering a fairy ring, trampling over its circumference as she goes. According to Jane Laing, the painting shows how the child's credibility and simple belief in fairies allows her to 'become part of their moonlit circle in the depths of the forest of the subconscious' (Laing 1995: 33). Laing's idealized reading of the painting is perhaps overly influenced by post-Victorian sanitization and is insufficiently attentive to the violent repercussions inflicted on humans interfering with this secret world, as explained above. Looking again at Greenaway's painting, we see that not only is the child's entry disruptive, it is violent: she has stepped on at least one fairy (there may be another under her rather ogre-ish boots) and is clutching another by the head: cruel retribution almost certainly awaits her. The look on her face seems crafty rather than unwitting and her entire demeanour is that of the precocious transgressor.

Even when accidental, Hartland provides many instances of humans stumbling across or into fairy rings who then 'disappear', such as in the case of two men from Pwllheli, North Wales, who 'went out to fetch cattle and came at dusk upon a party of fairies dancing' (Hartland 1891: 163). One man is captured and forced to dance incessantly inside the ring. His rescue is only attained when his friend returns for him a year and a day later, this being the usual prescribed period, finding him 'reduced to a mere skeleton' by the incessant dancing (Hartland 1891: 163). As so often in portal fantasy narratives, however, for the unwitting interloper time has stood still. In a similar story from Trefiw, again in North Wales, a man fell into a fairy ring wearing new shoes. When he

Figure 1.1 Kate Greenaway, *The Elf Ring*, Art and Picture Collection, The New York Public Library
Source: New York Public Library Digital Collections.

was retrieved a year and a day later, 'he could not be made to understand that he had been there more than five minutes until he was asked to look at his new shoes, which were by that time in pieces' (Hartland 1891: 164).

Irrespective of whether it is aimed at children or adults, while the plot details of the portal fantasy change, the narrative dynamics do not. So, an adult horror novel such as Clive Barker's *The Hellbound Heart* (1986), though dealing in graphic sexualized horror content, in narrative structure works identically to C.S. Lewis's *The Lion, the Witch and the Wardrobe* (1950). Both books depict protagonists who find themselves propelled into worlds they did not expect to find. Both narratives find those protagonists engaged in frightening and unanticipated scenarios which threaten to destroy them or their relatives. In structural terms, the only difference is that one portal is entered when the protagonist starts fiddling with a wooden box, and the other when a child starts fiddling with a wooden wardrobe.

Not all branches of fantasy work that simply, however. For Farah Mendlesohn, the portal fantasy is best understood as a version of quest narrative, 'because each assume[s] the same two movements: transition and exploration' (Mendlesohn 2008: 2). Portal fantasies, Mendlesohn argues, tend to require the reader to 'learn from a point of entry' (Mendlesohn 2008: xix), an observation that is certainly true of the horrors of *The Hellbound Heart,* though I remain unconvinced that it applies to *Alice in Wonderland.* Mendlesohn adopts the rather traditional view that fantasy is a morally coherent vision of 'world-building' (Mendlesohn 2008: 13), a perspective that leads her to the interesting recognition that portal fantasies originate in the Christian New Testament, for 'what else is a posthumous heaven … other than the ultimate in portals?' (Mendlesohn 2008: 3–4). Nevertheless, not all doorways are portals in fantasy narratives. In *The Rose and the Ring*, for example, a wonderfully comedic moment of fairy punishment results when Fairy Blackstick is prevented from attending the christening of the Princess Angelica by the haughty and dislikeable porter, Gruffanuff. Better still for the assembled child audience, 'Gruffanuff … made the *most odious vulgar sign* as he was going to slam the door' (Titmarsh 1855: 16), at which point the children's imagined giggling resonates clearly in the adult reader's head. Undeterred, Fairy Blackstick stops the door with her wand and punishes Gruffanuff by turning him into a door-knocker:

> he felt himself rising off the ground, and fluttering up against the door, and then, as if a screw ran into his stomach, he felt a dreadful pain there, and was pinned to the door; and then his arms flew up over his head; and his legs, after writhing about wildly, twisted under his body; and he felt cold, cold, growing over him, as if he was turning into metal, and he said 'O-o-H'm!' and could say no more, because he was dumb.
>
> (Titmarsh 1855: 17–18)

Doorways, then, can prevent as much as facilitate access to the fantasy world, but what of narrative returns? Edward Lear's nonsense sea-voyage narrative 'The Story of the Four Children who Went Round the World' (1867) opens with the traditional 'Once upon a time, a long while ago', but the place of embarkation is considered of no consequence, Lear being far more interested in the boat, which is 'painted blue with green spots, and the sail was yellow with red stripes' (Lear 2001: 220). Their return, however, is markedly more important. Through Lear's typical combination of logic and illogicality, the children 'sail quite round the world by sea', but 'come back on the other side by land' (Lear 2001: 220). *En route*, they find 'some land at a distance; and when they came to it, they found it was an island made of water quite surrounded by earth' (Lear 2001: 221). The final leg of their travels becomes *four*-legged, as they take a ride on the back of 'an elderly Rhinoceros' and, ungratefully, reward its pains by having it 'killed and stuffed directly, and then set him up outside the door of their father's house as a Diaphonous Doorscraper' (Lear 2001: 231–232). Lear's proclivity for alliterative nonsense may delight us, but we cannot miss the fact that, unlike in Thackeray's text, where the bad-tempered Gruffanuff is unlikely to elicit too much sympathy, this rhinoceros has been highly ill-used.

One of the freshest recent examples of portal fantasy is Ransom Riggs's *Miss Peregrine's Home for Peculiar Children*

(2011). In this novel, the first of a trilogy, the protagonist is Jacob/Jake Portman (note the port-al stem of his name), whose travels take him and his father to a remote Welsh island on which is located the ruin of an old children's home, wrongly believed to have been bombed during a World War II air raid. On first approach, Jake sees a wreck: 'What stood before me now was no refuge from monsters but a monster itself' (Riggs 2013: 83). The 'truth' of this house, however, lies within the mysteries of fantasy, in a temporal loop constructed by the Headmistress, Miss Peregrine, 'in which peculiar folk can live indefinitely' (Riggs 2013: 155).[2] Miss Peregrine is an 'ymbryne' or manipulator of time and the aforementioned 'loop' acts as a two-way membrane enabling characters to move back and forth into and from the 'ordinary' world.

What makes Riggs's portal distinct from Carroll's rabbit-hole or Lewis's wardrobe, is that the properties of the portal itself are innately intriguing; it is not a simple means of entry and egress. Before Jake finds his way inside it, he takes a trip to the local museum and views a 'bog body' of the kind Seamus Heaney writes about in his poetry of Northern Ireland.[3] Here is a truth that is stranger than fantasy, for the preservative qualities of the bog, 'where oxygen and bacteria can't exist', allow the corpse to be perfectly preserved over centuries. The museum curator informs Jake: 'His people believed that bogs – and our bog in particular – were entrances to the world of the gods, and so the perfect place to offer up their most precious gift: themselves' (Riggs 2013: 94). Thus, he continues, 'as doors to the next world go, a bog ain't a bad choice. It's not quite water and it's not quite land – it's an in-between place' (Riggs 2013: 94). This portal, then, is partly scientific and partly fantasy in structure. The fantasy aspect requires its consistency to be maintained by regular use. As Miss Peregrine tells Jake, 'One of us [ymbrynes] must cross through the entryway every so often. This keeps it pliable, you see. The ingress point is a bit like a hole in fresh dough; if you don't poke a finger into it now and then the thing may just close up on its own' (Riggs 2013: 160). It is this 'pliable' aspect of the portal in *Miss Peregrine's Home for Peculiar Children* that complicates Mendlesohn's view that portal fantasies render history 'inarguable', a claim she bases on the typical fictive idea that the two worlds within and beyond the portal are separated unassailably in time, thus making the pastness of 'reality' unalterable (Mendlesohn 2008: 14). In Riggs's novel, Jake is required to enter through the portal *precisely* in order to question the realist version of history attached to the children's home. The reality he discovers is one we would expect to connect with fantasy: the children were attacked and destroyed by monsters.

That emphasis on time differentials is common to many fantasy narratives, as we saw in relation to fairy-lore. When Lewis's Lucy returns to her siblings, telling them tales of her travels, one of the reasons they do not believe her is that, as far as they are concerned, she was gone 'less than a minute, and she pretended to have been away for hours' (Lewis 1972: 48). Ironically, it is the old Professor, whom they assume to be the embodiment of reason and who cherishes logic, who counters their disbelief: 'if, I say, she had gone into another world, I should not be at all surprised to find that the other world had a separate time of its own; so that however long you stayed there it would never take up any of *our* time' (Lewis 1972: 48). Lewis repeatedly engages directly with his child reader in the narrative, albeit sometimes rather heavy-handedly, such as when he repeatedly warns her/him that 'it is very foolish to shut oneself into any wardrobe' (Lewis 1972: 12). Having praised Lucy once for knowing 'that it is a very silly thing to shut oneself in a wardrobe' (Lewis 1972: 13), he repeats himself on her second visit, noting that 'She did not shut [the door] properly because she knew that it is very silly to shut oneself into a wardrobe, even if it is not a magic one' (Lewis 1972: 29–30). Conversely, he casts judgment on Edmund, when he pushes through behind Lucy, 'and shut the door, forgetting what a very foolish thing this is to do' (Lewis 1972: 30). Finally, when Peter enters the wardrobe later on, and 'held the door closed but did not shut it; for, of course, he remembered, as every sensible person does, that you should never never shut yourself up in a wardrobe' (Lewis 1972: 52), we correctly interpret Peter's caution as evidence that he will later prove himself responsible in more heroic ways.

DESIRE AND LOSS

Lewis's benign but admonishing voice in *The Lion, the Witch and the Wardrobe* positions him as a kind of surrogate parent. Fathers are often absent in fantasy narratives, from fairy tales onwards, but surrogates for them usually appear, not least grandfatherly figures such as Lewis's Professor, Tolkien's Gandalf and J.K. Rowling's Dumbledore. This surrogacy partly explains the attraction of the eponymous Mr Magorium in the fantasy film *Mr Magorium's Wonder Emporium* (dir. Zach Helm, 2007), starring Dustin Hoffman and Natalie Portman, a film partly about transition and death, but also partly about desire and loss. The opening scene of the film depicts an encounter on the street outside the shop, between Portman's character, Molly Mahoney, and Eric, a nine-year-old boy who is a friendless devotee of the toyshop. An equally avid collector of hats, this initial scene shows Eric's hat stuck on a flagpole above the shop door. Eric asks Mahoney how he can retrieve it and, when she suggests that he finds a ladder, replies 'Naah! I just need to jump higher.' Mahoney retorts: 'Eric, that's seven feet at least!' to which his final response is 'Do you think I should get a running start?' The comedy mismatch between aspiration and possibility is measured out in terms of overreaching the limits of the human, the same dynamic that determines the scale of the magic in the shop. Nevertheless, when Mahoney enters and 'wakes up' the toys, we can see behind her, through the window, that Eric has indeed grasped the flagpole and is swinging backwards and forwards on it. Similarly elongating the human scale, Mr Magorium claims to have been alive for 243 years and the shop-owner for 113 and the film details what happens on the day he 'departs', handing over the reins to Mahoney, an opening obviously echoing Tolkien's *Lord of the Rings Vol. I: The Fellowship of the Ring* (1954), in which Bilbo Baggins disappears, aged '*eleventy-one*, 111' at his birthday party, handing on his quest to his nephew, Frodo (Tolkien 1999a: 28).

While absent fathers/father surrogates can therefore operate as the explicit or implicit catalyst for action in children's fantasy, the loss of a mother deserves especial attention. Rowling's entire

Harry Potter series operates on the principle that nothing is more powerful than a mother's love for her child. Towards the end of volume 5, *Harry Potter and the Order of the Phoenix* (2003), Dumbledore explains to Harry his rationale for placing him under the care of the unsuitable and unsympathetic Dursley family, following his parents' deaths:

> I knew that Voldemort's knowledge of magic is perhaps more extensive than any wizard alive …
> But I knew, too, where Voldemort was weak … You would be protected by an ancient magic of which he knows, which he despises, and which he has always, therefore, underestimated – to his cost. I am speaking, of course, of the fact that your mother died to save you. She gave you a lingering protection he never expected, a protection that flows in your veins to this day. I put my trust, therefore, in your mother's blood. I delivered you to her sister …
>
> (Rowling 2003: 736)

On the face of it, Petunia Dursley has no sisterly affinity with the dead Lily, but in the opening pages of the final volume, *Harry Potter and the Deathly Hallows* (2007), as Harry persuades the Dursleys to leave their house for their own protection, Petunia 'stopped and looked back … [as if] she wanted to say something to him: she gave him an odd, tremulous look and seemed to teeter on the edge of speech' (Rowling 2007: 40–41). That unspoken 'teeter[ing]', located 'on the edge of speech', seems to offer up a bridging point between the realm of the unspeakable and the realm of decoy narratives. As a small child Harry was told, by the Dursleys, that his parents died in a car accident, but 'His aunt and uncle never spoke about them, and of course he was forbidden to ask questions' (Rowling 1997: 27). Again, a type of 'unspeaking' exists here, in the awareness of an enforced silence. Counteracting that unspoken presence, Harry carries with him a kind of trace memory: 'a strange vision: a blinding flash of green light and a burning pain on his forehead. This, he supposed, was the crash' (Rowling 1997: 27). No crash at all, what erupts from Harry's unconscious are fragments, traces, the remnants of Voldemort's murder of his parents and attempted murder of him. As Jackson observes, 'The fantastic is a literature which attempts to create a space for a discourse other than a conscious one' (Jackson 1988: 62) and it is from within this space for a discourse where none exists that Harry's wizarding education gradually fills the void with an explanation. No wonder Harry refuses to substitute the common euphemism 'He Who Cannot Be Named' for 'Voldemort'; the refusal to name has threatened to deny Harry a life narrative.

In her essay 'Revolution in Poetic Language' (1974), Julia Kristeva identifies the existence in infants of a pre-linguistic state, whereby 'Drives involve pre-Oedipal semiotic functions and energy discharges that connect and orient the body to the mother' (Moi 1986: 95). Harry's experience works as a perfect fictional illustration of Kristeva's ideas. Lily, even in her absence, roots Harry within a framework of belonging (Hogwarts, its staff and pupils) that even his abuse at the hands of the Dursleys cannot undermine. Thus Harry's eventual empowerment emerges from a pre-linguistic, originary 'unremembered' realm of *jouissance*: intra-uterine self-sufficiency, but here expressed through magic rather than psychoanalysis. Nor is the *Harry Potter* series the only fantasy narrative that works in this way. A similar recognition of unconscious desires linked to the lost mother leads Gray to identify the maternal drive as the biographical impetus underlying George MacDonald's *Phantastes: A Faerie Romance* (1905).

Twenty-one-year-old Anodos, MacDonald's protagonist, wakes to find a tiny woman in his room, 'as perfect in shape as if she had been a small Greek statuette' (MacDonald 2005: 3). She escorts him to fairyland, where an array of encounters awaits him. On looking into her eyes, Anodos's thoughts turn to that intra-uterine realm: 'They filled me with an unknown longing. I remembered somehow that my mother died when I was a baby. I looked deeper and deeper, till they spread around me like seas, and I sank in their waters' (MacDonald 2005: 4). According to Gray, MacDonald's entire creative impulse can be traced to mementos he kept of his mother:

> In a secret drawer in MacDonald's desk were found, after his death, a lock of his mother's hair and a letter by her containing the following

> reference to his premature weaning: 'I cannot help in my heart being very much grieved for him yet, for he has not forgot it ... he cryed desperate for a while in the first night, but he has cryed very little since and I hope the worst is over now.'
>
> (Gray 2008: 10)

Gray surely misses the point, here, as seems obvious to any woman who has breast-fed a child: one who *remembers* being weaned cannot have been 'prematurely' so, quite the opposite. The discovery of the letter surely says more about universal maternal anxiety than it does about childhood loss. A similar over-reaction involving weaning seems evident in Philip Pullman's response to Lewis's decision to kill off his protagonists at the end of the seven-volume *Chronicles of Narnia* rather than 'wean himself off them' more gently. Pullman exclaims: 'For the sake of taking them off to a perpetual school holiday or something, he kills them all in a train crash. I think that's ghastly. It's a horrible message' (Susan Roberts, cited in Rayment-Pickard 2004: 45). Here, Pullman seems to be conflating fictional characterization with actual childhood death. In narrative terms, all authors 'kill off' their characters when they stop writing about them and, in that sense, Lewis's child characters are not 'prematurely' killed at all. What Lewis does is strikingly similar to what the letter suggests MacDonald's mother did: he provides a sudden point of no return, to guard against the temptation to re-enter a phase that must end.

Mother loss is equally the driver in Barrie's *Kensington Gardens.* Peter first arrives in the Gardens by flying out of his nursery window and, as Barrie informs his young reader, 'It was wonderful that he could fly without wings, but the place itched tremendously, and – and – perhaps we could all fly if we were as dead-confident sure of our capacity to do it as was bold Peter' (Barrie 1999: 13). While flight meets flight of fancy, for Peter this is simply an excursion, not an escape: he always meant to return to his mother. Nevertheless, he keeps delaying doing so and other characters keep finding reasons to prevent him. When finally he does return, 'the window was closed, and there were iron bars on it, and peering inside he saw his mother sleeping peacefully with her arm round another little boy' (Barrie 1999: 40). Arguably, the Peter Pan narratives can be read as decoy dream-world narratives about death, loss and maternal desire. In this context, maternal grief over the loss of a child is re-written from Peter's point of view as the child's grieving loss for its mother.

MAGIC OR ILLUSION?

Overall, the relationship between children and fantasy is a complex one. Usually, most of us encounter fantasy narratives as children and these children's fantasies generally emphasize the satisfaction of wish-fulfilment desires. Enid Blyton's *The Faraway Tree Stories* (1939–1946) were the first books I remember self-reflectively reading as fantasy narratives and perhaps we should not overlook the fact that Blyton wrote them during World War II when, for a number of children evacuated from their homes and families, their daydreams and fantasies of home might feel very 'far away' indeed. In volume 1, *The Enchanted Wood*, three children, Joe, Beth and Frannie, move to the countryside as so many evacuated children did, setting in train the possibility of a magical encounter. Almost instantaneously, the lure of the countryside becomes imbued with fantasy: 'We might see fairies there!' (Blyton 2002: 1). Even father, returning from work, arrives with news that the nearby wood is 'called the Enchanted Wood' (Blyton 2002: 5). Managing possible parental scepticism early on, he adds, 'It's funny to hear things like this nowadays, and I don't expect there is really anything strange about the wood. But just be careful not to go too far into it, in case you get lost' (Blyton 2002: 5–6). Thus is the child reader hooked.

Once inside the wood the children encounter, as they hoped, elves, a gnome, a pixie and a small fairy called Silky, but they also encounter some intensely Lear-like characters, such as Moon-Face, a toffee-eating character who lives in the top of the Faraway Tree, and whose house is left via a 'slippery-slip that ran down the whole trunk … winding round and round like a spiral staircase', and Saucepan Man, who 'had saucepans and kettles hung all over him' and 'danc[ed] away, crashing his saucepans together' (Blyton 2002: 33, 78–79). For Blyton, as we shall later see in relation to her *Noddy* books, there is no incongruity in combining the world of fairy-lore with the world of toys, a point that reinforces the realization that, unlike so many of their adult counterparts, child readers waste no energy arguing over the 'proper' definition of fantasy, its sub-genres and/or the type of characters or scenarios it involves.

Certainly, magic plays an important role in many fantasy narratives and Tolkien goes so far as to assert that 'Faërie itself may perhaps most nearly be translated by Magic' (Tolkien 2001: 10). However, what actually constitutes magic is harder to define. For example, when David Rudd observes that he 'found magic' in Blyton's books (Rudd 2000: 2) we recognize that he is using the term in its more colloquial sense of 'wonder' or 'imaginative joy', despite the fact that some of her books depict enchanted objects and landscapes. What, then, is magic and is it enough for a fantasy narrative to contain a magician or a witch to make it so? Surely the answer to the last part of that question is 'No', at least in mature works of fantasy. Rowling's *Harry Potter* series and Terry Pratchett's *Discworld* series are arguably two of the most accomplished comparatively recent examples of magic-based fantasy and props such as wands, broomsticks, walking trunks and potions function centrally in them. Nevertheless, their achievement, in each case, relies on the narrative construction of competing worlds, not the existence of the paraphernalia of magic *per se*. The *Harry Potter* series is a portal fantasy, accessed from the 'real' world of modern transportation, namely Platform 9¾ of King's Cross railway station in London. Discworld, on the other hand, constitutes a separate world of its own, located on the back of 'Great A'Tuin the Turtle … swimming slowly through the interstellar gulf, hydrogen frost on his ponderous limbs' (Pratchett 1985: 11). Certainly Gandalf, in *The Lord of the Rings*, is a grand wizard in the epic fantasy tradition, capable both of great fun and great terror. At the start of *The Fellowship of the Ring*, he delights in his reputation with the children of the Shire as one 'skill[ed] with fires, smokes, and lights', but when his anger grows with Bilbo at the hobbit's reluctance to give up the ring, he warns him that he risks 'see[ing] Gandalf the Grey uncloaked' and, as he approaches him, Bilbo reflects that 'he seemed to grow tall and menacing; his shadow filled the little room' (Tolkien 1999a: 32, 44). Nevertheless, even here it is not Gandalf's magic alone that makes *Lord of the Rings* a fantasy trilogy; rather it is Tolkien's inventive creation of impossible species such as hobbits and orcs, the setting of the action in the carefully mapped-out inventive geography of Middle Earth and, in combination with both, the epic quest to Mount Doom with the totemic object of the One Ring. Indeed, no work of fantasy confounds further the often perceived requirement for magic to be present than Mervyn Peake's *Gormenghast* (1946), which contains no magic at all. In adapting the first two volumes of Peake's trilogy for television in 2000, Estelle Daniel described the aim of the production team being to show that fantasy can exist even when the characters 'don't fly around on wings [and] there are no trolls and dragons' (Daniel 2000: 61). What remains, again, is a vision of competing worlds, one existing in parallel to our own but characterized by the type of Medieval feudalism one also finds in *Lord of the Rings, Merlin* and *Game of Thrones.* The conclusion is clear: witches and wizards alone do not make fantasy.

Tolkien's view of the magic of faërie places it 'at the furthest pole from the vulgar devices of the laborious, scientific, magician' (Tolkien 2001: 10). Nevertheless, I would argue that a more useful way of conceptualizing the properties of fantasy, is to think less of magic *per se* and more of the stage magician. Few of us, when watching so-called 'magic shows' think that we are actually witnessing magic: we know we are witnessing an illusion created by a supreme inventor of imaginative trickery and play. This illusion is a much better way of conceptualizing fantasy: thus a (screen) writer or artist constructs a series of competing worlds in which the impossible becomes real or can be 'conjured up', as in music. As Tony Hassini of the International Magician's Society puts it, 'Long before advanced science and medicine, magicians created illusions, influencing the future scientists to turn those illusions into reality' (Hassini 2018: np). Thus, in both stage magic and fantasy writing, film or art, we sign up to what Samuel Taylor Coleridge described in *Biographia Literaria* (1817) as a 'willing suspension of disbelief' (Coleridge 1978: 518): namely that fairies, magicians, hobbits, talking animals, nymphs and jumblies *really* exist.

ANIMATION: THE CASE OF *TOY STORY 3*

Often, fantasy has suffered from a misconception that its importance lies in simply being a panacea to material reality, a charge that has also been levied at comic books. However, in his pioneering study of comics, Scott McCloud muses over the varying degrees of fantasy and realism that the graphic form uses. One might argue that his approach is similar to Hume's in that he sees fantasy and realism working together to produce animations which, depending on the balance between the two, will be more or less fantasy, more or less mimetic in form. He begins by contrasting comics with photographs, arguing that photographs are 'smaller, flatter, less detailed, they don't move, they lack color – but as pictorial icons go, they are pretty realistic' (McCloud 1994: 28). Similarly, of course, realist writing is 'smaller, flatter, less detailed' than reality. In that sense, all imaginative work is fantas-*tic*: creativity put through a filter of everyday experience. What differentiates fantasy from realism are the assumptions made about the fictional world portrayed. Too much distance between the fantasy creation and reality and the reader will find the connection too arduous to make; too little and it will fail to work as fantasy at all.

That balancing act is scrutinized continually in Disney Pixar's *Toy Story* series of animated films (1995–2019)[4] and tends to gain traction around the depiction of Andy, the human child/teenage protagonist. In animated images, something happens in the gaps between the realism and the non-realism of the pictorial representation of the cartoon image (a slashed line for a mouth, for instance) that enables the reader or viewer to interpret that over-simplified image as a human feature. This connection is essential for the viewer to identify with the animated character and, according to McCloud, 'viewer-identification is a specialty of cartooning' (McCloud 1994: 42). Careful attention to the opening sequences of *Toy Story 3* (2010) shows the interface between fantasy and realist animation working in a particularly fluid manner. The film opens with an embedded animated action sequence, involving a Western genre setting, in which a train is being robbed and a bridge crossing a gorge is blown up with dynamite. The train crashes into the gorge, leaving only a stricken Jessie on the brink of a precipice, mounted on Bullseye the horse. This sequence is then revealed to be a wholly enclosed fantasy play world as the animated setting shifts to Andy's room and we realize that what we have been watching is a game played by Andy, as he runs around the room, holding his toys. As the animation moves out again, taking in more of the room, we now realize we are watching a home-movie his mother has filmed of young Andy at play: time has moved on. The moment those enclosed boundaries of the original fantasy sequence are breached, so is the magic. Several home-movie scenes follow, with Andy progressively ageing until we reach the fictive present: seventeen-year-old Andy is on the brink of his own precipice, leaving home to go off to college.

That gradual ageing of Andy requires a shift in the relationship between animation, fantasy and realism. As a young boy subject of the home movie, his face is less naturalistically animated. His eyes are round like Woody's and, in a scene showing him hugging Woody in bed, their two faces alongside each other are mirrored by a lack of naturalistic detail. As he ages, Andy's eyes become increasingly elliptical, as human eyes are, and his facial features become increasingly naturalistic. The message is clear and consistent throughout the whole *Toy Story* series: fantasy belongs with play; and play belongs to the young. Thus, in the first three *Toy Story* movies Andy acts as the integer for mimesis throughout (he no longer appears in *Toy Story 4* (2019), except via a couple of fleeting flashbacks). Although those early scenes of *Toy Story 3* reveal a progression from fantasy to naturalistic animation, what remains constant throughout the first three films is the fact that, as soon as Andy picks up Buzz Lightyear, or any other toy, Buzz metamorphoses from being a fantasy hero to an animated plastic toy. Only when Andy puts him down again can Buzz aim for 'infinity and beyond'. There is a paradox here in which we all collude as viewers while knowing it to be impossible: the toys are 'really' alive, but pretend not to be, so that children's play can will them into a facsimile of life. Without children's attention they cannot be toys, instead they would be trapped as living but functionless figures. For an adult viewer of *Toy Story*, there is a trenchant self-recognition of loss in the need to identify with Andy, for he is the figure who moves inexorably from being a child who gives toys a reason to exist, to an adult whose maturity irreversibly renders his own existence futile, at least as far as his toys are concerned.

Perhaps this dual audience identification complicates the child-based status of the *Toy Story* franchise. For example, it may surprise us to discover that the first *Toy Story* film received a PG (Parental Guidance) rather than a U (for Universal) rating from the British Board of Film Classification, cautioning that it contains 'mild violence, scary scenes, dangerous behaviour'. However, perhaps following the extensive merchandising opportunities and clamour for a wider sales audience, supplemented by small-screen broadcasts which had already expanded the age-range of that original viewing audience, fears of harm to small children seem to have been tempered, *Toy Story 2* (1999), *Toy Story 3* and *Toy Story 4* all carrying U certificates, the British Board of Film Classification still cautioning that *Toy Story 3* 'contains mild violence and scary scenes' and *Toy Story 4* contains 'very mild violence, scary scenes'.[5] Alongside the child-adult dynamic of the films, however, there is another way in which the *Toy Story* narratives attain greater sophistication than might be expected in children's animation fantasy and that is in their innately postmodern treatment of subjectivity.

Despite Andy being the human protagonist and toy-owner in all the films, the question of which character constitutes the point of view protagonist for a child viewer is less obvious. Woody the cowboy doll is Andy's favourite toy, but do children identify with Woody when Andy is holding him? In *Toy Story 3*, Woody becomes separated from the rest of the toys, thereby allowing narrative point of view to pass from one toy to another. In fact, one of the most intriguing scenes in the film occurs when Mrs Potato Head, having left an eye under the bed in Woody's room after they have been sent off as a 'job lot' to the local day-nursery, is able to use that lost organ as a visual portal into Andy's room and can thereby console her toy friends that Andy is looking for them, thinking that they had been stored safely in the attic, when the toys had otherwise assumed that he had thrown them out. This variable identification between child viewer and Andy and/or

Woody and the other toys requires a much more interrogatory approach to viewing on the part of the audience and, along with it, an awareness of split subjectivity, a self-conscious portrayal of play as fantasy and a final sequence which is heart-rending for viewers of all ages.

Toy Story 3 leaves Andy at a pivotal moment in human existence: the point of no return when childhood is left behind and he drives away, over the horizon. In *Fantasy Fiction*, I identified the horizon as 'a symbol of simultaneous limit and infinity' (Armitt 2005: 4), a phrase that resonates with Buzz Lightyear's clarion call. What makes the horizon such a perfect metaphor for fantasy is that it is simultaneously absolutely 'there' and yet nowhere: our goal, although one that it is impossible to *real*-ize. That idea of moving beyond, as expressed in ballads such as 'Over the Rainbow' (Harold Arlen and Yip Harburg, 1939), written for Metro-Goldwyn-Mayer's musical *The Wizard of Oz* (dir. Fleming, 1939), engages directly with dreamscapes combined with flights of fancy: 'Somewhere over the rainbow skies are blue and the dreams that you dare to dream really do come true'. Similarly, the subterranean possibilities afforded by Jules Verne's *Twenty-Thousand Leagues Under the Sea* (1870) or circumnavigation possibilities afforded by his *Around the World in Eighty Days* (1873), capture perfectly the realist desire for travel to exotic lands, coupled with the impossible fantasies of what unearthly creatures and landscapes one might find there. That elongation of distance into the unknown takes our everyday world and transforms it into a geography of dreams and hyperbole, as in Lear's 'bong trees' or Carroll's 'bread-and-butter flies'.

Such elongations also apply themselves to the human scale. Once Alice finds herself in Wonderland, she contemplates: 'I seem to be shutting up like a telescope' (Carroll 1929: 7) or, later, 'It was much pleasanter at home … when one wasn't always growing larger and smaller, and being ordered about by mice and rabbits' (Carroll 1929: 28). Such elongations are not simply for effect; Alice's characterization as a young girl is both maintained and challenged through them: maintained in the sense that children's delight in pretend play is partly about wishing they were older, taller, stronger and more adept than they are, challenged in the sense that Alice's physical instability threatens her core identity. When her neck elongates so rapidly that she finds her head in the trees, a pigeon attacks her, mistaking her for a serpent. Alice's response is increasingly uncertain:

> 'But I'm *not* a serpent, I tell you!' ... I'm a – I'm a –'
> 'Well! *What* are you?' said the Pigeon. 'I can see you're trying to invent something!'
> 'I – I'm a little girl,' said Alice, rather doubtfully, as she remembered the number of changes she had gone through, that day.
>
> (Carroll 1929: 47)

That 'number of changes' incorporates sequences of animal fantasy, a quest narrative, political allegory, and unconscious desires or, in other words, the topics of all the subsequent chapters of this book. In Chapter 2, we will trace some of the key ways in which fantasy, too, has undergone a 'number of changes' from the time of Classical Antiquity to twenty-first-century digital gaming, beginning with Ovid's *Metamorphoses.*

NOTES

1 See Armitt (1996), especially chapter one: 'Structuralism, Genre and Beyond ...'; 17–38.
2 'Peculiar' in this sense means 'different'. The children here have what might be considered super-powers: the ability to levitate, self-imposed invisibility, superhuman strength.
3 See, for example, Seamus Heaney's 'The Tollund Man', in *Wintering Out* (Heaney 1972).
4 The original *Toy Story* movie was 'the first feature-length film entirely created using computer animation' (Blum 2010), arguably a fact that made it as interesting to adult film buffs as to its target child audience.
5 See www.bbfc.co.uk/releases/toy-story-1995 and www.bbfc.co.uk/releases/toy-story-3-2010-2.

2

A HISTORICAL OVERVIEW OF FANTASY

FROM OVID TO GAME BOY

As Gillian Polack observes, 'History, to be clear, is not the past but a cultural narrative that explains the past. Fantasy conventions and tales of a bitter feuding past are both ways in which one's understanding of history is shaped and a relationship with the past developed' (Polack 2015: 91). In other words, the history of fantasy has as much a shaping role to play in our understanding of history as it does our understanding of fantasy. This chapter will not pretend to provide an encyclopaedic history of fantasy. Instead, it identifies some of the key tales, tropes, genres and themes that recur across the centuries and find expression and adaptation in fantasy writing (popular and serious), music, illustration, film and theatre. So much modern fantasy derives its impetus from the ancient classics such as Ovid's *Metamorphoses*, in which we first encounter Pyramus and Thisbe, later given prominence in William Shakespeare's *A Midsummer Night's Dream* (1600); several monster narratives such as 'Perseus and the Sea Monster', the story of Medusa, the battle between Theseus and the Minotaur and arguably one of the most influential of all, the story of 'Orpheus and Eurydice' and their descent into the Underworld.

Ovid's *Metamorphoses* originally comprised a collection of short oral tales collated and authorized in Latin by Ovid in the first century AD, the English language version most of us read today having been translated by Arthur Golding in 1567. As Madeleine Forey observes, 'The classics were the raw material of the English Renaissance; to write in the sixteenth century meant to engage in dialogue with the great writers of ancient Greece and Rome' (Forey 2002: xi). In emphasizing the success and influence of Golding's translation, Forey continues by arguing that upon it 'rests the explosion of literary talent in the 1590s: of Marlowe, Donne, Spenser, Jonson and Shakespeare' (Forey 2002: xii). What we can extrapolate from Forey's observation is how heavily these writers also relied on fantasy for their success.

'ORPHEUS AND EURYDICE'

In Golding's translation of Ovid's 'Orpheus [Orphey] and Eurydice' we find a kind of classical alternative to the biblical Eden myth (Genesis 2:8–3:24). Young Eurydice, Orphey's bride, is bitten by a serpent on the ankle and dies. Orphey goes to the gods to plead for the restoration of her life, in response to which the gods summon her. As Ovid rather amusingly tells us, she 'was as yet among / The newcome ghosts and limpèd of her wound' (Ovid 2002: bk. 10, ll. 52–53), in other words injured, but not yet decomposed, a distinction we will see revisited in Monique Wittig's *The Lesbian Body* in Chapter 6. The bargain of the original text is that Orphey may lead Eurydice out of the underworld, provided he does not glance back at her *en route*. Just before they reach Limbo, the portal between earth and underworld, however, Orphey's nerve falters and he turns his head: 'Immediately she slippèd back. He, reaching out his hands, / Desirous to be caught and for to catch her grasping stands. / But nothing save the slippery air (unhappy man!) he caught' (Ovid 2002: bk. 10, ll. 61–63).

As we will see repeatedly, mythology readily embraces a range of fantasy bedfellows as these stories evolve and mutate across the centuries. In this sense the anonymously authored fourteenth-century text *Sir Orfeo* is typical, amalgamating material from the original Greek myth with Celtic fairy-lore of the Middle Ages. In *Sir Orfeo*, the Underworld is presented simply as a version of fairyland, with the rapacious King of the Fairies taking a fancy to Eurydice (here called Heurodis/Herodias) and abducting her, taking her back to his underground realm. In Ovid's version Orpheus seems to gain entry to the Underworld simply by sneaking in along with the newly dead. In *Sir Orfeo* it is felt that Orpheus's means of entry requires greater explanation, and such is provided by him disguising himself as a travelling minstrel, fairies being famously enticed by the pleasures of music. Once inside, his playing is judged so beautiful by the Fairy King and Queen that the King grants him a wish as a reward, in response to which he requests and is granted the return of his wife.

Perhaps not surprisingly, considering the emphasis placed upon Orpheus's musicianship, *Orpheus and Eurydice* has found some of its most popular expression across the centuries through classical music. It was made into a classical opera by Claudio Monteverdi in 1607, another by Christoph Gluck in 1762 and again by Joseph Haydn in 1791. Most popular of all, however, is the comic opera (or operetta) version written by the French composer Jacques Offenbach in 1858, titled 'Orpheus and the Underworld'. Whether classical or comic opera, as Dafydd Wood observes, several challenges face production companies trying to stage Orpheus's descent into the Underworld, because they need somehow to present the Underworld as having a different phenomenological status to the surface reality from which Orpheus travels and to which he will return: 'In Hades, Orpheus discovers its horrors ... From a dramatic standpoint something is needed to differentiate this place from anywhere else ... The easiest dramatic way of doing this is to add a character' (Wood 2008: 7). This new character (or characters) therefore represents the otherworldly element: 'the "Chorus of the Unburied Dead" in Haydn, the furies and remarkable "blessed spirits" of Gluck, [or] Cerberus and the train in Offenbach' (Wood 2008: 7).

This problem of how to stage the fantasy realm to convey its 'separateness' is one as old as theatre itself and, during the nineteenth century, Wood tells us that playwrights and librettists became so daunted by how to convey such a shift seriously that most 'shied away' from any attempt to do so, hence, he claims, why Offenbach writes his adaptation as 'an utter burlesque' (Wood 2008: 18). It is clear that Wood prefers classical versions to Offenbach's adaptation, but he acknowledges that, as entertainment, *Orpheus and the Underworld* was 'the 19th century equivalent of a Broadway smash hit or blockbuster' (Wood 2008: 20). Even now, most of us are familiar with the infamous (perhaps, for the time, scandalous) 'Can-Can' finale, and Kevin Clarke, of the Operetta Research Centre, Amsterdam, goes so far as to claim it to be 'part of our cultural DNA' (Clarke 2019). As Betsy Schwarm also observes, 'So marked was [Offenbach's] opera's fame, and so lasting, that in 1886 Camille Saint-Saëns satirized the satire by quoting the finale's cancan at a much slower tempo and assigning it to tortoises in *The Carnival of the Animals* (1886)' (Schwarm 2017).

Before Ovid, the origins of 'Orpheus and Eurydice' lay in oral storytelling. That such storytelling crossed geographical and cultural boundaries is to be expected from the common connection between travellers and storytellers, but it finds renewed interest during the late Victorian period, as post-Darwinian interest in refining society's understanding of the relationship between God and humanity extended to re-visiting our shared stories of Ancient Roman and Greek Gods. As Mary Douglas observes, 'How to explain the cruelties and irrationalities enshrined in mythology was one of the great puzzles of scholarship in the 1870–1910 period' (Douglas 1978: 10). In 1890, Sir James George Frazer wrote his landmark study of ancient religions and folklore, *The Golden Bough*, in which he pays close interest, among other things, to the influence fantasy has had, historically and concurrently, on the cultural development of indigenous communities worldwide, a focus requiring him to cover questions of philosophy, ritual, superstition and worship. Though Douglas accuses Frazer of 'churn[ing] gods and goblins impartially through the same analytical machine', clearly implying her preference for religion/mythology over folklore/fantasy, even she later acknowledges that 'Beliefs in fiends and gods, witches and mysterious powers of blessing and cursing make sense if we know the full context in which they are used' (Douglas 1978: 12, 14).

In fact, it is precisely the way in which mythological narratives adapt to folkloric superstition that provides one key piece of evidence for the cross-cultural interchange of fantasy across different periods. For example, one variant on the tale of 'Orpheus and Eurydice' was published in the *Irish Fireside* journal of January 1884 as a piece of local folklore. Though different names are attributed to the characters and the lost soul is a young boy rather than a wife, it retains its close family structure to the Greek original. In this version, a young boy is 'stolen by the fairies', they being another species of underground dweller, and swapped for a changeling. The Parish priest manages to capture the offending imp/goblin/elf (the terms are used interchangeably in the tale), which is 'dipped thrice' in the lake to produce 'a curl' on the surface, 'and up from the deep came the naked form of the boy' (Hartland 1891: 129). The family is then permitted to return home with the boy, provided it does so silently. According to Edwin Sidney Hartland, the mother 'accidentally spoke' and so the boy disappeared, but in this version the family is given a second chance and now 'the mother succeed[s] in holding her tongue' (Hartland 1891: 129). It is interesting to see how, by making this a story of fairy bargaining rather than mythology, castigation falls by inference upon the mother who, presumably, is sufficiently neglectful to allow the child to be stolen by the fairies in the first place and then cannot stop talking for long enough to secure his safety.

THE ONE THOUSAND AND ONE NIGHTS

Women's stereotypically perceived loquaciousness, however, can work to their advantage in fantasy, as the framing storytelling structure of *The One Thousand and One Nights* (sometimes known as *The Arabian Nights*) reveals. Our frame text tells us that King Shahriyar learns of his wife's infidelity, as a result of which he has her executed. Insuring against any further betrayal, from that time onwards he takes only virgins to bed and, in the morning, has each one beheaded. The ensuing reign of terror instigated among young women is interrupted only when Sheherazade volunteers to be the King's next bride. As Robert Irwin explains, she introduces a new condition: her sister Dunyazade must accompany her (Irwin 1994: 103). At the moment of defloration Dunyazade asks her sister for a story. Sheherazade obliges, but leaves the story unfinished and King Shahriyar, spellbound, insists the story is continued on the next and every subsequent night, thus prompting each successive tale of the collection. Eventually, King Shahriyar repents and the chain of tyranny is broken. Thus fantasy ensures the longevity, not just of Sheherazade but the next generation of young women.

Culturally, *The One Thousand and One Nights* collection is often believed to derive from 'the stock-in-trade of the professional street-corner storyteller' of the marketplaces of Middle-Eastern cities such as Marrakesh and Baghdad (Irwin 1994: 103). Historically, Kris Swank informs us that many of the stories are believed to be set during 'the Islamic golden age, the reign of Harun al-Rashid, caliph of Baghdad (786–809)' (Swank 2015: 164). The origins of the tales, far from being mono-cultural, however, derive from the storytelling traditions of 'ancient India and pharaonic Egypt' (Swank 2015: 163). In fact, and despite Western cultures' common usage of the alternative title *The Arabian Nights*, the tales were first translated into Arabic, under the title *Alf Layla* (literally *The Thousand Nights*), only as late as the early 1700s (Swank 2015: 163).

Around the same time in Britain, literacy really started to gather pace and cheap street pamphlets, known as chapbooks, had begun circulating freely among the public from the late seventeenth century onwards. To meet the growing demand for storybooks appropriate to a newly literate novice adult audience, chapbooks began to champion the 'everyday' hero outwitting the rich landowner, often depicting that landowner as a giant, the best-known example of which is 'Jack and the Giants', commonly known as 'Jack and the Beanstalk', published in chapbook form in the early eighteenth century. According to Swank, this moment is also when *The One Thousand and One Nights* is first brought to Europe, translated into French by Antoine Galland, who augmented the original collected tales with new ones. Ironically, it is

Galland's additions, not the original tales, that tend to be the ones we most closely associate with this collection: 'The Voyages of Sindbad', 'Ali Baba', and 'Aladdin' (Swank 2015: 164). The influence of *The One Thousand and One Nights*, however, is such that it affects not only popular but 'literary' culture and is reputed to have had a particularly shaping influence on Samuel Taylor Coleridge, who read it as a boy. According to Stephen Prickett, it 'so frightened him that he was … "haunted by spectres" whenever he was alone in the dark'. That early effect matured into a more aesthetically rounded influence which Coleridge, interestingly, connected with 'habituat[ion] to the Vast' (Prickett 2005: 6–7, quoting Coleridge), such 'vastness' featuring clearly in poems such as 'Kubla Kahn' (1816) ('In Xanadu did Kubla Kahn / A stately pleasure dome decree: / Where Alph, the sacred river, ran / Through caverns measureless to man'; ll. 1–4) and 'The Rime of the Ancient Mariner' (1817) ('Alone, alone, all, all alone, / Alone on a wide wide sea! / And never a saint took pity on / My soul in agony'; ll. 232–235).

From the twentieth century onwards, however, the greatest impact of *The One Thousand and One Nights* in British and American cultures has been cinematic, beginning in 1924 with the feature-length silent film, *Thief of Baghdad: An Arabian Nights Fantasy* (dir. Raoul Walsh, 1924), starring Douglas Fairbanks. This was not the first film to be made of the tales: David Butler reminds us that Georges Méliès, discussed in more detail below, directed *Le Palais des mille et une nuits/The Palace of a Thousand and One Nights* as early as 1905 (Butler 2009: 59); nevertheless, *The Thief of Baghdad* has proved the more influential on later adaptations. In the early days of cinema, in which the staging is clearly theatrical and stylized rather than naturalistic, and in which the voice work of theatrical performances had to be substituted by title cards, special effects must have provided early cinema with a much needed advantage over theatre and music hall. Walsh's lavish early film is certainly magical in theme and form but, as in many early films, it is careful to retain an overt connection with books and storytelling. In part this connection is maintained by the title cards establishing the location of individual scenes or inserting explicatory snippets of dialogue to explain plot shifts; in part it is secured because of the cautionary epigram which frames the opening and closing scenes and which retains the close moral connection with the Qu'ran: 'Happiness must be earned'.

Magic drives this film, the frame sequence focusing upon a sorcerer who conjures up magic dust, which rises up into the night sky to write the epigram in the stars. Internally, magic attaches itself to a series of objects: a magic basket, into which a small boy is placed before swords are thrust through it at various angles. A rope magically emerges from the top of the basket and snakes it way vertically into the air, becoming rigid. In an excellent early piece of cinema magic, out of nowhere the young boy miraculously appears, wholly intact, right at its top. Three foreign suitors for the Caliph of Bagdad's daughter travel in search of three more magic objects: a crystal ball, a flying carpet and a magic apple which restores life to the dead. Our 'hero', the eponymous thief, whose character is equally magically transformed by love for the Princess, also undertakes a quest in which he retrieves the magic dust which the viewer perceives to be that used by the frame sorcerer, and which enables him to grow a magic army from the ground, thus battling his way back into the palace and winning the Princess's heart. According to Swank, 'When Hollywood embraced *The Arabian Nights* in the twentieth century, it transformed merchants and traders like Sinbad and Ali Baba into action heroes' (Swank 2015: 174). Certainly, as Fairbanks himself jumps from a balcony to catch hold of the magic rope and climb down it, or as he and the Princess fly high above the assembled crowd of the palace on the magic carpet, that action heroism is fabulously realized.

Swank considers Walt Disney's plot for its animated movie *Aladdin* (dir. Ron Clements and John Musker, 1992) to be a 'recycl[ing]' of Fairbanks's *The Thief of Baghdad* (Swank 2015: 175), an assessment that seems a little harsh considering that some overlap in content is to be expected in two adaptations of one folktale. Certainly, in both films the title character is considered a thief, though in Disney's 1992 production, only out of hunger, and both main plots are anchored in the Sultan's daughter, Princess Jasmine, having to choose between suitors. As in *The*

Thief of Baghdad, in *Aladdin* none of these other suitors meets with Jasmine's approval, and in both films the thief play-acts being a Prince in order to attempt to win her hand. In *Aladdin*, the romance between Jasmine and Aladdin is obstructed by the King's evil adviser, Jafar, while in *The Thief of Baghdad* the same role is played by the empire-building Prince of the Mogols, both of whom are, of course, defeated. Magic retains its place at the centre of Disney's *Aladdin*, but works quite differently from *The Thief of Baghdad*. Crucially, in *Aladdin*, in a much closer connection with the original folktale, a genie appears in response to Aladdin's rubbing of the magic lamp; while, rather more in an echo of Disney's earlier representation of Kaa the snake in its animated classic film, *The Jungle Book* (dir. Wolfgang Reitherman, 1967) than anything to do with *The One Thousand and One Nights*, Jafar wields a magic staff in the shape of a cobra's head, its eyes becoming magically illuminated to hypnotize detractors into doing his bidding. The magic carpet ride is an essential component in any version of *Aladdin* and, as our hero and Jasmine take flight, the signature theme song of the film, 'A Whole New World' assures us that the romance of magic/the magic of romance will reveal to us 'A new fantastic point of view … A dazzling place I never knew', lines that surely encapsulate fantasy as well as any.

However, the major distinction between the two films is political and it is here where we instantly perceive that not all points of view are permitted to be either 'new' or 'fantastic', whatever the song might claim. Where Walsh's version is set in Baghdad, capital city of modern-day Iraq, the Disney adaptation is based in the entirely fictional setting of 'Agrabah', presumably in an attempt to avoid any direct association with a country and city that the United States air force had bombed only the previous year, in the military campaign now known as the first Gulf War.[1] Moreover, there are several uncomfortable Orientalist touches in Disney's 1992 adaptation that parody its cultural context: the superfluous inclusion of a man lying on a bed of nails in one street scene and a sword swallower in another, both of which seem to be there purely for parodic effect. Potentially offensive is the comedy song lyric 'Brush up your Sunday salaams', in an

Islamic culture in which the holy day of the week is Friday. In addition, the Islamic spiritual and moral context at the heart of *The Thief of Baghdad* is almost entirely erased in Disney's *Aladdin*, along with its moral message. There is no mention of the mosque which plays such an influential role on the title character of *The Thief of Baghdad*, and instead of a morally driven epigram, Disney's production simply opens by emphasizing the fantastic nature of its fictional setting, the frame narrator describing it simply as a 'city of mystery, of enchantment, and the finest merchandise this side of the River Jordan'. Fantasy, it seems, will overcome all divisions, with a little help from market forces.

Even the 2019 live-action Disney film *Aladdin* (dir. Guy Ritchie) does relatively little to remedy the cultural politics of the 1992 version. The setting of the film remains 'Agrabah' rather than Baghdad and the Islamic religious context is still totally erased, its only relic being the song lyric mentioned above, which has at least been amended to 'Brush up your Friday salaams'. There are moral messages in evidence, but they remain firmly secular and attached to property. Aladdin the thief has become more of a Robin Hood-style figure, stealing in order to feed the poor, although the class-based politics are undermined when Aladdin reprimands his monkey for stealing Princess Jasmine's bracelet, cautioning 'There's a time when we do steal and a time when we don't', presumably because of the impediment it causes to their romance. The most affecting observation made about theft in the film comes from Jafar, however. Telling Aladdin of how he, too, began as a street thief, he continues by advising him to aim big: 'Steal an apple and you're a thief; steal a kingdom and you're a statesman'. Regime change, it seems, is a natural extension of global capitalism.

THE FAIRY QUEEN

Kingdoms, nationalism and global politics are no strangers to works of fantasy. Edmund Spenser's *The Faerie Queene* (1590–1596) is one of the most famous fantasy works of English national politics and is frequently read as an allegorical paean in praise of Elizabeth I (1558–1603):

And she her selfe of beautie soveraigne Queene
Fair Venus seemed unto his bed to bring
Her, whom he waking evermore did weene
To be the chastest flower, that ay did spring
On earthly braunch, the daughter of a king,
(ll. 424–428)

Spenser was not the first to make this connection, however. Maureen Duffy explains that 'The metamorphosis of Elizabeth I into the Fairy Queen, and by extension England into Fairyland, began with her coronation' thirty years earlier (Duffy 1972: 109). Several things come together during this period to cement the connection between Elizabeth and folklore. Duffy claims that it was partly due to Elizabeth's 'untouchable' reputation as the Virgin Queen and partly the sixteenth-century fashion for the idealization of pastoral forms, such as is manifest in Sir Philip Sidney's prose poem *Arcadia* (1590), that the connection was forged. Equally, her 'love of dancing was another fairy attribute … [and i]n the pastoral convention she became Eliza, queen of shepherd and shepherdesses' (Duffy 1972: 116). Fairies conventionally live in an idealized version of the countryside, in accord with what Duffy calls 'the Golden Age and the Garden of Eden … the traditional English love of gardening' which was linked to 'the perfect pair without responsibility, when fruits and flowers bent to their hand and there was only one embargo' (Duffy 1972: 116). These easy slippages between Biblical Christianity and traditional folklore sit alongside each other happily in so many fantasy works over the centuries and Duffy, writing in the later twentieth century, is impatient with those for whom the fantasy content of *The Faerie Queene* should be diminished in favour of its politics: 'For some reason the deliberate use of fantasy and symbol in thought and life has become discreditable … Fortunately for us and for them the Elizabethans had no such inhibitions. They would have found us unsophisticated, and uneducated; our use of language and our thought processes dull and simplistic' (Duffy 1972: 110–111).

In fact, not only was the Fairy Queen of Elizabethan poetry rich and multi-layered, she became a key focus for a new and spectacular form of courtly entertainment, the masque. Arguably the originator of what we now think of as cinematic special effects, Inigo Jones (1573–1652) began his trade developing stylized masques for the Elizabethan Court, among them *The Faerie Queene*. For this extravaganza he 'sprinkled flowers in [Queen Elizabeth's] path … [and] she was awakened one morning by the Fairy Queen and her train dancing beneath her windows' (Harris et al. 1973: 22). Rather like Spenser's *The Faerie Queene*, Jones's masques typically comprised a mixture of fantasy, myth and political allegory, all commingled with the introduction of staged lighting and mechanical effects, such as 'curtains … and a rock lit by candles set behind glasses containing coloured liquid' (Harris et al. 1973: 33). Jones's technological skill began in the early years of the 1600s, when he is attributed with the invention of the proscenium arch which, in raising the actors above the audience, maximized the spectacular effect of his new stage engineering. In Ben Jonson's *The Masque of Blackness* (1605), Harris et al. inform us that Jones astounded his audience with the construction of '[a]n artificial sea with great sea-beasts and mermaids', while in *Hymenaei* (1606) he 'created a gigantic globe of gold and silver seemingly floating in mid-air, which turned to reveal the masquers seated in "a mine of light"' (Harris et al. 1973: 35). Throughout the course of his career Jones's ingenuity became more and more complex. By the time he produced the masque *Luminalia*, in 1638, he was able to utilize the 'fly-gallery' to produce 'not only the usual flying chariots, but also complex cloud effects revealing a whole city supported on a rainbow' (Harris et al. 1973: 90).

At the same time that Jones was beginning to develop his court masques, Shakespeare was writing and staging *A Midsummer Night's Dream*, another play in which the Fairy Queen features, here as Titania, and in which fantasy takes on a blend of magic and, via the midsummer setting, myth and folklore. As Marina Warner observes, 'Stagecraft [is] akin to magic' and, on stage, words form the stuff of sorcery:

> Magic is made by performative speech ... Puck recites a love spell ... to make Titania fall in love with Bottom when she wakes. The words

> 'chant', 'incantation' ... do not record or describe, they produce events, they inaugurate change, they effect conversion and transformation. Then performative projection narrows the gap between act and illusion.
>
> (Warner 2006a: 132, 136)

For all the enchantment and metamorphic transformations of Shakespeare's play, there is an argument for claiming that Puck is the character who most persistently embodies fantasy. Where all the other characters remain within or move between the competing worlds of the non-magical dukedom and the dreamscape of the enchanted wood, Puck is continually shape-shifting, at one moment a mischievous sprite who 'lurk[s] in a gossip's bowl / In very likeness of a roasted crab' (act II, sc. 1, ll. 47–48) and at another 'through bog, through bush, through brake, through briar; / Sometime a horse I'll be, sometime a hound' (act III, sc. 1, l. 102). In terms of the logic of impossibility, only Puck can overcome the boundaries of space and time to 'put a girdle round about the earth / In forty minutes' (act II, sc. 1, ll. 175–176) and, when he mistakenly enchants the wrong lover, responds to Oberon's command to rectify his error with 'About the wood go swifter than the wind, / And Helena of Athens look thou find', followed up by the assertion 'I go, I go, look how I go! / Swifter than arrow from a Tartar's bow' (act III, sc. 2, ll. 94–95, 100–101). In overcoming the space-time continuum, Puck lays the groundwork for much more modern-day fantasy sequences, such as we find in J.K. Rowling's novel *Harry Potter and the Prisoner of Azkaban* (1999), in which Hermione Grainger takes Harry back in time by means of an enchanted hour-glass, so that they can reverse the events leading up to the execution of Buckbeak, Hagrid's pet Hippogriff, thereby facilitating Sirius Black's escape from Professor Flitwick's office. As Hermione sets the hour-glass in motion, Harry 'had the sensation that he was flying, very fast, backwards. A blur of colours and shapes rushed past him … He tried to yell but couldn't hear his own voice' (Rowling 1999: 288). Time travel is only part of the enchanted shift: as they take shelter in a broom cupboard, they hear footsteps in the corridor and Hermione tells Harry 'I think it's us going down to Hagrids!' to which Harry can only respond 'Are you telling me … that we're here in this cupboard and we're out there, too?' (Rowling 1999: 289).

Despite Puck's conquering of the space-time continuum, Titania is never allowed to be upstaged and, though Oberon is Puck's master, Puck's concern for Titania is clear when he discovers the proximity of the carnivalesque 'play within a play' to her sleeping form: 'What hempen homespuns have we swaggering here, / So near the cradle of the Fairy Queen?' (act III, sc. 1, ll. 73–74). In fact, Titania's courtly sovereignty is never seriously under threat. She remains centre-stage throughout, accompanied by her fairy train: 'I serve the Fairy Queen, / To dew her orbs upon the green' (act II, sc. 1, ll. 8–9) as she at one moment calls for 'a roundel and a fairy song' (act II, sc. 2, l. 1), at another commanding Peaseblossom, Cobweb, Moth and Mustardseed to attend to Bottom by extension of their devotion to her. Those power relations are essential in a play written and presented while Elizabeth I was still Queen. Titania's enchanted plea to her donkey lover, 'I pray thee, gentle mortal, sing again:/Mine ear is much enamour'd of thy note' (act III, sc. 1, ll. 133–134) may subject her to a degree of teasing unheard of in Spenser's *The Faerie Queene*, but that same enchantment also plays to her vulnerability as a lady placed in a sexually compromising situation. Now even Oberon relents: 'Her dotage now I do begin to pity; / … I will release the fairy queen' (act IV, sc. 1, ll. 46, 69). As Ann Swinfen observes, 'The magic sleep is … often associated with heroes who will wake when help is needed' and so it proves here (Swinfen 1984: 45). By releasing Titania, Oberon prevents real sexual mischief from befalling her and he turns hero. In that regard, and a little like the teasing Puck, Shakespeare pushes the boundaries, but knows when to stop, most obviously in Puck's final abasing speech to the audience. All has been a dream, he assures us, and 'honest Puck … will make amends ere long' (act V, sc. 1, ll. 417, 420).

DANCE, MUSIC AND TOYS

That light playfulness of tone is retained, at the end of the seventeenth century, in Henry Purcell's semi-opera *The Fairy Queen* (1692), an adaptation not of Spenser's epic poem, as the title might suggest, but of *A Midsummer Night's Dream*. A mixture of opera, court masque, and theatre, Purcell's composition is an all-round sensory experience of sight, sound and spatial form. In that respect it provides the perfect 'dream-factor' combination of fantasy elements. As Allison Kay Deutermann suggests, the resulting amalgamation of ingredients is both the strength of Purcell's opera and the reason behind it going out of fashion at various moments in history, although she considers it superior to what she calls Shakespeare's 'mishmash of comedy and tragedy performed by the rude mechanicals' (Deutermann 2010: 61). One might argue that Purcell's *The Fairy Queen* sets a kind of early precedent for musical theatre and, as in musical theatre, individual songs from the original play-book were bought to give to friends or kept as souvenirs. Most interesting for our purposes, however, is the way in which Purcell reintegrates the respective worlds of the 'mortals and fairies', where Shakespeare concludes *A Midsummer Night's Dream* with them 'retreating to their separate spheres' (Deutermann 2010: 63). That decision positions the fantasy content differently in each case.

Shakespeare's *A Midsummer Night's Dream* presents us with a series of concentric rings within which the dream vision is safely contained. This outer layer comprises Theseus, Duke of Athens, and his betrothed, Hippolyta, 'Queen of the Amazons', who in their god-like roles establish the frame for pre-nuptial discord within the two inner circles which theirs contains. The second is the 'realist' courtly circle, represented by Hermia, Helena, Lysander and Demetrius, whose various romantic attractions and mishaps are first imposed by Egeus's realist refusal to allow his daughter, Hermia, to marry Lysander, later augmented by Puck's muddled magical meddling with the eye drops. Inside that layer we find Oberon and Titania and their followers, locked into their own marital dispute. Right at the heart of the play is the festival entertainment provided by the aforementioned 'hempen homespuns': Quince, Snug, Bottom, Flute, Snout and Starveling, tradesmen recruited as amateur actors. Although much of the action involves one layer bleeding into another, often at Puck or Oberon's request, the fact that even those in the outer layer bear the names of Gods prevents this play's spectacle from ever genuinely evoking reality. Purcell, on the other hand, allows parts of his opera to 'spill', both spatially and sensorily.

In a 2009 Glyndebourne production of Purcell's adaptation, the amateur actors are workmen rather than tradesmen and they, rather than Puck, become the glue that holds the various layers of the play together for a twenty-first-century audience. Arguably, the workmen are the stars of this production, as they repeatedly soften up the audience, particularly following the austere opening scene between Egeus and the young lovers. Their arrival onstage is as stage-hands, discussing how to establish the set, including the special effects required to bring moonlight onto the stage. To the audience's delight, this scene gradually morphs into an ensemble musical dance number with brooms. Comic effect is therefore maximized on a realist level before bringing on the spirits and other mythical beings. Having been reluctantly enlisted into the production he thought they were setting, even the transformation of Bottom takes place via realist, if ridiculous visual means. The actor re-appears onstage wearing two large men's shoes for ears and a tomato for a nose. That decision to connect the actors with comic realism rather than fantasy suggests a degree of embarrassment at the fantasy content and, in truth, at times the audience is right to be embarrassed. In places the fantasy elements of the Glyndebourne production are clumsily handled, such as in the 'Masque of Seduction' in act III, in which the actors are dressed from head to toe in cuddly rabbit suits while simulating copulation, simultaneously rendering the performance explicitly sexual and strangely childish. At others, however, the dream structure is conveyed well, as when one of the singers stands, a pillow attached to her head suggesting she is lying down, or in the ever-popular usage of staged flying with a harness, which remains one of the best ways of conveying to a modern-day theatre audience the magical world of fairies and mythology.

As we have already seen in the context of Offenbach's *Orpheus and the Underworld*, the connection between classical music and fantastic spectacle becomes highly popular during the Victorian period, and arguably never more so than in the context of Pyotr Ilych Tchaikovsky's ballet *The Nutcracker Suite*, first 'presented to the Russian court in 1892' (Balanchine and Mason 1954: 387;

cited in Roth 1997: 40) and based on E.T.A. Hoffmann's story 'The Nutcracker and the Mouse King' (1816). Linked, like *A Midsummer Night's Dream*, to the concept of festival, *The Nutcracker Suite* is set at Christmas as Clara's godfather, Drosselmeyer, brings her the present of a nutcracker soldier doll. After all have gone to bed, the toys come to life and a series of vignettes allow solo performers from the various toys to take place, most famously the dance of the sugar plum fairy from the top of the Christmas tree. The mechanical ingenuity we often attach to Victorian toymakers and which certainly informs Tchaikovsky's ballet actually originates a century earlier. As Ronald Taylor writes, 'Cultured circles in eighteenth-century Europe were much taken with the mechanical figures which ingenious and often unscrupulous inventors were offering for their entertainment – society eagerly received any novel demonstration of man's apparent control over the ... powers of nature' (Taylor 1963: 82). Such ingenuity and unscrupulousness continues to appeal to those writing fantasy entertainment for children, as is even evident in the otherwise escapist cinematic adaptation of Ian Fleming's *Chitty Chitty Bang Bang: The Magical Car* (1964) for cinema (dir. Ken Hughes, 1968). In Hughes's film, Baron Bomburst of Vulgaria is as childish in his adoration of toys and presents as he is evil and dictatorial towards actual children, all of whom are removed from their families and forced to work underground. Most villainous of all, however, is the sublimely terrifying character of the Child-Catcher, played in this film by Robert Helpmann, an Australian ballet dancer who had already co-starred in Michael Powell and Emeric Pressberger's film adaptation of Offenbach's *The Tales of Hoffmann* (1951). Such edginess might explain the ongoing appeal of *The Nutcracker Suite*, for however playful and escapist these fantasy figures are, the surrounding dangers of an adult-focused nocturnal world and its pleasurable appeal for a developing young girl renders the ballet suitable for at least two different generations of spectator.

Occasionally, the relationship developed between music, toys and fantasy is one of pure wish fulfilment, such as is the case in *Mr Magorium's Wonder Emporium* (dir. Zach Helm, 2007). Molly Mahoney is a musical child prodigy, seemingly destined for stardom as a classical pianist and/or composer. Gradually she realizes that she is falling behind in her destiny, an awakening that begins to provoke in her self-doubts regarding her role in the shop. In fact, Mahoney embodies magic – an aptitude which manifests itself in music spilling from her fingers as she 'air-plays' the piano on the bus and everywhere she goes. In the end, what she is looking for is 'sparkle', something she later learns to differentiate from 'twinkle' (the shop accountant's word) or 'quirk' (her own). Such purity is rare in adult fantasy. In her novel *The Magic Toyshop* (1967), Angela Carter depicts an evil toymaker and puppeteer with the ironic name Phillip Flower, who takes in his orphaned nieces and nephew after the death of their parents in a plane crash. Flower's toyshop is a 'crazy world … [of] men and women dwarfed by toys and puppets, where even the birds were mechanical and the few human figures went masked and played musical instruments in the small and terrible hours of the night' (Carter 1981: 68). Here, in a superficially innocent world of toys, Melanie will become the object of Uncle Phillip's leering perversity. Also here, toys come under the sub-category of the uncanny that Sigmund Freud calls 'eerie, weird, arousing gruesome fear' (Freud 1990: 345) and indeed there are moments when Carter's novel reads as a fictional version of Freud's 'The "Uncanny"'. Hence, when Melanie spies 'a wooden-leg factory *Walpurgisnacht* of carved and severed limbs' (Carter 1981: 66), we recall Freud's description of 'Dismembered limbs, a severed head, a hand cut off at the wrist' as examples of uncanny objects (Freud 1990: 366). Indeed, Melanie does later find a 'freshly severed hand, all bloody at the roots' in the kitchen dresser drawer (Carter 1981: 118).

EARLY CINEMA AND SPECIAL EFFECTS

The kind of mechanical ingenuity that inspired composers such as Tchaikovsky also inspired early film-makers and fantasy is at the kernel of cinematographic invention. Like Inigo Jones, the early French filmmaker, Georges Méliès (1861–1938), was an expert at stage mechanics and played his own significant role in the development of what we now call special effects. He had previously been a magician and illusionist and his interest in film is believed to have derived, in part, from a perceived opportunity to screen his illusions to a larger audience. As Butler informs us, Méliès's fantasy film career began 'as early as 1897 with *La Cigale et la fourmi* from Aesop's fable "The Grasshopper and the Ant"', followed by three films based on stories by Charles Perrault: *Cendrillon/Cinderella* (1899), *Le Petit chaperon rouge/Little Red Riding Hood* (1901) and *Barbe-bleue/Bluebeard* (1901) (Butler 2009: 48–49); he also directed *Le Royaume des fées/The Kingdom of Fairies* in 1903. Above all, however, it is his adventure films such as *Le Voyage dans la lune/A Trip to the Moon* (1902), *Voyage à travers l'impossible/The Impossible Voyage* (1904) and Á *la Conquete du pôle/The Conquest of the Pole* (1912) that have played such an influential role in the development of fantasy cinema.

Méliès's own influences return us to the nineteenth century and composers such as Offenbach, whose light operetta *A Trip to the Moon* (1875) was a musical adaptation of Jules Verne's *From the Earth to the Moon* (1865). Verne's novel and its sequel, *Around the Moon* (1870), alongside H.G. Wells's novel *The First Men in the Moon* (1901), are also believed to have inspired Méliès's filmic vision. Because Méliès viewed cinema as a new form of illusionism, early special effects came quickly to the fore, the most obvious of these, in *A Trip to the Moon*, being the moon landing itself. In truth, more of a splat than a landing, Méliès's camera switches its attention instantly from the rocket's unlikely launchpad (it is fired from a cannon), to a full image of the moon, suspended in the night sky. Gradually Méliès expands the moon's size, giving the illusion of it nearing, or, perhaps, the rocket nearing it. To add to the non-scientific approach, as the moon's surface nears, Méliès adds a human face to its surface, re-connecting with the urban myth of the Man in the Moon. The rocket then plunges from screen left into the right eye of that face, in a manner suggestive of a human hand actually forcing it in, although that hand is edited out. Again, the fantasy element returns, as the resulting displaced material (the above-mentioned splat) is shown to resemble soft cheese rather than rock or moondust, although subsequent hand-colouring of the plates renders it, in technicolour, more graphically and injuriously blood-red. For our purposes, what is interesting is Méliès's utilization of scientific advancement, both in terms of space research and cinema technology, for magic, illusory and fantasy effects.

It is this emphasis on illusion and camera trickery that prevents Méliès's *A Trip to the Moon* from being science fiction, something that might also be said of *The Impossible Voyage.* As James Walters observes, Méliès depicts 'spectacular machinery that can take its passengers on astonishing journeys across the earth's terrain, beneath the seas and into the skies above', but he 'shapes these facts of mechanized progress so that they become fantasy machines within his narrative: a train that can fly into space or a submarine that can fall from the skies' (Walters 2011: 42–43). Arguably, nevertheless, it was Méliès's commitment to fantasy that caused his downfall, as the tastes of the viewing public started to shift away from illusion towards naturalism, gathering around the new documentary and journalistic style of film-making. That shift very soon became linked to other types of advance, such as the British Antarctic Expedition in 1910, led by Robert Falcon Scott. In 1912, Méliès directed *The Conquest of the Pole,* but again created it in an antithetical style to the documentary. Strikingly similar in structure to *A Trip to the Moon*, its comedy content is of the slapstick variety, the first scene of *The Conquest of the Pole* beginning with an animated discussion between scientists about how best to achieve their goal. Dressed lavishly, evenly outlandishly, in a variety of costumes reflective of different nationalities, they are soon interrupted by a group of suffragettes, demanding their right to set off for the Pole too. During the protracted voyage, the travellers encounter many of the same celestial props we spotted in *A Trip to the Moon* and, on arrival, are confronted by the huge head and shoulders of a monstrous man, whom the party attacks with snowballs before one of the men is eaten, only to be regurgitated when a cannon (perhaps also the one that launched the rocket in *A Trip to the Moon*) is fired. The whole riotous extravaganza is designed to demonstrate Méliès's mechanical ingenuity, but clearly did not appeal to those who saw such films as disrespectful of real life human endeavour and, in the case of Scott's fatal expedition, tragedy.

The second great debt that film-making owes to nineteenth-century culture is the renewed interest that arose in monster narratives, inspired by scientific discoveries of what would later come to be known as dinosaur bones. Not only did these finds inspire the imagination of creative writers and artists, the scientific advances in knowledge they enabled transformed our visual expectations of monsters. Before the dinosaur bone discoveries, Prickett tells us that illustrations of monsters were 'clearly descended from the half-human species of classical mythology – fauns, centaurs, and tritons. Though they have scales and claws and often tails, their scale is essentially a human one. They even have human faces' (Prickett 2005: 78). Afterwards, 'Images of horror which had always leaned toward the slimy and scaly became more specifically reptilian' and he notes that even Tenniel's illustration of the Jabberwocky for Lewis Carroll's nonsense poem of the same name (1871) combined 'the leathery wings of a pterodactyl and the long scaly neck and tail of a sauropod' (Prickett 2005: 78–79, 80). The most obvious monster descendant of a post-Darwinian age, however, is no reptilian hybrid, but Marian C. Cooper and Ernest B. Schoedsack's *King Kong* (1933). Where, only a decade earlier, Walsh utilized a chained giant ape in *The Thief of Baghdad* as a means of punishment, criminals being torn limb from limb by the beast, in *King Kong* the audience develops a much stronger affinity with an ape that is shown to be an emotional as much as a physical giant. In terms of its effect on its first audiences, Butler quotes the awed response of a variety of newspaper reviewers, who described the film variously as 'a marvel of screen entertainment', something that 'defies the laws of possibility, dares to try the impossible', and 'the most fantastic [film] that has ever been put on the screen' (Butler 2009: 1).

The special effects technique used in *King Kong* came to be known as 'stop motion' or later 'stop-frame photography', in which models and puppets with 'universal joints, corresponding to human joints' are set against static backgrounds and then 'moved a fraction of an inch, then photographed, moved a fraction more, and shot again … at perhaps 25 frames per second' (Ash 1988: 73). As Russell Ash observes, this technique later became a mainstay of several successful BBC children's television series of the 1960s and 1970s, such *The Herbs* (1968–1972), *The Magic Roundabout* (1965–1977) and *The Wombles* (1973–1975) (Ash 1988: 73). In cinema, that stop motion technique gradually led to the development of 'Dynamation', a process pioneered by Ray Harryhausen (1920–2013) and which Butler considers an 'outstanding combination of live-action performers and stop-motion models interacting in the same frame' (Butler 2009: 77). By using a split screen, parts of the film could be blocked out, thus remaining undeveloped, and were then re-used, enabling the superimposition of live actors onto stop motion fantasy effects. Harryhausen's technique became particularly effective in 1950s monster movies such as *The Beast from 20,000 Fathoms* (dir. Eugène Lourié, 1953) and *It Came from Beneath the Sea* (dir. Robert Gordon, 1955) but, as Butler observes, it also featured in adventure narratives based on adaptations of *The One Thousand and One Nights*, such as *The 7th Voyage of Sinbad* (dir. Nathan H. Juran, 1958), in which Dynamation allowed the filmmakers to present an iconic duel between 'a swashbuckling human being and an equally swashbuckling skeleton' (Butler 2009: 77).

In the later twentieth century, the invention of computer-generated imagery (CGI) revolutionized the relationship between fantasy and cinematic naturalism. Whereas, in children's television, stop motion techniques required children to suspend disbelief in a more actively bookish or theatrical manner, CGI gives fantasy the illusion of being real. Again, monster movies such as *Jurassic Park* (dir. Steven Spielberg, 1993) and the 2005 remake of *King Kong* (dir. Peter Jackson) are at the forefront of this technique but, when it comes to Jackson's directing of the *Lord of the Rings* film trilogy (2001, 2002 and 2003), Butler explains that an even newer technique was required:

> Massive (Multiple Agent Simulation System in Virtual Environment), a 3-D animation system developed ... to provide the trilogy with large-scale battles involving hundreds of thousands of digitally-animated characters, each of which moves and interacts in relation to the characters around them.
>
> (Butler 2009: 81–82)

According to Kristen Moana Thompson, such a visual sense of awe might be seen as appropriate in a project which took 'eight years to plan and shoot, with twenty-eight leads, 100 speaking parts, a cast and crew which totaled 2500, and thousands of additional extras' (Thompson 2006: 284). Walters, in his own discussion of Jackson's first of the three films, The *Fellowship of the Ring*, places particular emphasis on the manner in which extremities of scale are enabled by this new interface between real landscape shots of the topography of New Zealand and its enhancement through special effects. Set against the vast backdrop of Saruman's lair, its 'colossal struts and stairways, huge heavy machinery, the glow of furnaces and endless numbers of workers dedicated to the operation of this industrial monstrosity', into the foreground flies a tiny moth (Walters 2011: 127). Suddenly, in what Walters describes as the 'virtuos[ity] ... of the camera's unbridled movement', the helicopter-borne camera traces out its agile flight, sweeping above the landscape (Walters 2011: 126). Accompanying everything is a 'single soprano voice', rising clearly above the machinery's industrial din, reinforcing the significance of the small individual and one hobbit's courage in this epic fantasy quest (Walters 2011: 127).

FANTASY TELEVISION AND THE HAND-HELD SCREEN

Walters identifies, in twenty-first-century cinema,

> a marked recent resurgence in fantasy film, ranging from large-scale (and large-budget) Hollywood franchises such as the *Harry Potter* ... *Chronicles of Narnia* ... and *His Dark Materials* ... series, to international and independent titles such as *Pan's Labyrinth* (Guillermo del Toro, 2006) and *The Imaginarium of Doctor Parnassus* (Terry Gilliam, 2009).
>
> (Walters 2011: 31)

Fantasy is certainly a connecting factor here, but so is medievalism, more specifically neo-medievalism, which Amy Kaufman defines as 'not a dream of the Middle Ages, but a dream of someone else's medievalism. It is medievalism doubled up upon itself' (Kaufman 2010: 4). In television fantasy drama, too, there has been a fascination with the neo-medievalist genre, from the Tiger Aspect/BBC production of *Robin Hood* (2006–2009), to the Shine/BBC Wales production of *Merlin* (2008–2012), to the Home Box Office (HBO) production *Game of Thrones* (2011–2019), itself an adaptation of five in a planned seven-volume epic fantasy series, *A Song of Ice and Fire,* written by George R.R. Martin (1991–present).

When Mervyn Peake's *Gormenghast* was televised in 2000, its producer Estelle Daniel observes that

> There was no question of making *Gormenghast* before the turn of the century as it struck us all as being the perfect story for then. An ancient world threatened with change, a fading aristocracy, a reluctant prince coming of age versus a villain who seems to embody the history of the century.
>
> (Daniel 2000: 19)

There *is* something about the turn of a new century that seems to encourage us to reflect on what has gone, as much as what is to come. It is a type of nostalgia for something that, in truth, we have never known, a perception that some kind of old order has passed and cannot be retrieved. It is, in that sense, a perfect impetus for fantasy. In season 2 of *Game of Thrones,* the young boy Bran discusses with Maester Luwen, his mentor, the content of his dreams. As the scene opens, the camera takes us from outside to inside in a series of stages, first through an external archway into an inner courtyard, where we are greeted by the servant, Hodor; then Maester Luwen arrives and the camera, now adopting Maester Luwen's point of view, takes us inside, as we follow Hodor's heavy tread up the stairs and into Bran's chamber, finding the boy in bed. Now point of view switches to Bran, and through his eyes we see a wolf on his chest, staring into his eyes as Bran stares back. That cinematographic shift from outside to inside is psychological as much as physical and takes the viewer to that most intimate of places, not the bedchamber but the meeting of minds: except that now we are shut out of that intimacy. There is a moment of mutual regard between the boy and the wolf (and temporarily the camera places the viewer in the position of the wolf as the boy stares directly into camera), but we have no understanding at all of what passes between them. That lack of insight is an essential preparation for what follows, as Bran start to tells Maester Luwen the content of his dreams, in an exchange that obviously reaches for a similar degree of empathy from his mentor to that which he enjoys with the wolf: 'Every night it's the same; I'm walking, I'm running, but I'm not, I'm not me … I'm sniffing the dirt, tasting blood in my mouth when I've made a fresh kill …' What Bran will later learn is that he is a warg, somebody who can enter the consciousness of a dog or wolf and already he suspects this to be the case. Maester Luwen refuses to engage with that instinct, however, insisting 'These are dreams, Bran, nothing more', before moving to a larger-scale dismissal: 'Maybe magic once was a mighty force in the world, but not anymore.' Bran's neutral response suggests that he is not convinced and neither are we. In miniature, what we are given in this scene is a 'taste', to use Bran's word, of what appeals to us about fantasy: we have a sense of having lost something we cannot quite grasp, but we know for sure that realism cannot provide it.

Despite that wistful glance back at the past, there is nothing romanticized about *Game of Thrones*: it is set in a harsh, bleak landscape and the lighting on set emphasizes a murky gloom. On a superficial level, Andrew B.R. Elliott summarizes the appeal of the series as one typical of 'the era of cable television', namely in which 'the Middle Ages are often characterized by a seemingly formulaic obsession with sex, violence, power, and dirtiness' (Elliott 2015: 97). That aspect is undoubtedly present, but there is a less obvious, more psychological appeal inherent in the series: the medieval content presents itself as a refuge, no matter how stark and taxing its elemental conditions, from our advanced digital/consumer age. When Walters focuses upon the juxtaposition, in Jackson's *The Lord of the Rings*, between a sublime topographical backdrop upon which is superimposed the tininess of an insect that can simultaneously soar to great heights and dive to the lowest valley floors, we recognize just how much perspective is lost, once we reduce everything to the size of a hand-held digital screen.

That hand-held culture certainly predominates in children's digital toys such as *Tamagotchi* and *Pokémon*, the latter being originally manufactured for a Game Boy interface. As Anne Allison observes, it is the portability of these toys and the fantasy worlds children construct around them that enables them to 'find meaning, connection and intimacy in everyday life [through] commodified apparatuses (goods/machines)' (Allison 2006: 13), even to the detriment of real human friendships. Yet, as in *Game of Thrones*, both *Pokémon* and *Tamagotchi* capture humanity's curiosity and the perceived necessity of being able to establish a relationship with fantasy species; in this case utilizing the concept of monstrosity, Pokémon itself being an abbreviation of 'pocket monsters'. Simultaneously monstrous and 'cute', in the case of the *Tamagotchi*, its very appearance embodies the concept of impossibility: 'a masked head perched on stick legs, a big-lipped octopus sporting a beret wired with a periscope' (Allison 2006: 22). It is here, perhaps, that the specifically postmodern element of contemporary digital toy culture comes to the fore. Where Disney's 'pet-like' characters such as Mickey and Minnie Mouse, Goofy and Pluto look remarkably *unlike* real mice or dogs, we nevertheless recognize those animal species to be the originals from which these stylized animations are seen to derive. To evoke Jean Baudrillard's concept of the simulacrum, the *Tamagotchi* constitutes 'the generation by models of a real without origin or reality' (Baudrillard 1983: 2), for rather like the moth superimposed upon Jackson's sublime backdrop, its embedded creature only appears virtually and in miniature as a fuzzy digital image at the centre of a very small computer screen, surrounded by a solid shell of gaudily coloured plastic.

In the sense of being a replica without an original, *Game of Thrones* does not really convince us that life during the medieval period was 'like that'. What it does emphasize, in absolute opposition to Japanese toy culture, is the importance of reconnecting physically with the elements, animals and the environment if we are to survive as a species. The brutality of the setting in *Game of Thrones* perhaps encapsulates the true scale of the struggle ahead, but however difficult, it remains a struggle we must face. In the first episode of season 1, Bran loses the use of his legs when, in a scene not unlike Steerpike's ascent of Gormenghast Castle (of which more in Chapter 4), he demonstrates his innate talents as a superb climber by scaling the vertical stone wall of a tower and looking into the window of a bedchamber, spying Cersei and Jaime, a sister and brother, engaged in incestuous sexual intercourse. Finding them exposed, Jaime pushes Bran violently to the ground, presuming him dead. Though Bran survives, he loses the use of both legs; later, as so often in epic quest narratives, however, that loss provides the impetus for his new role within the community. In season 4, re-opening the conversation he had with Maester Luwen in season 2, Bran confides in another young boy, Jojen, telling him about his dreams. Here we find the meeting of minds lacking in Bran's earlier conversation with Maester Luwen and Jojen reveals that Bran's destiny requires him to seek out the Weirwood Tree. Both characters set off across the icy wastes, accompanied by others, Bran being pulled on a sled by Hodor. Suddenly, we see the tree illuminated by a roseate glow and, after a fearful battle with a group of zombie skeletons, which emerges out of a snowfield, and during which battle Jojen loses his life, Hodor carries Bran to the tree's heart. Here he discovers an old man entrapped in its trunk, whom Brandon recognizes as 'the three-eyed raven'. The man/raven reveals the epic scale of Bran's destiny when he notes that he has 'been watching you, all of you, all of your lives, with a thousand eyes and one' (echoing, of course, *The One Thousand and One Nights*). Then addressing Bran specifically, he explains that Jojen's death was foreseen: 'He died so you can have what you lost'. Thinking the raven means to restore his legs, Bran's hopes are raised and then qualified in an instant: 'You'll never walk again, but you will fly.' Flight, as we have seen, has been the key wish-fulfillment fantasy trope right across the ages, recurring in narratives about fairies, magic carpet rides, in Jones's ingenious stage mechanics, Fleming's magical car and even Méliès's moon rocket fired from a cannon. In *Game of Thrones*, the young Bran's destiny reverses his boyhood fall from the tower, endowing him with the title 'three eyed raven' and, along with it, a bird's eye view of what lies ahead for all. In Chapter 3, we develop that relationship between young characters, birds and fantasy animals more fully, examining the field of animal fantasy for children.

NOTE

1 The NATO bombing raids of Iraq took place in January and February 1991. In name, Agrabah closely resembles the Indian city of Agra, site of the Taj Mahal, further removing the Middle Eastern cultural connection from Disney's *Aladdin*.

3

ANIMAL FANTASY FOR CHILDREN

As Ann Swinfen observes, animal fantasy 'has one of the longest and strongest traditions' (Swinfen 1984: 12), and an especially close link exists between fantasy for children and animal characters. Even when children's fantasy deals primarily with human characters, scenes of animal fantasy intrude. Take, for example, William Thackeray's *The Rose and the Ring* (1855), published under the pseudonym M.A. Titmarsh, in which the Princess Rosalba is thrown into a dungeon. Thackeray describes it as:

> a most awful black hole, full of bats, rats, mice, toads, frogs, mosquitoes, bugs, fleas, serpents ... No light was let into it, otherwise the gaolers might have seen her and fallen in love ... as an owl that lived up in the roof of the tower did, and a cat you know, who can see in the dark, and having set its green eyes on Rosalba never would be got to go back to the turnkey's wife to whom it belonged. And the toads in the dungeon came and kissed her feet, and the vipers wound round her neck and arms, and never hurt her, so charming was this poor Princess in the midst of her misfortunes.
>
> (Titmarsh 1855: 81)

The animals here, though described in broadly naturalistic terms, relate to the princess in a manner wholly typical of animal fantasy. In that sense, this scene is worth comparing with Walt Disney's *Cinderella* (dir. Clyde Geronimi, Wilfred Jackson and Hamilton Luske, 1950), which is superficially a human romance tale, but one wholly reliant on animal characters; for most of the film, Cinderella has no human friends at all. Continually ordered to sweep and clean the house and feed and clothe her sisters, it is the birds that she befriends who make her bed and the mice who sing the lament, 'Every time she finds a minute, that's when they begin it [issuing instructions] …' When Cinderella retrieves her dead mother's evening dress, hoping to wear it to the ball, those same mice embellish it with discarded sashes, lace and unwanted beads, albeit that the sisters later tear it to shreds, accusing Cinderella of stealing their unwanted trimmings.

As we saw in Chapter 2, the ideology of Disney films is not always as progressive as it might be and, in *Cinderella*, we may wish to reflect on the suggestion, not only that a young woman can never trust her 'sisters', but that no young woman needs any female friends at all, provided she has her prince. Western patriarchal capitalism would have it that *Cinderella*, above all other narratives, is the epitome of every young girl's wish-fulfilment fantasy. She is as much a cherished trophy as any glass slipper and no ambition beyond the securing of a handsome man is required. Moreover, any Western 'real-life' rags-to-riches story would probably substitute these singing mice and happily tweeting birds with human maids who are poorer, less fortunate, perhaps less physically attractive than Cinderella and/or of non-Western ethnicity. Disney's use of magical animals makes it far more difficult for any child reader to worry about such political imbalances, thus perpetuating the legacy of patriarchal capitalist romance and its duplicitous promises.

MICKEY MOUSE

No animated animal character has ever attained greater universal appeal than Disney's Mickey Mouse. Although not Disney's first animated animal character (Les Daniels reminds us that this was

Oswald the Rabbit, which appeared in an animated film in 1927), he has and continues to be Disney's flagship character; or, as Daniels puts it, 'the first "star" in the movies who needed no salary' (Daniels 1971: 51). In 1928, Mickey Mouse appeared in the 'sound cartoon' *Steamboat Willie* (dir. Walt Disney and Ub Iwerks) as a crew member of a boat captained by a large, ferocious cat who physically abuses him in a slapstick animation which establishes a clear hierarchy of animals, those judged inferior being subjected to violent abuse by their 'betters'. Deploying the mode of caricatured animation himself, Mickey, aided by a female prototype for the later Minnie, utilizes a goat as a barrel-organ, jamming open its mouth as a kind of gramophone speaker, while the 'Minnie prototype' turns its tail to play a tune. Similar fates befall a cow, whose teeth are played by Mickey hitting them with xylophone sticks, and a sow, whose suckling piglets are squeezed in turn by Mickey to produce different notes. The following year, in *The Karnival Kid* (dir. Walt Disney and Ub Iwerks, 1929), set in a fairground, Minnie makes her first appearance as 'Minnie the Shimmy Dancer' and the film follows Mickey's attempts to court her attentions. In both these early cartoons, much of the comedy derives from fantasy manipulations of the various animals' bodies, and we do laugh, despite our reservations. In *The Karnival Kid*, the large ferocious cat reappears as the impresario of Minnie's act and rival to Mickey, who is now a hot dog seller. In a heated exchange, the large cat pulls Mickey's nose so hard it droops to the floor like a loop of elastic. After a momentary outburst of weeping, Mickey realizes that if he pulls his own tail, his nose will return to its usual size. In both *Steamboat Willie* and *The Karnival Kid*, music motivates what little plot there is and is put to maximum comic effect, although in *The Karnival Kid* the animals are now musicians, no longer instruments to be 'played'. The hot dog sausages take the place of what were animated animals in *Steamboat Willie*, undergoing an ongoing variety of metamorphoses. It is here that our twenty-first-century anxieties about child protection undermine the comedy. When Minnie chooses her hot dog, the sausage jumps out of its bun and becomes a naughty, frightened child. As Mickey pulls down its 'trousers' (sausage skin) and spanks it into contrition, today's audience feels too uncomfortable to laugh.

However, by the time we encounter Mickey Mouse in an enclosed sequence in *Fantasia*, titled 'The Sorcerer's Apprentice' (dir. James Algar, 1940), the power relations have been reversed. Here he appears Cinderella-style, struggling along with two buckets of water, set to the accompaniment of Paul Dukas's orchestral composition of 'The Sorcerer's Apprentice' (1897). When the Sorcerer goes to bed, Mickey dons the wizard's hat and starts to conjure the broom to do his work. An embedded dream sequence follows, Mickey believing himself able to tame the elements, harnessing a spectacular light show from a night sky of shooting stars, which tip into the sea to form sweeping tidal waves. Unbeknownst to Mickey, however, these tidal waves have been created by the broomstick's ongoing activity, such that Mickey awakes surrounded by a flood. Turning to the slapstick vengeance that saved him in earlier films, Mickey chops up the broomstick, but now the broom and the flood water multiply many-fold. Only as the sorcerer returns is the flood abated, Mickey learning that it takes more than a magician's hat to quell the elements and, as he leaves, the sorcerer beats him along with the broom, in an interesting reversal of Mickey's former punishment of the sausage in *The Karnival Kid*.

Magic and music combine in *Fantasia*, in a set of sequences that are sometimes lightly comic, as in the movement depicting animated ostrich, hippopotamus and elephant ballerinas dancing to Amilcare Ponchielli's 'Dance of the Hours' from his opera *La Gioconda* (1876), and sometimes darkly gothic. 'The Sorcerer's Apprentice', set halfway through, carefully adopts the tone of potentially dark, but ultimately safe elemental chaos, in which an adult character returns to restore order, even if through harsh discipline. Between 2006 and 2016, that intermingling of magic, music and fantasy returned in a much tamer television series for small children, the *Mickey Mouse Clubhouse*. In this series, Mickey's clubhouse is built on a shared belief in magic and viewer participation is encouraged as the magic words 'Meeska Mooska Mickey Mouse' recur like a mantra, bringing into being the Clubhouse itself. All the usual animal characters appear: Mickey and Minnie, Donald and Daisy Duck, Goofy and Pluto, along with supporting characters such as Pete, who appears in a variety of guises, and Willy the Giant. These cartoons combine entertainment and education, utilizing fantasy as the 'glue'. In 'Donald of the Desert' (2013), Mickey Mouse and friends want to build sandcastles, but finding their sandpit empty, they travel to the desert. There Donald digs up a table lamp, which Goofy immediately and correctly identifies as a magic lamp capable of summoning a Genie. In this episode Pete is the Genie and, having granted Donald a wish and cautioned him to reserve it for something special, he then conjures up a magic blanket/carpet to take them home. Unfortunately the sand refuses to let Pete leave, so Donald uses his wish to free him and all fly back together. The lesson here is moral in kind: putting one's friends' needs before one's own will make for better fun.

'Quest for the Crystal Mickey' (2013) is a *Mickey Mouse Clubhouse* cartoon story loosely inspired by the fantasy adventure film *Indiana Jones and the Crystal Skull* (dir. Steven Spielberg, 2008). Mickey dresses up as Indiana Jones and he and his friends set off in search of the 'Crystal Mickey', a glass ornament in the form of Mickey's iconic head, stolen by Pete (here called Plunderin' Pete). Its theft removes the magic from the Clubhouse and, consequently, the house starts to disappear: only a fantasy adventure can save it. *En route*, various traps are laid, overcome by magic 'Mouseketools' and Pete is confronted in an ancient temple in a remote forest, only accessible using an amphibious vehicle. So much is resonant of the original Indiana Jones adventure; rather less so is Pete's relative willingness to agree that friendship is more important than greed. Once Pete learns that his act poses a threat to Mickey's clubhouse, he quickly returns his ill-gotten gains. Thus do we see, over the course of almost one hundred years of Mickey's cartoon existence, how his character mellows and matures incrementally, from a carnivalesque 'Kid' whose comedy relies on the exploitation of other animals, to a hapless apprentice tyrannized by a terrifying adult, to a reassuring, well-behaved, lovable cartoon friend to little children. So might we argue that Disney's Mickey Mouse features as the twentieth century's equivalent to Victorian fairies, which mutated from naughty, spiteful, secretive figures of rural folklore into charmingly safe nursery companions.

That animated animal characters hold a particular attraction for child readers and viewers of film and television fantasy is clear and they are endowed persistently with human characteristics to aid in the identification process. Especially attractive to young children are baby animals, as the simple one-word titling of the films *Dumbo* (dir. Samuel Armstrong et al., 1941) and *Bambi* (dir. James Algar et al., 1942), or the television series *Pingu* (1986–2006) demonstrates. The explanation for that popularity may derive from the ease with which alliances are formed between the animals that undermine or challenge adult authority. Almost without exception, Disney animals are more intelligent than the adult characters, outwitting them at every turn. Perhaps, for example, it is more manageable for a child reader/viewer of Disney's *The Lion King* (dir. Rob Minkoff and Roger Allers, 1994) to realize that Scar, a lion, wishes harm to Simba, his nephew, than it would be to watch an adult man wishing equal harm to a small boy. Contrastingly, the most villainous of all Disney characters are those humans who wish harm to baby animals. The stepmother in Disney's *Snow White and the Seven Dwarfs* (dir. William Cottrill et al., 1937) may be terrifying, but Cruella De Vil in *One Hundred and One Dalmations* (dir. Clyde Geronimi et al., 1961) is surely, as her very name suggests, the most (d)evil creation of all.

FANTASY ANIMALS AS MORAL INSTRUCTORS

In their identification with fantasy animals, children are clearly working through their fears in relation to adult humans, whether those be separation anxieties caused by their mothers leaving them at the school gate or dying early (*Dumbo* and *Bambi*), or the terror of getting to know a new primary school teacher (Ursula, the mythical hybrid of squid and octopus, found in Disney's *The Little Mermaid*, dir. Ron Clements and John Musker, 1989). These childhood landmark moments stay with us for life and fantasy narratives, which often render events *larger* than life, help the child to anchor her/himself within the seemingly less extreme real world. Nevertheless, it is important to remind ourselves that not all animal-centred narratives for children are told through fantasy. In Anna Sewell's *Black Beauty* (1877), despite it being narrated 'from the horse's mouth', the focus is otherwise realist. That realism enables two different lessons to be communicated directly to its child reader. Firstly, we become much more fully aware of a repetitive cycle of exploitation and abuse inflicted on horses by human characters of all classes. Secondly, the narrative operates as a direct means of instruction, whereby Beauty provides a mouthpiece for social indoctrination. Thus, as a young colt, finding the other young horses rough, Beauty is told by his mother that 'they are cart-horse colts, and, of course, they have not learned manners. You have been well bred and well born …' (Sewell n.d.: 12). Although many children continue to love horses, we need to remember that historical shifts may have made it easier to write a nineteenth-century realist novel using a talking-horse narrator than it would be today. In 1877, the horse-drawn carriage was still an everyday form of transport, rendering the relationship between horses and humanity common. Since the mass-production of the motor vehicle (see below), horses have become both more distant from that everyday world and more closely associated with dreams of wish-fulfilment, hence fantasy. It is interesting that, when Michael Morpugo wrote *War Horse* in 1982, he set it in a period in which horses were commonly used, both to work farmland and fight on the front line. Today, neither pertains, which means that when *War Horse* was adapted for the stage by Nick Stafford in 2007, the horse was more appropriately animated through technologically-advanced puppetry, making it less a direct descendent of *Black Beauty* and more of Inigo Jones who, as we saw in Chapter 2, 'employ[ed] complex machinery, elaborate lighting effects, and illusionistic settings' for the production of spectacle rather than verisimilitude (Harris et al. 1973: 35).

In C.S. Lewis's *The Lion, the Witch and the Wardrobe* (1950), animals are certainly creatures of fantasy, but they never lose their realist attributes. Lewis's depiction of Aslan the lion is most applicable here. Although, in allegorical terms, Aslan is a symbolic embodiment of Jesus Christ, Lewis never allows that metaphorical function to detract from his existence as King of the Beasts. In the following passage, depicting Lucy and Susan riding on Aslan's back, Lewis, in his guise of narrator, enquires of the reader:

> Have you ever had a gallop on a horse? Think of that; and then take away the heavy noise of the hoofs and the jingle of the bits and imagine instead the almost noiseless padding of the great paws. Then imagine ... the soft roughness of golden fur, and the mane flying back in the wind. And then imagine you are going about twice as fast as the fastest racehorse. But this is a mount that doesn't need to be guided and never grows tired.
>
> (Lewis 1972: 149–150)

Several lengths are undertaken, here, to engage the child reader with the verisimilitude of the passage, reinforced by the dialogic phrasing ('Have you ever …?'; 'Think of that …'; 'And then imagine …'). Aslan metamorphoses, during the passage, from tamed horse to wild creature, shedding a bit and bridle and galloping 'about twice as fast as the fastest racehorse'. According to the *Guinness World Records* website, the fastest speed ever recorded for a racehorse was 70.76 kilometres per hour (43.97 mph) over two furlongs (Guinness World of Records 2016), so our imagination would need to place Aslan's speed in excess of 80 miles per hour, twenty miles per hour faster than a cheetah. At the same time, that Aslan is being ridden at all, albeit at his own invitation, renders him far more docile than any real lion. Here, fantasy combines wish-fulfilment with the thrill of danger as Aslan's oxymoronic depiction reveals him simultaneously as tamed and untamed, mode of transport and lion, messiah and beast, saviour and pet.

The question of proximity between humans and animals threatens to upturn the frequently presumed hierarchy of human superiority over animals. James Frazer tells us:

> The Greeks thought that a garment made from the fleece of a sheep that has been torn by a wolf would hurt the wearer, setting up an itch or irritation in his skin ... [and] if a stone that had been bitten by a dog were dropped in wine, it would make all who drank of that wine fall out among themselves.
>
> (Frazer 1978: 41)

One can see how easily such superstitions develop into cautionary tales such as those in Aesop's *Fables*, also originating during the ancient Greek period. One such is 'Androcles and the Lion', in which an escaping slave, Androcles, encounters a wounded lion in the forest. He removes a thorn from the lion's paw and, in return, the lion gives him sanctuary in his lair: hence slave and lion become united against the established human hierarchy. Later recaptured, Androcles's punishment is to be thrown to the lion for public spectacle, but the lion recognizes him and refuses to attack. When the Emperor hears Androcles's story, he frees him from slavery and the lion from captivity. Androcles and the lion therefore retain their equal standing and shared fate throughout, although one should note that neither offers any genuine challenge to the existing political order; the Emperor retains his seat of judgement over both.

ANIMAL TRICKSTERS

From the Medieval period onwards, however, more complex roles become attributed to animal characters, enabling a more subject-led rather than object-led portrayal to develop. In the popular culture of nineteenth-century America, for instance, characters such as Brer Rabbit and Brer Bear, both of whom appear in Joel Chandler Harris's *Uncle Remus* tales (1880), develop as part of a long tradition of trickster narratives, first derived from African oral folklore, and thought to have travelled to North America along with the slave trade, although stories such as 'Mr Rabbit Finds his Match at Last' also have roots in Aesop's 'The Hare and the Tortoise'. Irrespective of its precise origins, 'Mr Rabbit Finds his Match at Last' re-emerges in twentieth-century popular culture in the form of the comic book, film and television cartoon figure Bugs Bunny (1939–). Principal character of the Warner Brothers' 'Loony Tunes' cartoon series, Bugs's 'spirited defences of his home and his person, conducted with a wise-cracking air of confidence, have been cited for making a contribution to boosting morale during the troubled days of the Second World War', at least according to Les Daniels (1971: 52).

In 'Tortoise Beats Hare' (1941) Bugs is outwitted by Cecil Turtle, who telephones all his apparently identical relatives, persuading them to arrive at various points of the race's course and baffle the swifter Bugs. Where Aesop's tale is both cautionary and moral, supporting the maxim 'slow and steady wins the race', the Bugs Bunny version is much craftier. Cecil cheats to win, but is applauded for outwitting Bugs, 'fair play' effectively being scorned. Certainly, the trickster figure is rarely an admirable character, but its comedic value contributes directly to its morale-boosting, carnivalesque effect. Thus, when Harold Scheub informs us that 'the hero and the trickster are the most durable of storytelling figures, ancient, unchanging, adapting to contemporary realities but ever the same' (Scheub 2012: 11), we realize that the trickster *is* a hero of sorts: usually winning against the odds and against the establishment, even if doing so through underhand means.

Chandler Harris's *Uncle Remus* stories, though influential, are ideologically problematic. The eponymous frame narrator is an old Black slave, telling stories to a plantation owner's young white son. Certainly the boy is enthralled and declared to be 'in thorough sympathy with all the whims and humors of the old man', repeatedly returning for more, lured in as Uncle Remus starts to recount his stories aloud to himself (Chandler Harris 2015: 111); nevertheless, we recall the political limitations of Androcles's empathy with the lion. Both may cleave together, but neither effectively undermines the social hierarchy. Further political consequences emerge from the white author's decision to write Uncle Remus's storytelling voice in Black slave dialect and the deeply problematic story 'Why the Negro is Black' makes for wholly unacceptable reading. The embedded animal tales themselves, however, retain their importance for a variety of cultures and, because Uncle Remus continually establishes a set of progressive duels or contests between different animal species, thus making the storytelling outcome less predictable, he offers a kind of narrative equivalent of the game 'Stone, Paper, Scissors', which keeps adding to the reader's interest as we try to predict, in each case, who the victor will be. As in several of the aforementioned animal narratives, Chandler Harris offers up two hierarchical layers of animal characters: his principal animal subjects carry the prefix 'Brer' ('Brother'), but accompanying them in some stories are 'lesser' animals, usually described simply by species type: crayfish, frogs, tadpoles. While Brer Rabbit is, arguably, the primary character, both in terms of frequency and victory, the animals' main influence is collective: together they offer up a kind of metamorphic chain reaction, the trickster taking on first one form and then another. That shape-shifting aspect of the traditional trickster positions it well to adapt to different cultures and animal types and helps explain its ongoing appeal for children down the ages. On the one hand, as Scheub informs us, 'the trickster is almost always physically inferior to the dupe: he is a diminutive human, perhaps, or a hare, spider, tortoise'. On the other, the trickster 'moves into the world like a child newly born, trying out his considerable powers on everyone and every-thing he meets' (Scheub 2012: 24, 12).

The point about greater size not necessarily equating to dominance is particularly interesting in 'The End of Mr Bear'. This story has a clear moral code: boasting like 'swell-head folks' will cause one's downfall (Chandler Harris 2015: 111). Brer Rabbit and Brer Bear are already on bad terms by the start of this story, owing to a previous encounter in another tale. Now Brer Rabbit convinces Brer Bear he has found a 'bee-tree' dripping with honey. Enticed by the prospect, Brer Bear climbs the tree while Brer Rabbit promises him that he (Rabbit) will poke it with a stick to help loosen the honey. Of course, what Brer Rabbit has really spotted in the tree is a bees' nest, into which Brer Bear promptly forces his head, while Brer Rabbit hits the nest with his stick, deliberately aggravating the bees to sting Brer Bear's face. Depending on how one reads the last few lines of the story, the end result is bleak indeed. Brer Bear's head swells up larger than a 'dinner-pot', so that not only is he unable to remove it from the nest of stinging bees, but he is left hanging by the neck while Brer Rabbit celebrates below.

FANTASY BEARS

Chandler Harris's 'The End of Mr Bear' echoes far more tamely in A.A. Milne's first Winnie-the-Pooh story, 'Winnie-the-Pooh and Some Bees' (1926). Similarly attracted to a tree containing a bees' nest in the aim of obtaining honey, Pooh (unlike Brer Bear) finds his tree-climbing skills inadequate to the task, a deficiency that proves advantageous by comparison. Pooh's unsuccessfully outlandish attempt to trick the bees out of their honey involves floating into the tree attached to a balloon, attempting disguise as 'a small black cloud'. Succeeding only in being stung on the nose, Pooh asks Christopher Robin to shoot the balloon with his pop-gun, enabling him to descend. Where Brer Bear is hanged by the neck, Pooh suffers the rather gentler fate of 'his arms [being] so stiff from holding on to the string of the balloon all that time that they stayed up straight in the air for more than a week' (Milne 2002: 19, 23). Milne's stories attract a rather gentler child than Chandler Harris's, it seems.

Favourite among the many fantasy animals appealing to children, surely, is the bear. Russell Ash reminds us that the storytelling origins of fantasy bears probably lie with 'Bruin in twelfth-century fables', continuing through 'Goldilocks and the Three Bears' and the Uncle Remus tales, before flourishing in the twentieth century with 'Mary Plain, Rupert, Winnie-the-Pooh, Teddy Robinson, SuperTed, Sooty and Yogi Bear' (Ash 1988: 31). In part, the popularity of all these twentieth-century bear characters derives from the core importance of teddy bear toys for children. As is well known, the teddy bear was invented in 1902, in honour of President Theodore (Teddy) Roosevelt of the United States of America. Embarrassed at the president having been unsuccessful as guest of honour on a Mississippi hunting trip, other members of the party 'cornered and tied a black bear to a willow tree', inviting the president to shoot it. Deeming the act unsporting, Roosevelt refused, at which point the story circulated in the media. A toy-maker decided to make a cuddly toy out of 'Teddy's bear' and the name entered popular culture (National Park Service 2018).

Despite Winnie-the-Pooh being the subject rather than the object of Milne's stories, he is most certainly a toy teddy bear, hence his initial introduction: 'Here is Edward Bear, coming downstairs now, bump, bump, bump, on the back of his head, behind Christopher Robin', illustrated by E.H. Shepard's drawing, the teddy bear's right hand gripped firmly in the boy's left, while he drags it backwards along behind him (Milne 2002: 9). In fact, the fantasy aspect of Milne's creation relies on the child reader's awareness that Pooh, Eeyore, Piglet and Roo are really toys who come to life only in Christopher Robin's imagination, sometimes encouraged by the presence of a first-person narrator, intermittently voiced in the frame of the story as an adult storyteller:

> ('What does "under the name" mean?' asked Christopher Robin.
> 'It means he had the name over the door in gold letters and lived under it.'
> 'Winnie-the-Pooh wasn't quite sure,' said Christopher Robin.
> 'Now I am,' said a growly voice.
> 'Then I will go on,' said I.)
>
> (Milne 2002: 11)

That toy bear status differentiates Winnie-the-Pooh from the later Paddington. Michael Bond, Paddington's creator, originally intended him as a fantasy bear, not a fantasy *toy* bear, a distinction that Ash argues required the correction of an early error in Paddington's origin story. According to Ash, when Bond first submitted *A Bear Called Paddington* for publication, Paddington was said to hail from 'Darkest Africa' (Ash 1988: 16). While the editor liked the manuscript, he added:

> there are no bears in Africa, darkest or otherwise. The race of bears in the Atlas mountains has been extinct for centuries. Children either know this or should know this and I suggest that you make suitable amends, for which purpose I am returning herewith the script. There are plenty of bears in Asia, Europe and America, and quite a few on the stock exchange.
>
> (Ash 1988: 18)

Paddington's existence as a fantasy character, then, emanates from an important foundation of zoological authenticity. Accordingly, while the fantasy element derives partly from Paddington's existence as a talking animal, summarily it emanates from a more general anthropomorphism: his role within the human Brown family. Ash asks the inevitable question deriving from the commingling of animal and human features: 'Which is he … child or adult, animal or human? Is he a family pet, the youngest member of the family, the troublesome younger brother?' (Ash 1988: 49) Despite Bond's early fastidiousness in relation to species authenticity, Paddington's development over the decades has resulted in an increasing level of ambivalence in relation to his relationship with the human world. When the merchandising licenser, Paddington and Company, wanted to take steps to quell applications for 'inappropriate' products, they produced a dossier for Paddington, containing a range of characteristics 'not in line with his image', which included an embargo on him 'associat[ing] with other woodland creatures' (Ash 1988: 92). In fact, Paddington only converses with humans and, when other animals are included, it is as household pets – a relationship which secures Paddington's difference from them.

Swinfen begins her discussion of animal fantasy by noting that 'the desire to enter the skin of the animal and assume his very nature and individuality' is precisely what drives our interest in animal characters (Swinfen 1984: 14). Even animal research scientists struggle with questions of anthropomorphism. Randall Lockwood, an animal psychologist, reflects on his changing view of this connection across his career: 'When I first entered the world of … animal behaviour almost twenty years ago, I was given the distinct impression that it was time to put away my teddy bears and memories of Disney films and acquire the cold, hard, "objective" eye of the scientist' (Lockwood 1985: 185). In the intervening period, he acknowledges, the situation has shifted and new fields have emerged directly from anthropomorphic methodologies, such as 'The growing appreciation of the mental abilities of domestic animals, and the nature of their emotional bonds to humans and each other' (Lockwood 1985: 196–197).

HEDGEROW FANTASY

A careful combination of meticulous scientific detail and narrative 'flight of fancy' typifies Beatrix Potter's animal characters.[1] Though Peter Rabbit was the first and best-known of Potter's creations, 'The Tale of Mrs Tiggy-Winkle' (1905) is especially interesting for our purposes. A hedgehog laundress, Potter's illustrations of her perfectly combine the anatomy of the hedgehog, complete with prickles emerging from her cap and clothes, with humanoid characteristics. Narratively, too, while 'Her little black nose went sniffle, sniffle, snuffle' (Potter 2002: 90), her occupation enables Potter's child readers, both of the early twentieth century and now, to learn a great deal about traditional laundry duties. Thus, Mrs Tiggy-winkle proudly asserts 'I'm an excellent clear-starcher', while utilizing equipment such as an 'ironing blanket' and 'a clothes-horse', not to mention 'fetch[ing] another hot iron from the fire' in those days before electric irons. So archaic are some of Mrs Tiggy-winkle's skills that when she 'goffer[s]' the clothes (Potter 2002: 91–93), the author of this book had to consult the *Collins English Dictionary* to learn that to 'goffer' is 'to press pleats into (a frill)'.

What I am calling 'hedgerow fantasy' focuses upon animals in a wild habitat unspoiled by human intervention. In that respect, although Mrs Tiggy-winkle's laundry duties position her as remarkably anthropomorphized on one level, she relates to humans as equals, not as a threat to be avoided. That equality of engagement may derive partly from the fact that, according to the anonymous editor of 'the original and authorized edition' of *Beatrix Potter: The Complete Tales*, Mrs Tiggy-winkle's character 'was inspired by Kitty McDonald, an old Scottish washerwoman', whom Potter herself described as 'a comical, round little old woman, as brown as a berry and wear[ing] a multitude of petticoats' (Potter 2002: 86). Furthermore, the frame protagonist of Mrs Tiggy-winkle's tale is a young girl called Lucie, based on a real life friend of Potter's, 'Lucie Carr, daughter of the Vicar of Newlands'. Lucie has lost 'Three handkins and a pinny!' and meets Mrs Tiggy-winkle when she sets out to find them; in fact, it is Lucie's handkins Mrs Tiggy-winkle is goffering (Potter 2002: 86–87). Similarities in structure exist between 'The Tale of Mrs Tiggy-Winkle' and Lewis Carroll's *Alice in Wonderland*, both in the sense that they each require the girl protagonist to engage with a series of fantasy animal characters *en-route* to her destination and, because both are based on real-life child friends of the author. One key difference, however, is that where Alice's story is predominantly about her, once the reader encounters Mrs Tiggy-winkle, Lucie becomes easily forgettable by comparison.

Another important distinction between Potter's and Carroll's narratives lies in the differential motivations driving the two child protagonists' adventures, for these affect their respective relationships with animals. Where Alice's adventures are prompted by boredom, enabling her to disappear into a world of often intellectually challenging surrealism, Lucie's tale is prompted by loss, requiring her to defer to the animals she meets: 'Have *you* seen them, Tabby Kitten?'; 'Sally Henny-penny, have *you* found three pocket-handkins?' Importantly, Potter's animals maintain that superior distance: 'The kitten went on washing her white paws … [and] the speckled hen ran into a barn, clucking', even though Potter adds anthropomorphizing speech-rhythms to Sally Henny-penny's departure: 'I go barefoot, barefoot, barefoot!'. Footprints similarly lead the way to Mrs Tiggy-winkle, for so Lucie discovers 'a tin can upon a stone to catch the water – but the water was already running over, for the can was no bigger than an egg-cup! And where the sand upon the path was wet – there were footmarks of a *very* small person' (Potter 2002: 87, 89). The question of competing scales and dimensions is a crucial aspect of animal fantasy narratives for children, especially when comparing child and animal characters and, by inference, child and adult characters. To a hedgehog, an egg-cup would be of comparable size to a human sink to an adult and because small children often struggle to reach sinks because they are situated too high on a wall, one sees how the child reader's empathy with Mrs Tiggy-winkle is facilitated.

It is Mrs Tiggy-winkle's presence, or more particularly her voice, that prompts the shift into full anthropomorphism, for she is also a singing hedgehog: 'Lily-white and clean, oh!/ With little frills between, oh! … '. As Lucie gingerly enters her home, she has to retrospectively revise her earlier view of Sally Henny-penny and Tabby Kitten, for no longer *just* a hen and a kitten, both are now revealed as the owners of laundry items: 'a pair of stockings' and 'a pair of mittens' respectively (Potter 2002: 89, 91–94 *passim*). Intriguingly, Mrs Tiggy-winkle is also laundering items belonging to two characters not otherwise in this story, but title characters in their own tales, written in 1902 and 1903 respectively: Peter Rabbit and Squirrel Nutkin. This playful writerly conceit enables Potter to construct a wider community for her characters, adding in the process an environment of fictive verisimilitude to her fantasy creations. Her final claim for authoritative control over her characters returns her reader to questions of fantasy versus realism:

> Now some people say that little Lucie had been asleep upon the stile – but then how could she have found three clean pocket handkins and a pinny, pinned with a silver safety-pin?
> And besides – *I* have seen that door into the back of the hill called Cat Bells – and besides *I* am very well acquainted with dear Mrs. Tiggy-winkle!
>
> (Potter 2002: 100)

Kenneth Grahame's *The Wind in the Willows* (1908) opens with housework, too. This time Mole is spring-cleaning and, being a far more reluctant housekeeper than Mrs Tiggy-winkle, he expostulates 'Bother!' and 'O blow!' and 'Hang spring-cleaning!' before seizing his escape upwards onto the surface in a delightfully onomatopoeic manner: 'So he scraped and scratched and scrabbled and scrooged, and then he scrooged again and scrabbled and scratched and scraped' (Grahame 1983: 1). Fantasy and mimesis mingle and meld together in this combination, for onomatopoeia, particularly of this accumulating serial kind, aims to capture the reality of sound, while simultaneously inserting a degree of imaginative distance into it.

Where the class aspect of Potter's 'The Tale of Mrs Tiggy-Winkle' is intrinsic to it, yet implicit, Grahame's is unapologetically overtly stratified. Mole and Ratty, the creatures with whom we most easily identify, are middle-class; comfortable, sensible and respectable. The stoats and weasels are working-class ruffians, with 'evil wedge-shaped face[s]', who invade Toad Hall in Toad's absence, 'Eating [his] grub, and drinking [his] drink, and making bad jokes ... and singing vulgar songs'. Toad is upper-class, indolent, 'pleasure-bent' and self-centred. While living in Toad Hall, he can afford to indulge himself in a leisure trip in a horse-drawn gypsy caravan, but in a manner that demonstrates absolutely no empathy with genuine travelling communities (Grahame 1983: 126–127, 15). Transport itself, however, comes under much closer scrutiny, for Grahame has caught his animals at a very specific cultural moment. Trotting along on horseback,

> far behind [the three companions] they heard a faint warning hum, like the drone of a distant bee. Glancing back, they saw a small cloud of dust, with a dark centre of energy, advancing on them at incredible speed, while from out of the dust a faint 'Poop-poop!' wailed like an uneasy animal in pain ... [I]n an instant (as it seemed) the peaceful scene was changed, and with a blast of wind and a whirl of sound that made them jump for the nearest ditch, it was on them! The 'poop-poop' rang with a brazen shout in their ears ... and the magnificent motor-car, immense, breath-snatching, passionate, with its pilot tense and hugging his wheel, possessed all earth and air for the fraction of a second, flung an enveloping cloud of dust that blinded and enwrapped them utterly, and then dwindled to a speck in the far distance, changed back into a droning bee once more.
>
> (Grahame 1983: 19)

First note the use of animal metaphors in the passage. The first and last impressions created by the car are framed by the distinctive buzz of a bee. Thus, even to other animals, the bee is established as dangerous by comparison. Again, the sound of the horn 'wail[s] like an uneasy animal in pain', thereby differentiating between the unspecified animal alluded to here, the three named animals in the caravan, the nameless horse which draws it, and the bee which threatens it metaphorically. It would appear that not all animals inhabit the same relationship to fantasy in Grahame's text. Second, defamiliarization drives Grahame's choice of figures of speech here. The passage begins with synecdoche, as the 'small cloud of dust' stands in for the thing, at that point invisible, that is creating it. Onomatopoeia then intrudes, followed quickly by an elemental disturbance ('a blast of wind and a whirl of sound'), as if the very composition of the atmosphere is under threat, which, of course, it will be later in the century, with the urban pollution created by diesel and leaded petrol fumes. Finally, its driver is rendered ontologically distinct from the three animal protagonists. Though we know 'he' is male, we are not told if he is animal or human. In the process he becomes neither, reduced to a kind of cyborgian extension of his machine. Grahame's narrative was first published in 1908, when the motor-car was a comparatively rare phenomenon on country roads, mass produced motor cars not being developed until 1913.[2] Nevertheless, even for us, that defamiliarization continues to work *as* defamiliarization, perhaps because motor cars and their dangers, their speeds and their polluting properties, continue to have *real* consequences today.

There are also, of course, consequences for the protagonists themselves, as 'their' horse (literally a dumb beast) rears out of control and the caravan is smashed to pieces as it crashes into a ditch. While Rat and Mole bellow and gesticulate at the retreating motor vehicle, Toad sits entranced, longing to emulate their destroyer's antics and rebuffing Rat's suggestion that he should contact the police. The next they hear, Toad has ordered 'a large and very expensive motor-car'. Several reported crashes follow, but what is clear in the reportage is the role played by capital in the class structure of Grahame's narrative. In a conversation with Badger, Rat tells him: 'Toad's rich, we all know; but he's not a millionaire. And he's a hopelessly bad driver, and quite regardless of law and order. Killed or ruined – it's got to be one of the two things, sooner or later' (Grahame 1983: 22 and 37). Destruction is as much collateral as corporeal, here.

The hierarchy of animal characters in *The Wind in the Willows*, both class-based and (un)speaking reaches its pinnacle through Mr Toad for, as in 'The Tale of Mrs Tiggy-Winkle', he is able to engage with talking humans without receiving from them any sense of species inequality. The human Magistrate, in conjunction with his equally human Clerk of Court, may sentence Toad to twenty years' imprisonment for stealing a motor car, driving dangerously and 'gross impertinence to the rural police', but no allusion is made to his bestiality (Grahame 1983: 69). Similarly, a human engine-driver helps Toad to abscond from prison, while a human barge-woman employs Toad to do her washing for her. Here, the comparison with Potter's tale becomes especially interesting, since, while Toad is clearly no Mrs Tiggy-winkle, his ineptitude as a washerwoman is attributed to his class, not his species. Failing miserably and 'mutter[ing] under his breath words that should never pass the lips of either washerwomen or Toads,' the barge-woman responds with derision. Now Toad reveals his grotesque class-consciousness: 'You common, low, *fat* barge-woman … don't you dare talk to your betters like that! … I am a Toad, a very well-known respected, distinguished Toad!' (Grahame 1983: 112). In *The Wind in the Willows*, it is not the animal/human species division but one's class identification that determines one's place on the social hierarchy.

FARMYARD AND FIELD FANTASY

Farmyard and field fantasy is a coinage I am adopting for narratives in which humans form the dominant species, but whose presence, husbandry (in the agricultural sense) and management of the land poses a direct threat of death to the animal characters. Perhaps because the presence of death is made clear from the start of these narratives, there is a tendency for the author to move incrementally from initial realism into animal fantasy, humans belonging more 'properly' to realism. E.B. White's *Charlotte's Web* (1952) takes us on an especially gradual journey in this respect. Our original point of view character is Fern, an eight-year-old girl given permission to hand-rear the runt of a new pig litter, whom she names Wilbur. At this point in the narrative the closest we come to fantasy is pretend play, as Fern wheels Wilbur around in her toy pram. By chapter three, however, Wilbur has reached five weeks old and is sold to a neighbouring farm. Now Wilbur's interaction with other animals endows him simultaneously with narrative point of view and the accompanying ability to speak.

The educative aspect of *Charlotte's Web* is subtly but insistently drummed into its child reader: the attainment of language both unlocks the door to imaginative freedom and is intrinsic to the development of full subjectivity. According to Karen Coates, 'children tend to learn the personal pronouns in the order "mine", "me", and then "I", suggesting a grammatical progression from knowing what bounds them, to recognizing their object status, to finally assuming a subject position' (Coates 2004: 19). While I recall my own children going through these phases, and agree with the order in which Coates positions pronoun acquisition, I interpret at least the initial stage of that acquisition differently. Small children are especially preoccupied by property and its relationship to their own boundaries. 'Mine' is the triumphant or insistent exclamation of a child who clutches an object or person tightly to him/herself and, in the process, affirms his/her *subjectivity*, both as the owner of and as a person distinct from that object. To possess is, therefore, to have agency over one's immediate environment, a fact that differentiates the young child fundamentally from its former infant self. As D.W. Winnicott observes, 'There is no such thing as a baby – meaning that if you set out to describe a baby, you will find you are describing a baby and someone. A baby cannot exist alone, but is essentially part of a relationship' (Winnicott cited in Davis and Wallbridge 1990: 31). In a world in which the small child is controlled, placed, moved, dressed and fed, 'mine' is an essential assertion of self-control. However, that very young stage of childhood is also one at which the child remains self-obsessed and views others as presences to be tolerated or made to serve and entertain: s/he is and remains the central protagonist of his/her own drama. By the time that child has matured sufficiently to read *Charlotte's Web*, on the other hand, her boundaries should have become more 'porous', to use Coates's term (Coates 2004: 4), a fact that pertains to the more complex, progressive point of view structure White adopts.

Despite the novel bearing the title *Charlotte's Web*, we do not encounter Charlotte herself until chapter five. Furthermore, her initial depiction seems unpromising for reader identification, initially privileging realism over fantasy. As Wilbur watches her dive on, wrap up and stun a fly for her breakfast, his response is 'horror. He could hardly believe what he was seeing' (White 2003: 49). Only as the animal fantasy aspect of her character starts to come to the fore and White increasingly emphasizes Charlotte's ingenuity and loyalty as a friend, does the reader begin to recognize her potential as the narrative heroine of the book. Thereby the child reader is encouraged to be both open-minded and considered in his/her view of others: physical traits alone are not what counts. Where others, including Fern, show themselves unequal to the task of saving Wilbur's life, this tiny spider succeeds and she does so through literacy. Her weaving into her web of the simple phrase 'some pig' provides another educational lesson: the ability to read is not in itself enough, one must also learn to *think* about what we read. 'Some pig' is a simple, monosyllabic phrase, but when the farm hand reads it, he misinterprets it, unthinkingly taking the message at face value, reading it as proof of Wilbur's specialness. Only Mrs Zuckerman reads it insightfully: 'you're a little way off. It seems to me we have no ordinary *spider*' (White 2003: 106). Where *Charlotte's Web* differs from so many children's narratives, however, is that White confronts children with the uncomfortable realization that while untimely death might be avoided, natural death is inescapable: Charlotte can save Wilbur, but she cannot save herself. While Wilbur is at the height of his powers, winning a medal at the local fair, Charlotte lays her egg sac, announces she is dying and does so unnoticed: 'No one was with her when she died' (White 2003: 226). Indeed, just as we had to wait five chapters for her to appear, the novel continues for a final, lengthy chapter after her death. Though it seems strange that a book bearing the name of a character can begin and end without her, we see how this peripheral departure forms the next stage in the child reader's understanding of the self: we may be the essential component in our own life narrative, but we remain unnecessary to everybody else's.

Dick King-Smith's novel *The Sheep-Pig* (1983) covers very similar thematic terrain to *Charlotte's Web*, except for the narrative oddity that this pig also learns to herd sheep. Indeed, it would be considered entirely realist in form, were it not for the fact that all the farm-animals talk to each other. Its film adaptation *Babe* (dir. Chris Noonan, 1995), however, is much more obviously fantasy in category and, actually, a more satisfying work. The fantasy frame is established in the opening credits, which are animated and provide a kind of 'nursery-style' tone, with framed portraits on the wall and mechanical animal figures.

Music, which (as we saw in Chapter 2) plays a key role in the development of fantasy across the centuries, features centrally in this film too, and the opening sequence is accompanied by the sound of a musical box, supporting the nursery theme, playing what becomes the film's signature tune: Camille Saint-Saën's Symphony No. 3 in C minor, Op. 78 (1886), which he composed in the same year as his own animal fantasy suite, *The Carnival of the Animals*. While a movement from *The Carnival of the Animals* might have been a more obvious choice for this film, none of Saint-Saën's animal subjects are pigs, the only farmyard creatures represented being 'Cocks and Hens' (Movement III). What makes Symphony No. 3 in C minor a more multi-layered choice is that, in 1978, popular song lyrics were added by Jonathan Hodge and it was successfully released as a single under the title 'If I had Words'. For those familiar with classical music, the association with *The Carnival of the Animals* is maintained through the choice of Saint-Saën as composer, but for a much wider, film-going audience, many of whom will be familiar with the song, the words are playing through their minds even as the musical box strikes up its lonely tune, eventually being augmented by a full orchestral score. There are indeed 'no words' at the start, an irony functioning on two levels. First, one might presume the animals to have no words, although the film reveals otherwise. Second, Farmer Hoggett is a man of very few words and only through his developing relationship with Babe does he find a voice, crooning the song quietly to Babe on his knee, as he nurses him back to health in his living room. By the closing credits, the tune has been completed by Hodge's lyrics, sung by a mouse chorus, whose high-pitched warbling also reads out the title cards that are inserted at intervals throughout the film, including 'Pork's a Nice, Sweet Meat', accompanied by giggling, and 'A Tragic Day', said in a sad voice. Generally speaking, the mice exist only as voices, but at the end they are shown centre-screen, as if to give them their own credit, their toy-like cuteness reaffirming and extending the happy resolution of the film.

The opening scene of *Babe*, however, could not be more different in tone from the end. It begins by showing a battery farm in which pigs are housed in continual darkness, only interrupted as the doors open to allow entry to the lorry which will take them to slaughter. The human voiceover adopts the viewpoint of the pigs, explaining the pigs' belief that this lorry represents an escape or release from continual darkness, transporting them (in both senses) to a new paradisal existence from which none have ever chosen to return. Rather like White's instruction to the child about the inevitability of death, this child viewer recognizes the lie inherent in the frame narrator's claims, an untruth that establishes a conflict between the human decision to rear animals for meat and the encouragement, through fantasy, of the viewer to identify more closely with the animals than the humans. On more than one occasion in this film we see Babe cry, a behavioural characteristic we might interpret as pure animal fantasy, until we learn from pig specialists that 'Pigs that are sad or grieving are known to cry real tears' (Anon 2018). Those real tears are, themselves, a critique of the human characters, as we watch Farmer Hoggett's brattish granddaughter burst into ungrateful 'crocodile' tears on unwrapping the dolls' house he has painstakingly crafted for her as a Christmas present: 'It's the wrong one! I want the house I saw on the television!'

In many of the more respected works of animal fantasy for children those child viewers are encouraged to reflect politically and/or philosophically on their content, especially in relation to animal-human interaction. When, in *Babe*, the cow tells the duck 'The only way you'll find happiness is to accept that the way things are is the way things are', not only does she articulate a point of view *Babe* itself challenges, all fantasy challenges it. After all, fantasy presents us persistently with the way things *aren't* and requires us to accept it. Richard Adams's *Watership Down* (1972) similarly engages its child reader in some thought-provoking content, in part linked to the scientific foundation for his narrative and in part its linguistic experimentation.

In the 1950s, tens of thousands of rabbits were killed across Britain by Myxomatosis, a parasitic disease fatal to rabbits. Controversially, it was widely suspected that the outbreak had been encouraged and perhaps even started by farmers, as pest control. According to Colin Willock, amid this outbreak 'the distinguished biologist and field naturalist', Ronald Mathias (R.M.)

Lockley, undertook a four-year study into rabbit colonies on behalf of Nature Conservancy and, in 1964, published his highly influential book, *The Private Life of the Rabbit* (Willock 1964: np). What made Lockley a controversial figure was his belief that he could communicate directly with animals and, though there are no overt claims of that kind in *The Private Life of the Rabbit*, his interest in fantasy certainly erupts through its opening:

> Why does the rabbit amuse and charm us? ... The rabbit has a baby face, of rounded outlines, snub nose, enormous ears and eyes ... Like children, the rabbits in garden, field and hutch endear themselves to us ... Small wonder that in the traditional nursery tales the rabbit is both the *enfant terrible* and the lovable character. Beatrix Potter and a hundred other authors have created the acceptable image of careless, cheerful, clever Rabbit. Those enchanting Little People, the gnomes, goblins, elves and pixies, have long rabbit-like ears. Uncle Remus's Br'er Rabbit always wins in the battle of wits with Br'er Fox; Baby-face triumphs once more over Long-Nose.
>
> (Lockley 1964: 11–12)

Lockley's rabbits are, overall, characters rather than objects of study and it is easy to see how this otherwise scientific work would prove so influential to a novelist of animal fantasy. It is widely accepted that Adams's *Watership Down* derives much of its understanding of rabbits from Lockley's work. Here we identify the key distinction between *Watership Down* and the writers to whom Lockley refers above. Potter and Chandler Harris write stories around one individual creature: 'The Tale of Peter Rabbit' (1902), or 'Uncle Remus and Brer Rabbit' (1907), while both Lockley and Adams focus upon the entire rabbit colony, its power relations and anthropology.

In order to explore this interaction between rabbits, Adams goes to the impressive lengths of devising a new rabbit language, usually glossed for the child by means of authorial footnotes. In so doing, he offers both a 'translation' into English and an anthropological context. Thus, when Hazel explains that Fiver acquires his name from there being 'Five in the litter, you know; he was the last – and the smallest', Adams adds the following expansive footnote:

> Rabbits can count up to four. Any number above four is *Hrair* – 'a lot', or 'a thousand'. Thus they say *U Hrair* – 'The Thousand' – to mean, collectively, all the enemies (or *elil*, as they call them) of rabbits – fox, stoat, weasel, cat, owl, man, etc. There were probably more than five rabbits in the litter when Fiver was born, but his name, *Hrairoo*, means 'Little Thousand', i.e. the little one of a lot or, as they say of pigs, 'the runt'.
>
> (Adams 1974: 16–17n)

The footnote requires an actively thoughtful response from the child reader. By telling us that rabbits can count, but only up to four, we surmise that ability to have a bodily foundation (rabbits have four paws). By extension, a child might realize that our own ten fingers are the likely foundation for decimal calculations. Moreover, Adams encourages the child to reflect on how *all* languages work. By adding a definite article 'U' ('The') to 'Hrair' and also an affectionate diminutive suffix ('-oo'), the child starts to understand language not just as a set of words, but as building blocks for social understanding.

Michael Rosen's 1978 film adaptation of *Watership Down* cannot hope to replicate the linguistic experimentation of Adams's original, but it does open with a storytelling sequence which makes the same claim for a rabbit mythology. The wording tends towards a biblical and thus a philosophical depth. In the Book of Genesis, we are told that 'In the beginning God created the heaven and the earth … And God made the firmament … And God said let there be lights in the firmament … And God said let the earth bring forth the living creatures … cattle, and creeping things … ' (Genesis 1:1–25 *passim*). At the start of Rosen's film, the narrator tells us that 'Long ago, the great Frith made the world. He made all the stars, and the world lived among the stars. Frith made all the animals and birds and at first made them all the same.' The same anxiety about carnivorous eating that predominates in *Babe* arises here. Initially, Frith only creates herbivorous animals, but as the rabbits multiply and eat all the grass, he introduces carnivores as his own form of pest control: 'To each of them Frith gave a fierce desire to hunt and slay the children of El-ahrairah'. As Walters observes,

> The animation in this [opening] sequence is unsophisticated, line drawn, self-consciously cartoonish in its two dimensionality. It has a child's picture-book quality, a feature complemented by the casting of Michael Horden as Frith, his voice recognizable as that of the excellent narrator of the British *Paddington Bear* television series for children.
>
> (Walters 2011: 123)

That lack of sophistication might be argued to contribute to a kind of storybook structure, except that the graphics are even more simplistic than Walter suggests, bearing closer relation to the artistry of ancient cave paintings and, as such, making an implied claim for a type of ancient tribal folklore. Once we shift into the main storyline, the animation moves to the other extreme, becoming almost startlingly naturalistic for its time as it pans over meadowland, rolling hills, fences and pylons, attesting to the interface between human and animal communities. As the first close-up of Hazel appears, animation settles for a midway point, bearing a similar degree of stylization to Disney animations of the same period, such as *The Jungle Book* (1967) or *The Aristocats* (1970), both directed by Wolfgang Reitherman. As soon as fears of housing development occur, however, that unsophisticated animation is back, breaking in like an ancient curse.

Towards the end of Rosen's film Fiver says to Hazel, 'If we meet again … we'll have the making of the best story ever', to which Hazel replies 'And you'll be the one to tell it'. The dialogue echoes Sam and Frodo's conversation, in J.R.R. Tolkien's *The Return of the King* (1955), after they have destroyed the One Ring in the fires of Mount Doom and are on their way back. Exhausted and trapped by lava flows, death seems inevitable, but Sam, tending to his adored friend like a child, 'hold[s] his master's hand [and] caressed it … "What a tale we have been in, Mr Frodo, haven't we? I wish I could hear it told! … and I wonder how it will go on after our part"' (Tolkien 1999c: 272–273). At the start of *Watership Down*, the rabbits look out across the countryside and spy out a far hill where they plan to settle again, well away from humanity and all other fears. At that point, the landscape seems almost of Middle Earth-like vastness to a rabbit. The rabbits' story is, above all, a journey narrative which, through its claim for a larger rabbit mythology, a link to ancient times and small individuals representing an entire community, offers the closest one will find, in animal fantasy, to an epic quest struggle. Animal fantasy, as we have seen, supports the child reader in her/his understanding of developing subjectivity, moral and political reasoning, animal/human relationships, and our relationship to the immensity and dangers of the environment. In Chapter 4, we consider some of the most influential fantasy quest narratives of all, beginning with a quest with no apparent destination: the ongoing search for the Holy Grail.

NOTES

1 Beatrix Potter was herself an amateur botanist of some repute.

2 According to the Daimler motor company, the very first patented automobile was produced in 1885–1886, quickly followed by the three-wheeler 'Velocipede' in 1886, but four-wheeled motorized transport only emerged in 1894. According to the Ford motor company, Henry Ford's 'Quadricycle' was first produced in 1896, though he did not develop his 'first moving assembly line' until 1913. See www.daimler.com/company/tradition/company-history/1886-1920.html, www.ford.co.uk/experience-ford/Heritage and www.ford.co.uk/experience-ford/Heritage/EvolutionOfMassProduction (all accessed 13 January 2017).

4

FANTASY QUESTS

At its simplest, a quest is a journey, but fundamentally one searching for knowledge or understanding. Although the direction of travel may take the character forward in time and distance, the knowledge sought often takes the same character back in thought. Perhaps one of the reasons why quest narratives so frequently involve fantasy is due to this multi-layered understanding of time and space. Historically, quests carry either religious connotations, such as the quest for the Holy Grail, of which more below, or moral and ethical connotations in which an adventurer undergoes a series of challenges in order to bring justice, prestige and security to (usually his) country. Literal journeys are a key requirement and the impetus for those journeys is, not infrequently, loss, actual or perceived: a lost object; a lost or threatened community; lost parents; the search for ancient civilizations and their stories; ancient faiths and their origins; anthropological excavations and their rituals.

THE EPIC QUEST

Quest narratives are as old as civilization itself, but as readers we are most likely to associate their origins with the Ancient Greeks and Romans, the Bible, or Norse sagas brought to Britain by the Vikings. Crucially, quest narratives, always popular as oral tales, gained even more traction with the writing of the earliest manuscripts and the invention of the printing press. Thus the quest for the Holy Grail, purportedly a narrative about searching for the chalice from which Christ invokes his disciples to drink his 'blood' at the Last Supper (Matthew 26:28; Mark 14:24; Luke 22:20), is really a Medieval chivalric romance, often attributed to the twelfth-century poet Chrétien de Troyes, through whom it also becomes connected to Arthurian legend, partly as a way of endowing King Arthur with a Christ-like resemblance. When Pauline Matarosso tells us that 'The knights of the Round Table were forever setting out on quests, forever meeting with adventures of a more or less "marvellous" nature' (Matarosso 1969: 15), we again see how inseparably fantasy, here expressed as the marvellous, attaches itself to these legendary journeys, even when based on supposed biblical truths and a real geographical route between the Holy Land and Britain.

That fantasy aspect is intrinsic to the appetite for the search, sometimes expressed as a desire to prove doubters wrong. Robert Rouse and Cory Rushton structure their book, *The Medieval Quest for Arthur*, around a series of relics, including the round table at Winchester, Arthur's tomb at Glastonbury Abbey and the sword Excalibur. Consistently, they reiterate a paradox: that the probable inauthenticity of all these relics and their associated stories proved no natural deterrent to the readiness of readers/listeners to believe them: 'Although the 1191 discovery of Arthur's body may seem like an obvious fraud to a modern reader … the story seems to have been largely accepted by the chroniclers of the time' (Rouse and Rushton 2016: 59). The issue is not, I think, that twelfth-century chroniclers were more gullible than us, but that twelfth-century chroniclers saw the social and political advantages in a good story. So might we: without them, we would have neither Alfred Tennyson's *Idylls of the King* (1859), nor Mark Twain's *A Connecticut Yankee at King Arthur's Court* (1889), nor T.H. White's *The Once and Future King* (1958), nor Mary Stewart's *The Crystal Cave* (1970). Similarly, there would be no Walt Disney's *The Sword in the Stone* (dir. Wolfgang

Reitherman, 1963), no *First Knight* (dir. Jerry Zucker, 1995), nor the *Merlin* television drama, broadcast on British television in 2008–2012.

As the above-mentioned list reveals, the popularity of Arthurian and other quest myths has remained ebullient across the last 160 years. Although first Geoffrey of Monmouth (1095–1155) and then Sir Thomas Malory (1415–1471) played the essential role of documenting the Arthurian quest myth, our more modern understanding of Arthur, much like our knowledge of fairy tales, relies heavily on nineteenth-century writers and artists, who found renewed fascination with the Arthurian tales, perhaps because the Victorians, too, lived during an age of supreme monarchical influence. As Clare Simmons puts it, the attraction of Arthurian legend invokes 'the quest for origins; the relationship between religion and nationalism; and the model of an ordered or idyllic society' (Simmons 2001: 1). Nevertheless, those evocations of the past take on the form, in quest narratives, of journeys in and related to the present day. Thus, much like the myths of the ancient Greeks and Romans, they present an alternative world that is simultaneously impossibly removed from and impossible *to* remove from our own.

Sir James Frazer's *The Golden Bough* (1890) reveals how a thirst for knowledge can become a quest in itself. Writing as an armchair traveller into the unknown, as he observes in his Preface to the 1911 edition:

> When I originally conceived the idea ... I thought that it might be adequately set forth within the compass of a small volume. But I soon found that in attempting to settle one question I had raised many more: wider and wider prospects opened out before me; and thus step by step I was lured on into far-spreading fields of primitive thought which had been but little explored by my predecessors.
>
> (Frazer 1978: 16)

Here, the rhetoric of exploration on foot ('set forth', 'compass', 'step by step') combines with an ever-expansive landscape ('wider and wider prospects', 'far-spreading fields', 'little explored') in a manner wholly in keeping with fantasy quest narratives. In the

BBC television fantasy series *Merlin,* the first episode opens with the title character approaching on foot. What initially looks like a walk towards the beach across sand dunes and/or sandy soil quickly switches to a view of our hero pursuing an inland mountain path. Though seemingly incongruously edited, the mere suggestion of coast which turns out to be a mountain path introduces scale and distance in a way that is hard to encapsulate otherwise, in a shot framed by and for the small screen. Instantly the viewer makes assumptions that prove correct: the character is an incomer, he is embarking on a new phase in his young life, he is alone (for which read 'singular'), he is on a quest. In fact, the first episode of *Merlin* never uses the word 'quest', though it uses 'destiny' more than once. Merlin has magical powers in an Arthurian world in which Uther Pendragon, then King, hates magic. Indeed, the opening scene details the execution of a young male sorcerer and the subsequent curse placed upon Uther by his mother, a witch: 'An eye for an eye, a tooth for a tooth, a son for a son', she intones. Similarly, we learn early on that Merlin is the nephew of Gaius the healer and has been sent to him by his mother, for safety. If Gaius's quest is to keep Merlin safe, Merlin's quest is to survive as a warlock in this hostile regime, despite being given the role of manservant to the unruly Prince Arthur. As the viewer already knows, Merlin's destiny is wholly entangled in what will become Arthur's own quest: like so many chivalric romances of the Middle Ages, it will prove a quest of and for kingship.

J.R.R. Tolkien's trilogy, *The Lord of the Rings* (1954–1955), is also a quest of kingship, hence the title of his final volume, *The Return of the King* (1955). So immense is the landscape and cartography of Middle Earth, however, subsequently reinforced through the visual addition of the maps that he and his son Christopher drew, that even Kings become diminished in scale by comparison. Aragorn's marriage to Arwen 'in the City of the Kings upon the day of Midsummer' (Tolkien 1999c: 302) may seal the hobbits' triumph, but in that context it is worth remembering that Aragorn is a man, not an elf, dwarf or hobbit: Tolkien ensures that the species hierarchy never genuinely threatens humanity's supremacy. Nevertheless, that wedding does not signal the 'happy ever after' resolution to the quest, which still relies on the hobbits and their return to the Shire. For most readers, the quest has been to save the land: it is a topographical victory for which Frodo must, in Christ-like mode, die:

> I tried to save the Shire, and it has been saved, but not for me. It must often be so, Sam, when things are in danger: some one has to give them up, lose them, so that others may keep them. But you are my heir: all that I had and might have I leave to you.
>
> (Tolkien 1999c: 376)

So keen is Tolkien to reset the scale of his quest narrative to the dimensions of a single footprint, however, that he gradually peels back the layers of grandeur as we near the end. With Frodo removed, the three remaining companions return. Merry and Pippin take their leave of Sam at the turn in the road for Buckland, 'singing again as they went' (Tolkien 1999c: 378) and it is now that Tolkien enforces Sam's unlikely marriage to Rosie Cotton, as he ends the narrative devoid of male companionship, 'alone' with wife and baby: 'He drew a deep breath. "Well, I'm back," he said' (Tolkien 1999c: 378). A clumsily enforced victory for domesticated heterosexuality prevents any awkward residue of Sam's yearning grief for Frodo, though that marital resolution is easily the least credible element of the entire quest. Nevertheless, the return to one small protagonist and his footprint on the Shire brings us full circle to where the first volume, *The Fellowship of the Ring* (1954), begins, and we see how this original departure point mirrors so closely Frazer's aforementioned words in his preface:

> The light grew clearer as they went forward. Suddenly they came out of the trees and found themselves in a wide circular space ... There was a sky above them, blue and clear to their surprise, for down under the Forest-roof they had not been able to see the rising morning and the lifting of the mist. The sun was not, however, high enough yet to shine down into the clearing, though its light was on the tree-tops.
>
> (Tolkien 1999a: 147–148)

In both Tolkien's and Frazer's descriptions, sight, perspective and obstructions adopt a cognitive aspect. So often in epic fantasy, landscape proves the backdrop to philosophical enquiry: 'Where are we going?' 'Why are we going there?' 'What are the consequences?' These are life questions, applicable not just to individuals but communities, nations and across periods. Frazer's study operates on many layers simultaneously, but so does *Lord of the Rings*. Tolkien, in creating Middle Earth, creates a world beyond known time and space, but one which resembles, in geography, our own. It is both the landscape of pastoral idyll and of modern threat.

In C.S. Lewis's *The Lion, the Witch and the Wardrobe* (1950), landscape not only forms the backdrop for philosophical enquiry, but takes shape as pathetic fallacy. Though the Witch/Queen brings sadness, the landscape she inhabits remains sublime, almost in mimicry of her own cold beauty. Edmund, searching for her, slips and slides through an Alpine landscape of frosted hills and valleys but, when they travel together towards a Narnia to which Aslan has returned, Spring erupts:

> Every moment the patches of green grew bigger and the patches of snow grew smaller. Every moment more and more of the trees shook off their robes of snow ... Then the mist turned from white to gold and presently cleared away altogether. Shafts of delicious sunlight struck down on to the forest floor and overhead you could see a blue sky ...
>
> (Lewis 1972: 110)

For Edmund, loveliness comes in fits and starts, meted out, glimpse after glimpse. By contrast, when Aslan takes Peter aside, just a few pages later, and shows him the same landscape as a form of inheritance, elongation extends the horizon into the distance:

> [T]he whole country below them lay in the evening light – forest and hills and valleys and, winding away like a silver snake, the lower part of the great river. And beyond all this, miles away, was the sea, and beyond the sea the sky, full of clouds ... [and] the sunset. But just

> where the land of Narnia met the sea – in fact, at the mouth of the great river – there was something on a little hill, shining. It was shining because it was a castle and of course the sunlight was reflected from all the windows which looked towards Peter and the sunset ...
>
> (Lewis 1972: 118–119)

We begin by looking down here, but comparatively close. Gradually our perspective takes on greater and greater distance, becoming a sustained study of the 'beyond'. From our hilltop location we overlook tree-tops and the crests of smaller hills, reaching out and further away. We have already seen more forests, hills and valleys (plural) before we see the river 'winding away'; in other words we see *beyond* the river itself, taking in its course for some distance. Only then do we read 'And beyond' again, before elongating still further to what is normally considered the end-point: the coast. Now verticality flattens out and becomes part of the horizon(tal), as the sky is no longer 'overhead', as it was for Edmund, but simply, once more, 'beyond', as we extend still further from the planet's surface to conclude with 'the sunset'. Only then does the focus retract, as Lewis pulls us into sight of the castle, at the meeting-point of sea and land and, then, further in again, for now we are no longer looking at the castle, it is looking at us ('the windows which looked towards Peter'), claiming its rightful heir, a feature integral to the epic fantasy structure, whereby seemingly inanimate objects seem to gain temporary agency for the purposes of affirming a character's right to rule. Thus we see how, in both Tolkien and Lewis's writing, elongation and magnification of scale are essential overtures to a return to the diminutive. Epic fantasy quests must also retain their human scale in order to maintain the conviction that a journey outwards is also a journey inwards and that self-knowledge is the ultimate destiny. Hence the emphasis on a one-to-one correspondence between reading pace and walking pace, for thus is the reader enabled to make the protagonist's quest hers. Equally, that juxtaposition of the small and the immense reminds us that no quest is worthwhile without physical duress.

So far, we have prioritized the horizontal axis in measuring epic distance, even when journeying over undulating or hilly terrain. However, towards the start of Mervyn Peake's first volume of the *Gormenghast* trilogy, *Titus Groan* (1946), we encounter a vertical climb of equal derring-do, when Steerpike, whom we first encounter as an oppressed and ill-suited kitchen hand, sets off on a quest which, in actual distance, is comparatively small, but in dimensions of height, duration and endurance, remains dizzying. *Gormenghast* is a quest for feudal power and, utilizing as a cover the festive celebrations linked to the birth of a new heir, Steerpike escapes the kitchen and begins to explore the castle's upper floors. Spying through the keyhole of Titus's birth-chamber, he witnesses Doctor Prunesquallor's pronouncement of Titus's ugliness, in response to which Flay, Lord Sepulchrave's manservant, locks Steerpike in a room high up in the castle walls. Lacking any alternative means of exit, this social climber removes his boots, splays his fingers and begins to scale the wall, 'refus[ing] to allow himself to think of the sickening drop' (Peake 1999: 90).

If we, as readers, feel a sense of one-to-one identification with a walking protagonist, how much more closely do we hold our breath as Steerpike ascends slowly, fingertip by fingertip, stone by stone, until safely sitting astride the apex roof. Now he follows, in his mind's eye, the horizontal line of ridge-tiles, mapping the next stage. The castle roof is built

> in a wide curve to where in the west it was broken by the first of four towers. Beyond [it] the swoop of roof continued to complete a half circle far to his right ... surrounding which, though at a lower level, were the heavy, rotting structures of adjacent roofs and towers, and between these could be seen other roofs far away, and other towers.
>
> (Peake 1999: 91)

Initially, generalized elongation takes precedence over precise dimensions, but soon Steerpike begins to quantify perspective. Identifying an 'area the size of a field' on the roof 'a league away', it takes him 'over an hour' to arrive, this time crawling (Peake 1999: 91). It turns out to be a rooftop flagstone pavement, wholly enclosed and seemingly inaccessible by other means. What appeared a destination now serves as a stopping-point, as Steerpike spends a frozen night there, searching in vain for any means of egress. After enduring 'twelve to fifteen hours' on the roof, at daylight he drops 'nine feet from the parapet' to another sloping roof, descends 'a small winding stone staircase … across a gap between two high walls' and gingerly finds his way around 'a cluster of conical roofs' (Peake 1999: 94–95). Still he is confronted by a seemingly impenetrable vertical drop. Peake tells us that Steerpike 'had made a hundred imaginary journeys' before espying 'a high window in the Western Wing', which turns out to lead him into Fuchsia's secret attic. At this, the final leg of his epic rooftop quest, the measurements come thick and fast: 'It was now two o'clock in the afternoon' and '[t]he next three hours made him repent that he had ever left the kitchens'; it has been 'twenty-four hours after he had lain above the prison room on the sloping roof of slates' and it is 'three hours' since he had first spotted the window. He is now 'midway between the ground two hundred feet below him and the window'. Tellingly, however, as he nears the window all measurement and scale disappears, and the narrator tells us that 'Distance, even more than time, had ceased to have any meaning for him'. Only at the very last stage do measurements reappear, as he realizes that the ivy he has been using to approach the window is now 'Only a foot or two in depth' and he has to squeeze his fingers between it and the wall to gain any kind of purchase, moving 'inch by inch' (Peake 1999: 101–102).

Such an emphasis on eccentric travel is perhaps easier to accomplish in fantasy narratives than classical realism. As Mary Douglas observes of Frazer, the authenticity of *The Golden Bough* might be argued to have been compromised by him not having travelled to most of the regions about which he wrote. Conversely, Tolkien can invent unapologetically a world as extensive as Middle Earth, precisely because he would never need to go there. That is not to say, however, that fantasy cartography has no connection with actual geography. In Charles Kingsley's *The Water-Babies* (1863), as his boy protagonist, Tom, flees from his Master Sweep, Grimes, and embarks on a journey that will transform him from victimized child sweep to industrial engineer and man of influence, Kingsley ensures that the early sections of the narrative are set against a backdrop which emerges from the actual topography of rural northern England:

> The name of the place is Vendale; and if you want to see it for yourself, you must go up into the High Craven, and search from Bolland Forest north by Ingleborough, to the Nine Standards and Cross Fell; and if you have not found it, you must turn south, and search the Lake Mountains, down to Scaw Fell and the sea; and then, if you have not found it, you must go northward again by merry Carlisle, and search the Cheviots all across, from Annan Water to Berwick Law; and then, whether you have found Vendale or not, you will have found such a country, and such a people, as ought to make you proud of being a British boy.
>
> (Kingsley 2016: 17)

The Forest of Bowland (here 'Bolland Forest'), Ingleborough, the Nine Standards Rigg, Cross Fell and Scafell Pike (here 'Scaw Fell') are actual geographical landmarks of the Pennines, North Yorkshire, North Lancashire and the Lake District respectively. Nevertheless, the extent of the terrain covered here is more substantial than any child could travel on foot, Nine Standards Rigg lying ninety miles east of Scafell Pike, and Ingleborough being twenty-seven miles north of the Forest of Bowland. Moreover, as Vendale is purely fictional, no traveller, however assiduously s/he followed Kingsley's directions, could ever hope to find it. That combination of precision and impossibility, as we saw in *Gormenghast*, arguably defines the fantasy quest narrative. Geography is an essential aspect of the journey and it must be sufficiently convincing and detailed to give credence to the otherwise extraordinary feats of endurance and derring-do that characterize fantasy narratives, but it is almost never fully 'real'.

QUESTS FOR SELF-KNOWLEDGE AND SOCIAL KNOWLEDGE

The genuinely educative inclusion of recent scientific discovery as an element of quest fantasy recurs across the Victorian period. The ideas of two major scientists dominate in *The Water-Babies*: Charles Darwin and Karl Linnaeus. Kingsley took a close interest in Darwin's work on evolution, and Stephen Prickett has noted that he wrote a letter of congratulation to Darwin on the publication of *The Origin of Species* (1859) (Prickett 2005: 150).

Linnaeus's system of taxonomy enabled scientists to attribute clear Latinate species labels to all known varieties of plants and animals; the system remains in wide use today and looms large in *The Water-Babies.* Here Kingsley amalgamates science and fantasy, as alongside the scientific species of water-dwellers such as Holothurians, Cephalopods, lobsters and otters, live the water-babies, a particular brand of fairy unique to Kingsley's book and one he classifies along Linnaean principles: 'Amphibious. Adjective, derived from two Greek words, *amphi*, a fish, and *bios*, a beast. An animal supposed by our ignorant ancestors to be compounded of a fish and a beast; which therefore, like the hippopotamus, can't live on the land, and dies in the water' (Kingsley 2016: 1). Kingsley's invention of a hybrid creature, both fairy and water-dweller, in part plays on the fantastic array of flora and fauna that Linnaeus is able to classify, confusing in the mind of the ordinary reader questions of fact and fantasy. It is precisely the same combination that Jules Verne will come on to employ in *Twenty Thousand Leagues Under the Sea* (1870), in which his central protagonist, Professor Pierre Aronnax, observes: 'The great ocean depths are totally unknown to us … .What kinds of creatures live and are able to live 12 or 15 miles beneath the surface of the water? What is the organic nature of such forms of life? We can barely guess' (Verne 2018: 14).

Fittingly, then, it is within water that Kingsley situates his competing fantasy realm, as Tom stumbles into a stream and finds himself swept along by the current. Prickett confirms that 'No fictional fantasy could equal the variety and peculiarity of the life [Kingsley] found teeming in the rivers and sea; there was no need to pass through any looking glass beyond that of our own world' (Prickett 2005: 145). Nevertheless, Kingsley does not rely wholly on the wondrous water-dwelling species to convey the fantasy elements; instantly Tom is submerged, his physiognomy is diminished to being 'about four inches or – that I may be accurate – 3.87902 inches long and having round the parotid region of his fauces [the back of the mouth] a set of external gills … just like those of a sucking eft' (Kingsley 2016: 25).

Such a dual interleaving of the enticements of fantasy with scientific scrutiny befits Kingsley's overall emphasis on societal reform. Although we would find many of Kingsley's views on race and ethnicity abhorrent today (of which more in Chapter 5), his views on child chimney-sweeps were progressive, humanitarian and sustained and, in part, his novel is an authorial quest for social justice. Although, as his full title *The Water-Babies: A Fairy Tale for a Land Baby* suggests, Kingsley initially wrote his narrative to entertain his youngest son, Greville, its subsequent publication ensured that Kingsley's views on child sweeps would reach a much wider audience than did his political essays. Such messages were crucial: as Prickett informs us, quite aside from the respiratory horrors and other dangers innate to scaling the inner walls of chimneys, 'Cancer of the scrotum was common in the boys – caused by crawling naked through the sooty flues' (Prickett 2005: 150). Within one year of the novel's publication, 'the Chimney Sweepers Regulation Act became law,' rendering illegal the employment of child sweeps in Britain (Prickett 2005: 150).

Tom's origins as a boy sweep remind us that his underwater journey is not the first time he has had to navigate an alternative world from that of daylight reality. Early on in the narrative we watch him on a different kind of quest, negotiating his way through the 'pitchy darkness' of the labyrinthine chimneys of Harthover House, 'as a mole is underground' (Kingsley 2016: 9). Unlike Carroll's Alice, who plummets underground and stays there for the duration of the text until she returns to the river bank, Tom's quest begins in an upward vertical direction from land to what would be air, if only he could breathe properly. Returning to the combined perspectives of vertical and horizontal axes, where Alice's journey is a simpler descent and return, Tom's is much more meandering. Alice is a knowledgeable, even precocious child, whose self-assurance comes from the complacency of social privilege. Tom's journey is longer and more tortuous precisely because he lacks social advantage, and the amalgamation of vertical and horizontal trajectories up and down chimney flues, up and down hillsides, into and under water enables that struggle to become visualized more clearly.

This same interface between vertical and horizontal trajectories meets its match metaphorically in Kingsley's treatment of both Darwin's theory of evolution and the anti-Darwinian concept of social degeneration, both of which manifest themselves centrally in the novel.[1] Tom's fairy godmother, Mrs Bedonebyasyoudid, shows him a vision, much as the three Spirits do to Scrooge in Charles Dickens's *A Christmas Carol* (1843), written twenty years earlier. Yet where Scrooge's warning concerns the harm he could do to the poor and needy, the visions shown to Tom reveal a degenerative future caused by collective social inertia which will have grave consequences for children like him. The result is a community named 'the Doasyoulikes', destroyed by a volcano because its citizens refuse to heed warnings about its dangers. Five hundred years later, this same community is 'liv[ing] miserably on roots and nuts'; five hundred years later still, it is 'living up in trees, and making nests to keep off the rain'. In another five hundred, 'their feet had changed shape very oddly, for they laid hold of the branches with their great toes' and, another half millennia on, they have become hirsute, run by a 'hairy chief [who] had had hairy children, and they hairier children still … for the climate was growing so damp that none but the hairy ones could live' (Kingsley 2016: 87, 88, 89). Thus Kingsley introduces a note of moral caution into social Darwinism: individual agency will prove the key to Tom's social elevation. Early on in the novel, things happen *to* Tom: 'he tumbled himself as quick as he could into the clear cool stream … he fell fast asleep … [and] The reason of his falling into such a delightful sleep … was merely that the fairies took him' (Kingsley 2016: 22). Literally washed clean in the water, it is easy to connect Kingsley's work as a Church of England Rector with Tom's immersion and read it as a kind of baptismal experience, except for the fact that such an approach would devolve responsibility for Tom's fate to God. Tom gradually has to learn that true transformation comes from self-agency or, as the popular social maxim might have it, 'God helps those who help themselves.'

Like Kingsley, George MacDonald employs a female guide for his questing protagonist Anodos, in *Phantastes: A Faerie Romance* (1858). In Chapter 1, we discussed the importance of maternal loss to MacDonald's creativity, but here we will consider it as the impetus for quest. When Anodos finds the tiny woman in his bedchamber, he looks into her eyes 'deeper and deeper, till they spread around me like seas, and I sank in their waters' (MacDonald 2005: 4). As in *The Water-Babies*, water is the magical element in *Phantastes* and no sooner does Anodos allow this woman to immerse him in fairyland than he finds his bed located beside a river and his washbasin 'overflowing like a spring' (MacDonald 2005: 6). By extension, the flowers on his patterned carpet have metamorphosed into actual flora, his wooden furniture has returned to its arboreal origins and a footpath becomes discernible, which Anodos identifies as 'the path into Fairy Land' (MacDonald 2005: 8).

Phantastes, of course, pre-dates the work of Sigmund Freud and Carl Jung by several decades. Freud set up his own practice in 1886, working with Anna O. in the same year, but did not publish *Studies in Hysteria* until 1895; Jung published *Psychology of the Unconscious* in 1912. While one cannot, therefore, argue that Anodos's quest is *motivated* by a desire to unearth the secrets of his unconscious, using Fairy Land as its geographical manifestation, one can claim that *Phantastes* demonstrates the pre-existence of desires later claimed as unconscious, Anodos's quest gradually exhuming some of its buried secrets. The effect can also work for the reader. William Reaper, MacDonald's biographer, claims that rather than depicting characters, MacDonald works through 'a series of encounters, as in a night of dreams', in which the various episodes are less with characters than 'symbols … [which] remain, working their way into us after we have finished reading' (Reaper 1987: 145 and 153). *Phantastes* reminds us that quest narratives do not always have to carry a wider moral message; they may function as a means for introspection. Such interiorization explains why Anodos, whose name translates from the Greek as 'pathless', lacks a clear goal or destination for his quest.

Instead, one can identify in Anodos's journey a presiding pattern of compulsive repetition, which Freud will later come to identify as one aspect of the uncanny and which, in *Phantastes*, oscillates around Anodos's encounters with women. Irrespective of whether it is the tiny woman in his bedchamber, the marble lady, the sweet old woman in the cottage or the dangerously alluring Alder-maiden, all prove to be unstable shape-shifters, enticing or consoling one minute and dangerous the next.

William Gray, we recall from Chapter 1, believes that maternal yearning drives MacDonald's imaginative vision and certainly when Anodos enters the old lady's cottage in Chapter Nineteen, her face is 'older than any countenance I had ever looked upon', but her eyes are 'absolutely young – those of a woman of five-and-twenty' (MacDonald 2005: 141). For an author whose mother, at the time he wrote *Phantastes*, had been long dead and who had died young, such an apparition seems wholly in keeping with this desire for a maternal re-connection, one clearly achieved in the text when she feeds Anodos from a spoon like an infant, 'with one arm round [him], till [he] looked up in her face and smiled' (MacDonald 2005: 142).

DEATH AND THE SHADOW-SELF

In a similarly feminized location, a cave, which proves to be a portal into a floral idyll, Anodos finds clear water which he drinks in a manner which, depending on one's perspective, evokes either Christ's promise of the blood of the new covenant at the Last Supper, or mother's milk, '[feeling] as if I knew what the elixir of life must be' (MacDonald 2005: 35). Slipping into a satiated dream state, what Anodos then experiences surely encapsulates the perfection for which all fantasy quests strive:

> [A]ll lovely forms, and colours, and sounds seemed to use my brain as a common hall, where they could come and go, unbidden and unexcused. I have never imagined that such capacity for simple happiness lay in me, as was now awakened by this assembly of forms and spiritual sensations, which yet were far too vague to admit of being translated into any shape common to my own and another mind.
>
> (MacDonald 2005: 35–36)

Whether one calls what Anodos experiences nirvana, *jouissance*, intoxication, intra-uterine bliss or spiritual ecstasy, the synaesthesia of this description is something hard to express through realism. Nevertheless, such bliss is short-lived, for MacDonald gradually interlaces wish-fulfilment with horror, as if to recognize the futility of such escapist goals. According to Tolkien, 'Death is the theme that most inspired … MacDonald', a drive which Tolkien identifies as 'the oldest and deepest desire, the Great Escape' (Tolkien 2001: 68) and which Reaper further qualifies by reminding us that death frames all quests, for 'Death is what gives meaning to life' (Reaper 1987: 148). In my opinion, however, it is less death *per se* and more its shadow that haunts *Phantastes.* Anodos, wandering through a wood in Chapter Four, experiences 'a vague sense of discomfort … as if some evil thing were wandering about in my neighbourhood'. Paradoxically, as his path continues, the form both takes shape and evades clear outline: 'I saw the strangest figure; vague, shadowy, almost transparent, in the central parts, and gradually deepening in substance towards the outside, until it ended in extremities capable of casting such a shadow as fell from the hand'. Perhaps this known but unknowable presence encapsulates our collective preoccupation with, and lack of comprehension of, death. Here, the gothic intrudes most clearly into Fairy Land, as Anodos decides that 'It reminded me of what I had heard of vampires; for the face resembled that of a corpse more than anything else I can think of' (MacDonald 2005: 25–27).

That shadowy threat gathers intensity and begins, again, to mutate along feminine lines. Seemingly at the opposite extreme of what will later become the good mother's eyes, Anodos finds himself peering into eyes which 'were alive, yet not with life. They seemed lighted up with an infinite greed. A gnawing voracity, which devoured the devourer, seemed to be the indwelling and propelling power of the whole ghostly apparition' (MacDonald 2005: 27). Meredith Skura, discussing the 'fiercely ambivalent' unconscious dynamic existing between breast-feeding mothers and their infants describes a similarly vampiric co-dependency, as the baby 'is tied down, moved, filled, and emptied by someone too strong to resist – an invasion of the body which has its logical culmination in cannibalism and vampirism' (Skura 1981: 104). When Anodos confronts this shadowy predator by lying prone on the ground, his 'head within the form of [its] hand', we again perceive Anodos once more becoming self-infantilized, but now the dead mother returns in unwanted uncanny form (MacDonald 2005: 26). Rather than this part of the quest to Fairy Land being a dream in which Anodos longs to re-access mother's love, here he is confronted by the nightmare possibility of *never* escaping mother. After all, though Anodos, Peter Pan, Harry Potter and Snow White all mourn the loss of their mothers, their adventures require her death in order for them to attain full subjectivity.

Of course, mothers may harm while still alive. When Anodos enters the cottage of the ogre woman, she presents him with a Bluebeard-style prohibition not to open a particular door in her house, despite him sensing a powerful urge to do so. Giving in to temptation, Anodos finds himself peering into a closet with no back wall, MacDonald's influence on Lewis's *Chronicles of Narnia* being evident here.[2] Gradually he makes out a night sky, 'through the perspective of a narrow, dark passage' (MacDonald 2005: 61). Suddenly, from the depths of the darkness, a figure sprints towards him. As Anodos recoils, MacDonald simultaneously accelerates and decelerates time, as 'On and on it came, with a speedy approach but delayed arrival; till, at last, through the many gradations of approach, it seemed to come within the sphere of myself, rushed up to me, and passed me into the cottage' (MacDonald 2005: 61). Just as time both quickens and slows, so the oncoming assailant simultaneously passes *through* and passes *by*. The shadow, for so it proves, is both of Anodos and distinct from him, as all shadows are: 'Its motion was entirely noiseless, and might be called a gliding, were it not that it appeared that of a runner, but with ghostly feet' (MacDonald 2005: 61). Part outward projection, part inward introspection, this shadow is both literal and symbolic in quality, elongating and compressing in the sunlight, while depressing Anodos's mood. When MacDonald explains that 'rays of gloom issued from [it] … as from a black sun' (MacDonald 2005: 65), we find him anticipating the work of another psychoanalytic theorist, Julia Kristeva, who in her study of melancholia and depression, also titled *Black Sun*, identifies the shadow as something 'cast on the fragile self … The shadow of despair' (Kristeva 1989: 5).

MacDonald's treatment of the shadow may have been influenced by Hans Christian Andersen's story 'The Shadow' (1847). In Andersen's story, a man 'from the cold regions of the north' moves to a hotter culture. Struggling with the heat, he can only sit outside in the evening, when he becomes inquisitive about a seemingly uninhabited house across the street, in which 'flowers stood in the balcony' and 'music could be heard' playing inside. One evening, illuminated from behind by 'A light … in his own room', his shadow is projected onto the neighbour's wall and suddenly the fantasy possibility presents itself of sending his shadow, unaccompanied, into the house opposite, to spy out the identity of its inhabitant(s). What he does not realize until the following morning is that, as he turns away, his shadow does indeed disengage itself from his body and enter as bidden. It is a long time until it returns, by which time it has gained a third dimension, emulating the shape of a 'remarkably thin' man. Now it has made its fortune and wishes to be treated as an independent being in its own right, insisting that its former master now address it as 'you', the formal term used to address a superior, not the familiar 'thou', used for friends or social inferiors. Again the shadow disappears, but some years later returns 'quite fat and stout'. Now it insists on reversing the power hierarchy, addressing its former master as 'thou', while the former master continues to call it 'you'. The shadow meets and marries a princess, convincing her that his former master is deranged. The man is, he insists, *his* shadow claiming to be *his* master. Faced with such possible insurrection, the princess's response is swift and decisive, reflecting both the anxieties about revolution that dogged the ruling classes in the early nineteenth century and reminding us of the political foundations underlying so many traditional fantasy texts (of which more in Chapter 5): 'indeed, when I think how often people take the part of the lower class against the higher, in these days, it would be policy to put him out of the way quietly'. The last three sentences of the story, which would usually reach their climax in 'And they all lived happily ever after', instead read: 'It was indeed a grand wedding. The princess and the shadow stepped out on the balcony to show themselves, and to receive one cheer more. But the learned man heard nothing of all these festivities, for he had already been executed' (Andersen 1847). In Andersen's story, the shadow's quest has been to acquire full subjectivity, something it can only achieve by devouring his original. In the process the fate which befalls the shadow's former master resonates absolutely with the warnings articulated by Kristeva in *Black Sun.* Casting depression in the form of the shadow, she further defines it as, 'the hidden face of Narcissus, the face that is to bear him away into death, but of which he is unaware while he admires himself in a mirage' (Kristeva 1989: 5).

There are other readings of the shadow available in fantasy narratives, however. In 'The Uncanny', Freud observes that 'the "double" was originally an insurance against the destruction of the ego' (Freud 1990: 356), or, to put it another way: if we cast a visible shadow we know we exist. From this perspective we recall the opening scene of J.M. Barrie's play, *Peter Pan* (1904), in which Peter enters the Darling family's nursery at dead of night, looking for his shadow, accompanied by Tinkerbell. Though he finds it in a drawer, he cannot re-attach it to his body and, when Wendy wakes up, she finds him crying and stitches it back on. Instantly, the stage direction informs us, '*It awakes and is as glad to be back with him as he is to have it. He and his shadow dance together*' (Barrie 1995: act 1, scene 1, ll. 370–371). Here, shadow and self are seen to be mutually required for full subjectivity. *Peter Pan* is arguably a play about dead children, who go to live in Neverland ('Second to the right and then straight on till morning' (Barrie 1995: act 1, scene 1, l. 343) as a form of afterlife and, in denial, understand themselves only as 'Lost Boys'. In that sense they live a shadow existence, kept away from the nursery of living children by ever-vigilant parents, who seem to know that death is contagious, hence Peter's warning to Wendy 'No one must ever touch me', reinforced by the stage direction '(*He is never touched by any one in the play*)' (Barrie 1995: act 1, scene 1, ll. 353, 356). Though Peter knows he must not be touched, he does not know why, being too taken up with 'admir[ing] himself in a mirage' (to recall Kristeva's phrase) to realize he is dead, hence his otherwise redundant boast, later in the play, 'To die will be an awfully big adventure' (Barrie 1995: act 3, scene 1, l. 180). Peter's quest is one of self-knowledge: only by coming to know death can Peter transcend his stubborn identity as 'the boy who wouldn't grow up', to quote the phrase used as the play's original subtitle.

TOTEMIC OBJECTS

Peter Pan's search for his shadow introduces the concept of totemic objects, items which must be found or destroyed for the quest to be fulfilled. The most obvious example of such an object in a fantasy quest narrative is 'the One Ring' in Tolkien's *The Lord of the Rings*, an object so powerful in magic that Gandalf assures Frodo, before he sets out, that 'Even if you took it and struck it with a heavy sledge-hammer, it would make no dint in it. It cannot be unmade by your hands, or by mine' (Tolkien 1999a: 80). More recently J.K. Rowling, in her *Harry Potter* series (1997–2007), establishes a similarly robust set of magical quest objects, in the horcruxes into which Lord Voldemort subdivides and thus hides his soul. As Harry learns in *Harry Potter and the Half-Blood Prince* (2005), in an explanation clearly resonant of Gandalf's words to Frodo: 'even if one's body is attacked or destroyed, one cannot die, for part of the soul remains earthbound and undamaged' (Rowling 2005: 464–465). The horcruxes amounting to seven in total, that being 'the most powerful magical number' (Rowling 2005: 466), Harry's quest is to find and destroy them all, for only then will Voldemort perish. Much as in the case of the shadow selves explored above, however, it becomes increasingly clear that Harry's own life is attached to Voldemort's, such that in killing him there is a significant possibility that Harry will die also.

Retrospectively, we recognize that the search for the horcruxes explains the emphasis placed, in the earlier volumes of the *Harry Potter* series, on the fantasy game of Quidditch, the purpose of which is to locate and capture the Golden Snitch. These rules are meticulously described in volume 1, *Harry Potter and the Philosopher's Stone* (1997), in which the Snitch itself, 'tiny, about the size of a walnut … bright gold … [with] little fluttering silver wings' (Rowling 1997: 125) is notoriously difficult to locate, equally difficult to catch but, once caught, ends the game. Precious-looking (to echo Gollum's trademark view of the One Ring) and miniature, the snitch certainly has the appearance of a totemic object. When the eleven-year-old Harry is selected to play in the team position of Seeker, he is 'the youngest house player in … a century' to be so (Rowling 1997: 113). In part, this specialness is a simple wish-fulfilment narrative for the child reader, but it is also precisely the same dynamic that identifies the 'very small, and very uprooted, and well – desperate' hobbit Frodo in Tolkien's fantasy quest (Tolkien 1999a: 82).

The search for the third horcrux is worth discussing in more detail, since it involves a mini-quest in itself, one that ultimately proves as futile as Anodos's. To reach this totemic object, Salazar Slytherin's locket, Dumbledore and Harry journey together into a water-filled cave. Magic is needed to reach the location, as 'No Muggle could reach this rock unless they were uncommonly good mountaineers, and boats cannot approach the cliffs; the waters around them are too dangerous' (Rowling 2005: 519). Once there, a Muggle-like swim into a tunnel in the rock follows, before more magic is required to discern the concealed entrance. Much to Dumbledore's disgust, a donation of blood is spent as a kind of toll payment, before the magical summoning of a boat enables the two questing characters to reach an island at the centre of the underground lake. Next, Dumbledore must swallow a chalice of poison, in a profane reworking of the Grail legend, perhaps. Only after a horrific encounter with underwater zombies do the two attain what they think is the horcrux, later actually discovering that what they have retrieved is a fake.

Rowling's utilization of submerged corpses in this scene clearly echoes Tolkien's description of the Dead Marshes in *The Two Towers*, the second volume of *The Lord of the Rings* (1954). In Tolkien's book, Gollum guides Sam and Frodo across swampy terrain. As darkness falls, will-o'-the-wisps appear, which Gollum calls 'Candles of corpses' (Tolkien 1999b: 287) and, as Sam trips he falls flat on his face in the mud: 'Wrenching his hands out of the bog, he sprang back with a cry. "There are dead things, dead faces in the water … Dead faces!"' (Tolkien 1999b: 288). It is Gollum who provides an explanation rooted in epic struggle, in a rare articulation from the life of his former self:

> There was a great battle long ago, yes, so they told him when Sméagol was young, when I was young before the Precious came. It was a great battle. Tall men with long swords, and terrible Elves, and Orcses

> shrieking. They fought on the plain for days and months at the Black Gates. But the Marshes have grown since then, swallowed up the graves; always creeping, creeping.
>
> (Tolkien 1999b: 288–289)

First, we recollect that Gollum is a further example of the shadow/split self. In this passage he refers to himself, in consecutive sentences, as Sméagol (in his previous life) and I (Gollum). It is easy to read Gollum metaphorically as a drug-addict, driven by longing for something (the 'One Ring') that is and will continue to destroy him, separated from himself by that self-destructive quest. A shadow of his former self, only very rarely, as here, does Gollum see clearly. The epic battle he describes echoes the struggles of ancient tales from Norse or Old English traditions, but it is also overlaid with geological and topographical facts: peat bogs do preserve bodies perfectly and a submerged graveyard will yield up its corpses.

In Rowling's text, Harry has presumed that any underwater antagonists will take on a mythic or folkloric form: 'water-monsters, of giant serpents, of demons, kelpies and sprites' (Rowling 2005: 526), but being familiar with mythical creatures of all kinds he, like Sam and Frodo, is much more terrified by the thought of an encounter with the human dead. By the final volume in Rowling's series, *Harry Potter and the Deathly Hallows* (2007), a confrontation with death is the inevitable destination. According to Frazer, 'when a person's life is conceived as embodied in a particular object … the destruction of which involves his own, the object in question may be regarded and spoken of indifferently as his life or his death' (Frazer 1978: 242). The quest within a quest in this volume involves Hermione, Ron and Harry removing themselves from the rest of the wizarding community and setting up camp in a remote wood in which, fittingly, 'the Quidditch World Cup' had been held (Rowling 2007: 225). Thus is the circle complete: if Quidditch is a rehearsal for the final duel to the death, it is only fitting for that finale to be played out on a championship pitch. Narratologically, this removal into the wilds enables the three principal characters to fulfil their quest largely unaided, just as Frodo, Sam and Gollum fulfil their lonely quest to reach Mount Doom and destroy the One Ring. Following an earlier struggle in which Rowling's three characters were engaged before 'apparating' (appearing magically) in the wood, they now have the actual locket, but cannot work out how to open it. In the meantime, as Harry wears it around his neck, 'so cold against his skin it might just have emerged from icy water', resulting in a re-igniting of the pain in his scar, more evocations of Frodo emerge (Rowling 2007: 229). As Hermione and Harry visit the graveyard at Godric's Hollow, the place of Harry's parents' burial, they also find Dumbledore's family's grave, with its inscription: 'Where your treasure is, there will your heart be also' (Rowling 2007: 266). Though the phrase obviously recalls the horcruxes, what we might miss is that Rowling has taken the verse from the Bible (Matthew 6:21). We are, in this book, back to the search for the Holy Grail once more and, as the series reaches its climax, Rowling draws increasingly on the conventions of epic fantasy, never more so than when Harry finds the sword of Gryffindor (a clear echo of Excalibur) although, in Rowling's series, its rightful inheritor turns out to be Ron, not Harry.

MONSTERS

If the totemic object is the goal of the quest, *en route* we may expect our epic heroes to encounter one or more monsters whose role it is to prevent him/her reaching that destination. From Ovid's *Metamorphoses* onwards, monsters have often provided one of the most imaginative and exciting elements of the quest. Particularly in the earliest tales, questions of sexual perversion sometimes accrue around the monster's origins, just to insure against their victimization evoking sympathy in the reader/listener, and hybridity is commonly used as a visual shortcut to imply grotesque immorality. In Book VIII of *Metamorphoses*, both traits combine, as the minotaur that fights Theseus is reputed to be the offspring of Minos's mother, who 'play[s] the harlot with a bull and in her womb could bear/ A bairn in whom the shapes of man and beast confounded were' (Ovid 2002: bk. VIII, l. 175) and which is later described as being 'Of double shape, an ugly thing' (Ovid 2002: bk. VIII, l. 207). Nevertheless, no bestial form is more frequently utilized for monsters than that of the giant reptile. So, in book IV of *Metamorphoses*, Perseus saves Andromeda from a sea monster, with 'scaly neck', 'cruel teeth', and 'spindle-tail' (Ovid 2002: bk. IV, ll. 880, 881, 892), while in book I, Ovid writes a kind of creation myth in which the warmth of the sun (Phoebus) mingles with the 'lusty earth' to create 'sundry creatures sundry shapes' (Ovid 2002: bk. I, ll. 495, 507), among which is the Python. Though serpentine in name, the sheer size of this creature ensures that it is 'A terror to the new-made folk which never erst had known / So foul a dragon in their life, so monstrously forgrown, / So great a ground thy poison-paunch did underneath thee hide' (Ovid 2002: bk. I, ll. 527–529). Such monsters are there purely to be defeated and the Python is slain by Apollo, 'The god of shooting', who fires 'a thousand shafts well near' into the Python's side, thus 'forc[ing] forth the venomed blood along his sides to gon; / So that, his quiver almost void, he nailed him to the ground' (Ovid 2002: bk. I, ll. 530, 532, 534–535). Ovid's stories of gods and monsters are epic tales of good versus evil in which character development is subordinated to a clear moral victory as we observed in the case of Edmund Spenser's *The Faerie Queene*, book 1 (1590), also discussed in Chapter 2. This book of Spenser's epic poem marks the culmination of the Redcrosse Knight's heroism through the depiction of him slaying a colossal dragon, whose length 'of three furlongs does but little lack' (Spenser 1966: 227), and whose 'deepe devouring jawes / Wide gaped, like the grisly mouth of hell' (Spenser 1966: 228). Again it is included simply to be destroyed. When the dragon retaliates by snatching both the knight and his horse and flying off with them, though we enjoy the thrill of the struggle, the result is never seriously in doubt. Finally impaled on the Redcrosse Knight's sword, one imagines the cheers as 'A gushing river of blacke goarie blood, / That drowned all the land' (Spenser 1966: 231) bursts forth, the hyperbole reaching its climax in the suggestion of such a flood.

Spenser's portrayal of the dragon is conventional for such epic fantasy: it is immense, malicious, deadly and reptilian. On the one hand, it becomes easily identifiable as a version of the Old Testament manifestation of Satan in serpentine form, tempting

Eve in the Garden of Eden (Genesis 3:1–15), aiding an uncomplicated opposition to be established between the Redcrosse Knight as good and the dragon as evil. Simultaneously, Spenser's dragon's excessive size and grotesque appearance also emphasizes its fabular qualities, facilitating its existence not simply as an antagonist, but as a symbol within the terms of which 'otherness', strangeness and foreignness of species type easily translate into the 'otherness', strangeness and foreignness of other races. No sympathy must be wasted on either count, in the desire for colonialist expansion.

More recently, fantasy quest narratives have endowed their dragons with a more complex moral depth, symptomatic of a society in which animal rights are far more developed and in which national war-mongering attracts greater hostility, perhaps, than in former times. In the television series *Merlin*, the dragon is imprisoned in a dungeon to hide the existence of magic from the King's court and citizens. Despite being initially frightened on discovering it, perhaps more because of its *scale* than its *scales*, Merlin quickly realizes the dragon is a source of 'old wisdom', a phrase synonymous, here and elsewhere, with magic. By extension, it is the dragon who imparts to Merlin the nature of the hero's quest, rendering it monster and philosopher/adviser in one. It is therefore in the context of consulting the dragon that Merlin starts to question the very nature of monstrosity itself. If the dragon is a monster because of its magic, then what of himself: 'I'm not a monster, am I?' he asks Gaius.

Rowling strikes a kind of middle ground in her *Harry Potter* books, her dragons simultaneously existing as antagonists *and* exotic animals. In volume 4, *Harry Potter and the Goblet of Fire* (2000), the first task of the Triwizard Tournament involves each of the players evading a dragon in order to steal a golden egg from its nest. Harry faces a Hungarian Horntail, 'a monstrous, scaly black lizard thrashing her spike tail, leaving yard-long gouge marks in the hard ground'. This dragon is clearly an antagonist, though Harry's attempt to compare it in his mind with 'just another ugly opposing team' at a Quidditch match demonstrates his attempt to reduce rather than exacerbate its otherness. Certainly some characters express disgust at the dragons' presence, such as Madam Pomfrey the matron, who exclaims 'Last year Dementors, this year dragons, what are they going to bring into this school next?' (Rowling 2000: 309–310, 312). Others, such as Hagrid, adopt an excessively compassionate approach. For Hagrid, all creatures are beautiful and, from *Harry Potter and the Philosopher's Stone* onwards, dragons are shown to be his particular favourite. Harbouring a newly hatched baby dragon, he croons '"Isn't he *beautiful*?" … He reached out a hand to stroke the dragon's head. It snapped at his fingers, showing pointed fangs. "Bless him, look, he knows his mummy!" said Hagrid' (Rowling 1997: 172). When Ron voices an objection, he does so partly on legal grounds, partly on safety grounds, and partly for identical reasons to those depicted in *Merlin*: 'Dragon-breeding was outlawed by the Warlocks' Convention of 1709 … It's hard to stop Muggles noticing us if we're keeping dragons in the back garden – anyway, you can't tame dragons, it's dangerous' (Rowling 1997: 169). Perhaps, however, some additional concern attaches itself to the prohibition of domesticating a dragon: for creatures as ancient and (literally) fabulous as these, such practices seem as demeaning as lion-taming. As Susan Stewart observes:

> The comic image of the monster on a leash … the pet … dragon, illustrates the absolute inversion of the miniature which the gigantic presents … the pink elephant being the most incongruous mixture of nature and culture, a beast dreamed by an interior decorator.
>
> (Stewart 1993: 70)

In fantasy quests, as we have seen, the journey is intrinsic, be it literal or metaphorical, and questions of scale and contrasting scales predominate. From *Metamorphoses* to *Harry Potter* the quest has changed little in structure or theme, although the moral and ethical interpretations of the protagonists' actions have been transformed by societal change. As we saw in relation to *Phantastes*, psychoanalysis has enabled us to understand that quests can pursue an inward as well as an outward path and children are often as well suited to being their central protagonists as Arthurian knights. Towards the end of the chapter we also considered in brief some of the ways in which monsters can facilitate a politically charged interpretation malleable across time. In Chapter 5, we will consider in a more sustained manner the various ways in which fantasy narratives have been used as deliberate conduits for political change, as well as exploring some of the political debates they have unwittingly prompted in recent times.

NOTES

1 Although social degeneration was developed more fully by scientists and philosophers in the twenty years following the publication of *The Water-Babies*, the early seeds of it were being sown during the period when Kingsley was writing.
2 Lewis acknowledged that a copy of *Phantastes* which he bought at a railway station bookstall in 1916, played a landmark role in his conversion to Christianity (see Prickett 2005: 176).

5

FANTASY AND POLITICS

Most fantasy narratives, films, television and comics, with their apertures onto parallel worlds, use those vistas not simply as entry points into impossibility, but to confound our assumptions about real science, politics, environments and sexuality. Sometimes fantasy is written or scripted to be polemical intentionally, but some works find themselves unwittingly, perhaps decades later, at the centre of a heightened political controversy sparked by changing social attitudes towards gender, race and/or sexuality. Among these, children's narratives often come to the fore, due to concerns that children are impressionable readers less capable of offering up resisting readings than adults. Here, we begin by considering three children's fantasy narratives which have sparked such political controversy, before turning to narratives for adults that deliberately set out to utilize fantasy as a social and political critique of the world.

PROBLEMATIC POLITICS IN CLASSIC CHILDREN'S FANTASY

Charles Kingsley's *The Water-Babies* (1862), discussed in detail in Chapter 4 as a quest narrative, today reads as anti-Irish propaganda, written at a time when the whole of Ireland was a British colony.[1] Kingsley's racist observations begin when Tom, the protagonist, finds himself along a salmon river, next to which Kingsley depicts an imaginary Irishman called Dennis. Here, as elsewhere, Kingsley steps in as frame storyteller to address his child reader directly:

> Dennis [will tell] you strange stories of the Peishtamore, the great bogy-snake which lies in the black peat pools ... and puts his head out at night to snap at the cattle ... But you must not believe all that Dennis tells you ... [He] will look up at you with his handsome, sly, soft, sleepy, good-natured, untrustable Irish eyes ... because he is in the habit of giving pleasant answers: but, instead of being angry with him, you must remember that he is a poor Paddy, and knows no better; so you must just burst out laughing; and then he will burst out laughing too, and slave for you, and trot about after you ...
>
> (Kingsley 2016: 42–43)

Although an apparent mix of positive and negative attributes is offered here, Dennis being 'handsome' and 'good-natured' as well as 'sly' and 'untrustable', it quickly emerges that the positive qualities are included simply to make the negative ones sound credible. Thereby, as the passage develops and becomes progressively more offensive, the naïve child reader is more likely to 'tag along' with the narrator's views. Nor is it solely the Irish upon whom Kingsley vents his bigotry. On the same page, he goes on to compare this river with a

> Welsh salmon river, which is remarkable chiefly ... for containing no salmon, as they have all been poached out by the enlightened peasantry, to prevent the Cythrawl Sassenach (which means you, my little dear ...) from coming bothering into Wales, with good tackle, and ready money, and civilisation, and common honesty, and other like things of which the Cymry stand in no need whatsoever ...
>
> (Kingsley 2016: 43)

Kingsley's phrase 'Cythrawl Sassenach' only actually includes 'you, my little dear' if the reader in question is English, for the phrase, more properly written in Welsh as 'Cythrawl Saesneg', translates as 'English Devil'. Thus, what is elsewhere implied covertly is made explicit here: Kingsley's implied child reader is both English and Anglophile in his/her politics.

Perhaps not surprisingly, Kingsley's racist politics extend beyond Britain, as he compares a seal in the water to 'a fat old greasy negro with a gray pate' and describes Tom, the boy sweep, as 'a little black ape' (Kingsley 2016: 50, 10). While 'black', in this context, could be argued to refer to the soot rather than Tom's skin, subsidiary observations make clear Kingsley's colonialist views of other races, such as when Tom sees the picture of the crucified Christ in a young girl's bedroom at Hartover House and, not recognizing the image, reflects that 'Perhaps it was some kinsman of hers, who had been murdered by the savages in foreign parts' (Kingsley 2016: 10). As recently as 2017, Catherine Nealy Judd has offered a kind of apologia for Kingsley's politics, claiming that he was wrestling more tortuously than a twenty-first-century reader might realize with 'what were for him indissoluble social and political problems'. She notes his 'disquietude' over 'the Irish Famine, U.S. slavery, and the condition of the British working classes' (Judd 2017: 179), and later reiterates, 'Although he was both racist and politically conservative, he opposed slavery' (Judd 2017: 190). Nevertheless, it seems hard to defend Kingsley's extraordinary description of the Irish famine victims he encounters on a fishing trip: 'I am haunted by the human chimpanzees I saw along that hundred miles of horrible country … [T]o see white chimpanzees is dreadful; if they were black, one would not feel it so much, but their skins, except where tanned by exposure, are as white as ours' (Kingsley 1894: 107; cited in Judd 2017: 201). On the figures of speech linked to apes, Judd observes that 'Parallels drawn between Africans and simians were also a nineteenth-century commonplace' (Judd 2017: 197), as if this excuses Kingsley's attitudes on the grounds of Victorian norms. Evidently, Kingsley was an accomplished writer, whose use of terminology, rhetorical play and figures of speech are well-honed weapons in his ideological armoury. As we will come on to see, all writers of quality understand fully the role language plays in constructing a social and political worldview and Kingsley's responsibilities to his child reader will have been abundantly clear to him.

Two twentieth-century children's fantasy narratives have also found themselves at the centre of controversy in recent decades. The first is Jean de Brunhoff's *Histoire de Barbar/Barbar the Elephant* (1931), about a young elephant whose father is killed by a hunter and who is then caught, placed in captivity and brought to France. Numerous political problems attach themselves to the Imperialist assumptions inherent in de Brunhoff's story. Barbar is taught literacy, in a plot device clearly aimed at narrowing the division between the elephant and the primary-school aged reader. He starts to wear clothes, under the 'civilizing' patronage of a wealthy spinster, who then allows him to return to Africa for a holiday, accompanied by his female elephant friend Celeste, whereby both show their mothers how far they have come, in both senses of the term. The triumphalist ending depicts Barbar driving a motor car back into Paris, Celeste's and his own mother following behind.

In response to that final scene, Herbert Kohl reminisces about his response as a child, especially to de Brunhoff's accompanying illustrations: 'Babar, Celeste, and Arthur [are] dressed to kill ... while Celeste's and Arthur's mothers [are] naked as elephants'. The effect, he argues, is to give 'the civilized elephants ... personal identity and distinction: the natural elephants are portrayed as indistinguishable' (Kohl 1995: 10). The message for child readers is clear: Westernization transforms the unidentifiable savage into a defined individual. Speaking to a Black South African friend of his about *Barbar*, Kohl's friend's response was uncompromising: 'the analogy between the naked elephants and African people was so transparent and insulting as to make the book overtly racist and without redeeming factors' (Kohl 1995: 33). Not only is the story Imperialist in tone, it raises uncomfortable truths about respect for one's elders and, in particular, respect for older women. Kohl's view on this point has remained constant from childhood to adulthood: 'Every time I looked at the book as a child, I felt there was something here that wasn't right. The mothers weren't being treated fairly. They should have been the ones in the car and the children should have been running behind, or they should all have been together in the car'. He continues: 'Yet that wouldn't work either, since the idea of dressed and naked elephants riding together seemed embarrassing to me. That illustration was and is painful for me to look at' (Kohl 1995: 10).

Barbar was first translated into English by A.A. Milne, in 1933 and again by Enid Blyton, in 1941. Blyton's connection is ironic, for her books have perhaps attracted more political controversy over the last 40 years than any other writer's. As Blyton herself is reputed to have said, 'I do not write merely to entertain … My public do not possess matured minds … And my public, bless them, feel in my books a sense of security, an anchor, a sure knowledge that right is always right …' (Anon 1950: 2). The potential for political indoctrination is rife in these words and, as early as 1966, the *Guardian* journalist Lena Jeger argued that Blyton's early book, *Little Black Doll* (1965), was 'insidiously dangerous' on ideological grounds (Jeger 1966: 18). However, it is undoubtedly Blyton's *Noddy* books (1949–1963) that have reached the widest child audience across successive generations and have therefore attracted most notoriety in children's fantasy circles.[2] The *Noddy* series turns toys into characters with whom children identify directly, Noddy himself being the key point of view character, Big Ears a Grandad-like figure, Master Tubby the local naughty boy (in teddy bear form) and Bumpy-Dog his pet. At least in the original series, however, Noddy is also accompanied by a Golliwog, and it is this figure, above all, that has raised so much political anger. Bob Dixon is clear that the golliwog 'is a racial caricature, of an African type' (Dixon 1978a: 99), a point with which *The Guardian* newspaper journalist Cindy Matthews agrees: 'There is not much doubt in my mind that the golliwog … with its goggle eyes, spiky hair, and banana lips is in fact a distorted representation of a black person' (Matthews 1984; cited in Rudd 2000: 136). In terms of child empathy, Dixon argues that Blyton ensures her readers are given 'little opportunity to develop … affection' for her golliwogs, because they are 'usually "naughty" and constitute a threat to Noddy' (Dixon 1978a: 96).

David Rudd, however, is less convinced that child readers necessarily associate Blyton's golliwogs with Black people, nor does he agree that Blyton's golliwogs are any more naughty than her other characters. In fact, based on 'a *corpus* of 323 Blyton stories, randomly selected', Rudd observes that 'Nine per cent featured golliwogs, 25 of which ... were "good" and only four "bad". There do actually seem to be more naughty teddy stories than gollies ... In fact, the golliwog is often a character that comes up with solutions to problems ...' (Rudd 2000: 152). According to Rudd, most of the controversy was sparked by the fourth book, *Here Comes Noddy Again*! (1951), in which Noddy is attacked by a group of golliwogs. Certainly, Rudd accepts that one might read this attack scene as a racist warning of the social consequences of the newly cosmopolitan Britain and, equally clearly, we know that Blyton was fully aware of the colonial power politics inherent in her writing: 'Quite apart from my millions of English-speaking readers, I have to consider entirely different children – children of other races ... I am, perforce, bringing to them the ideas and ideals of a race of children alien to them, the British' (Anon 1950: 3). However, though Blyton's words here are certainly nationalistic, one has to ask if they are necessarily racist, written as they were in the immediate aftermath of World War II and evoking, as she goes on to do here, a number of European readers of various nations, including the Germans, 'who, oddly enough, are perhaps more taken with my books than any other foreign race' (Anon 1950: 3).

In reopening the case, Rudd conducts empirical research with groups of schoolchildren of a variety of ages and ethnicities. Beginning with the question of whether child readers of Blyton's stories consider 'golliwog equals ethnically black person', his observation is: 'All I can say is that, of the children who were not previously aware of the equation ... none made it' (Rudd 2000: 147). Following his explanation to the children, first that adults *had* made this connection and then had decided to edit out the golliwogs because of it, Rudd reports that the children became indignant, accusing the editors of 'reverse racism'. As two of his interviewees – 'two Asian boys (14-year-olds)' – observed: 'if they want to change a character, they could have changed a different one. Why [do] they have to deliberately remove that golliwog, or whatever?' (Rudd 2000: 151). On the basis of Rudd's far more extensive findings than I can accommodate, adult readers do seem to read Blyton's golliwog characters differently from child readers, but they are also deeply selective in their findings. Rudd continues, 'People who isolate the "mugging" of Noddy by golliwogs in *N[oddy]4* miss the fact that crime is rife in Toyland. The golliwogs aren't distinctive … Car thefts occur in five more books – none of which involves golliwogs – besides other thefts in seven further titles' (Rudd 2000: 85). One might argue that Rudd's approach is similar to Judd's, who acknowledges Kingsley's racism but explains it away. However, while Rudd accepts that Blyton 'was part of a society that was racist', he refuses to identify her as racist (Rudd 2000: 134). In similar vein to me tasking Kingsley with taking responsibility for the politics of his own language use, Rudd argues that 'Blyton, as a storyteller, was always refashioning her work'. If she had been aware of concerns about racism, he argues, 'She would have been the first to retell her stories without golliwogs … just as, had she lived, she would have updated her language from those rather passé days of "queer" and "gay" abandon' (Rudd 2000: 202).

COMICS AND GLOBAL ANIMOSITY

Dixon's negative view of Blyton's conservative politics is matched in his assessment of British children's comics of the 1970s, regarding them as conservative publications in which 'royalty and the aristocracy are thrust upon the reader' (Dixon 1978b: 7). Superman and similar comic superheroes, Dixon claims, construct national stereotypes 'by building fantasy upon feelings of inadequacy and by diverting frustration against authority on to acceptable hate-figures', to the extent that 'the fascist overtones of the superheroes are stressed' (Dixon 1978b: 41). Gershon Legman goes further, claiming that Superman 'is really peddling a philosophy of "hooded justice" in no way distinguishable from that of Hitler and the Ku Klux Klan' (Legman 1963; cited in Dixon 1978b: 41). While Dixon demurs from going that far, he is clear that the rise of the comic superhero in the 1930s coincides with the global rise of fascism: 'Even Superman himself, in 1938, was not the first of the line as Lee Falk created the Phantom, complete with black mask and purple tights, in 1936' (Dixon 1978b:

41). For Les Daniels, on the other hand, part of the success and importance of comics lies in their *counter*-cultural politics. Tarzan and Buck Rogers, he notes, were created in 1929, following the Wall Street Crash which led to the decade of the Great Depression in the United States and much of Western Europe. Thus Daniels identifies in the popularity of these two comic superheroes, 'a desire for escaping from the grim truth of the economic situation' (Daniels 1971: 6).

Certainly the connection between the creation of superhero figures and global political strife seems incontrovertible. In 1941, the year the United States entered World War II, Captain America emerged as a new comic book hero. Originally Steve Rogers, sole recipient of an experimental serum designed to 'turn ordinary men into superb mental and physical specimens (for the war effort of course)', once drafted into the Army he is Steve Rogers GI by day, but by night Captain America: 'clad in a red, white and blue costume and brandishing a bullet proof shield, he struck terror into the hearts of spies, saboteurs and fifth columnists everywhere' (Daniels 1971: 136). The nature of that transformation, however, is worthy of further comment. Unlike Superman or Batman, both of which had already appeared in print by this time, Captain America did not acquire superpowers; he 'could not fly and was not immortal', a feature Daniels considers important for military morale (Daniels 1971: 137). Nobody engaged in military conflict wants to hear that victory can only be secured by those endowed with superpowers.

The term 'superpowers', however, takes on a new political meaning after World War II, with the development of the Cold War between the United States of America and the Union of Soviet Socialist Republics (Soviet Union). During this period, such patriotism as was evident in the creation of Captain America was not sufficient to save comics from attack by Senator Joseph McCarthy (1947–1957), whose fervent belief that the political establishment of the United States had been infiltrated by Soviet spies (colloquially termed 'Reds under the beds') led to a systemic paranoia that spread to all sections of the arts. Comics were treated with especial suspicion, although McCarthyism was not their sole enemy. Daniels explores the equally negative influence of the German-American psychiatrist Frederic Wertham who, in his book *Seduction of the Innocent* (1954), claimed that 'comic books led children to crimes of lust, violence and anarchy' (Daniels 1971: 86).

Alongside its fears of Soviet infiltration, another of America's key political enemies during and after this period was Japan, a society that has since had a major impact on the development of fantasy toys, animation and comic-books. In her influential (though noticeably pro-American) study of Japanese toys, *anime* and technological fantasy creations, Anne Allison writes, controversially in my opinion, about the important role World War II played in the destruction and re-building of Japanese culture. Noting that it was Japan's own wartime government that depleted its toy manufacturing industry by restricting its use of metals only to the production of weapons, Allison claims that the wholesale destruction caused by allied forces' atomic bombing of the Japanese cities of Hiroshima and Nagasaki in 1945, somehow enabled Japan to rebuild its toy industry. Equally helpful, so Allison claims, was the amount of rubbish (such as tin cans) left strewn across Japan by departing occupying forces, because it provided Japanese toy manufacturers with the basic ingredients for that rebuilding. Allison does, nevertheless, acknowledge the extent of the animosity shown towards Japan by the United States of America in the post-War decade, describing the secret detonation in 1954 of

> a fifteen-megaton hydrogen bomb (750 times the atomic power of the bombs dropped on Hiroshima and Nagasaki) near Bikini Atoll in Micronesia. A Japanese trawler, the *Daigo Fukuryū Maru* (Lucky Dragon), fishing in nearby waters, was exposed to the fallout, and six members of the twenty-three-man crew died shortly afterward.
>
> (Allison 2006: 44–45)

In response, Japanese culture utilized such events as inspiration for the construction of several Japanese film and comic book heroes and monsters. One such is the eponymous *Gojira* (1954), a cinematic 'four-hundred-foot-tall amphibious monster awakened from his four-hundred-million-year hibernation at the bottom of the sea by nuclear testing conducted by Americans', resulting in the type of monstrous hybrid encountered in Chapter 4, in this case 'part dinosaur, part nuclear weapon' (Allison 2006: 42). The second is the construction of the *manga* character *Tetsuwan Atomu* (Astro Boy), in 1951, whose half-clad body and rocket-propelled boots combine what Allison calls the 'fetishization of the mechanical' with a 'playful and cute' appearance, 'a sensibility that has pervaded children's media, particularly that targeted [at] boys during the entire postwar period' (Allison 2006: 58–59). Unlike British and German toymakers, who traditionally specialized in toys 'miniaturizing adult life' through 'dolls' houses and vehicles', thereby emphasizing the realist aspects of pretend play, it was the aforementioned heroes of American comics around which Allison claims the Japanese toy industry was re-constructed (Allison 2006: xvi).

POLITICAL DYSTOPIAS I: *NINETEEN EIGHTY-FOUR* AND 'ESCAPE FROM SPIDERHEAD'

In a British post-World War II context, there is no more influential politically based narrative than George Orwell's *Nineteen Eighty-Four* (1949). Written as a political critique of all totalitarian regimes in direct response to the global rise of fascism and communism, even today it is striking just how many of Orwell's imagined dystopian changes have actually occurred. Just as Orwell invents a 'telescreen' that spies on those near to it, 'receiv[ing] and transmit[ing] simultaneously' (Orwell 1984: 8), so do we fear covert surveillance by phone app. (see Curran 2018). When Oceania, Orwell's dystopian society, invents a Lottery with a 'weekly pay-out of enormous prizes', even though its inhabitants suspect those prizes may prove 'largely imaginary', the panacea effect of our own National Lottery becomes clear (Orwell 1984: 77). Orwell's sustained emphasis on the role personal dejection plays in political oppression propels us into an experiential as much as an intellectual engagement with dystopia. We long for some alleviation to the bleakness of Winston Smith's life, sharing his desire for a separate space of fantasy within which he might secure some sensory respite.

Orwell's prescience unsettles a twenty-first-century reader in particular. Two of his coinages, 'Room 101' and 'Big Brother', have passed into common parlance in the form of popular television programmes. *Room 101* is a comedy panel show in which guests 'compete to banish their top peeve or worst nightmare' (Anon 2019c), while *Big Brother* 'follows a group of people living together in a house outfitted with dozens of high-definition cameras and microphones recording their every move, 24 hours a day' (Anon 2019a). Both programmes follow the basic function attributed to their title phrases in *Nineteen Eighty-Four*, except for the terrifying political intensity of the original. One cannot laugh at or immediately after reading Orwell's novel, whereas these television programmes trade in wry humour, not political horror and, in the process, demonstrate the complacent superiority of modern Western Democracy: nobody living in fear under a totalitarian dictatorship would find Orwell's concept the basis for light entertainment. Here is where the competing world of fantasy emerges, as we sit reading comfortably, reassuring ourselves that Orwell's vision is *only* a political dystopia. Similarly, despite our growing unease about digital surveillance, there is a particular irony for our purposes in *Big Brother* being marketed as a *reality* television programme, one definition of which is 'a genre of programming that purports to show the unscripted actions of everyday people, rather than prepared dialogue delivered by actors' (Allen 2019). As the use of the word 'purports' suggests, layers of fantasy accrue around reality television and its participants. Similarly, layers of fantasy are built up in *Nineteen Eighty-Four*, but in this case by its protagonist as a means of survival. In fact, Orwell's Room 101 does more than confront its victims with their greatest individual 'peeve' or 'nightmare': it uses that fear with the express aim of reducing them to inhuman wrecks begging for their loved ones to be tyrannized, tortured or maimed rather than themselves.

Two of the key words that we have come to associate with fantasy in this volume, the 'impossible' and 'nonsense' recur in Orwell's novel, but they do so as an internalized riddle, there only to reveal their redundancy. Winston tells O'Brien, a member of the Thought Police, that the desired vision to create 'a world of terror' is 'a dream. It is impossible,' to which O'Brien simply replies 'Nonsense' (Orwell 1984: 231). Elsewhere, Winston himself reminds us that Newspeak reduces everything to 'the substitution of one piece of nonsense for another' (Orwell 1984: 40). As he is employed to alter journalistic accounts of recent events to match the reality that the Party wishes to create, replacing one name with another, or changing the words to discredit one person or elevate another, Winston contemplates that 'Statistics were just as much fantasy in their original version as in their rectified version … Everything faded away into a shadow-world in which, finally, even the date of the year had become uncertain' (Orwell 1984: 40). As in Edward Lear's nonsense writings, discussed in Chapter 1, the political horror towards which the Party strives in Orwell's novel follows a logical pattern. As the fictional dissident Goldstein observes in his pamphlet: 'The Party intellectual knows … he is playing tricks with reality; but by the exercise of *doublethink* he also satisfies himself that reality is not violated' (Orwell 1984: 183).

Despite the odds, Winston clings to his belief in the existence of competing worlds, singling out the glass paperweight he buys in Mr Charrington's shop as a miniature object encapsulating that dream. The paperweight is a perfect symbol of fantasy, having no utilitarian value, but drawing one's imagination into the space on the other side of a transparent but impermeable glass membrane, inside which is a small piece of fragile beauty, here a fragment of pink coral. In association with the clandestine romantic relationship Winston develops with Julia, he allows himself to believe that 'The paperweight was the room he was in, and the coral was Julia's life and his own, fixed in a sort of eternity' (Orwell 1984: 130), but to position his love-affair inside the glass dome is to screen it off from Oceania which, despite its marine-like name, would have neither use nor interest in sea-coral. In this sense, too, Orwell is unwittingly prescient, for to us as twenty-first-century readers, coral has become a primary signifier of the dangers of advanced capitalism, as climate change causes it to bleach and die (World Wildlife Fund 2019). Again, Winston's optimism proves ill-founded; though he may talk of the room above the antique shop as 'a hiding-place that was truly their own', Mr

Charrington is also revealed as a member of the Thought Police (Orwell 1984: 123). Even the paperweight has been planted to inspire and then crush dreams, being snatched up and deliberately smashed as arresting guards burst in.

Nevertheless, Winston *is* a recurrent dreamer, although his dreams fail to attain their usual segregation from political reality. Instead of the Thought Police, Big Brother, the Party and O'Brien simply featuring as characters in dreams authored by Winston's unconscious, it is as if Winston's unconscious is being authored by them. Two dreams prove especially important, the first taking place in

> a pitch-dark room. And someone sitting to one side of him had said as he passed 'We shall meet in the place where there is no darkness.' ... What was curious was that at the time, in the dream, the words had not made much impression on him. It was only later and by degrees that they had seemed to take on significance. He could not now remember whether it was before or after having the dream that he had seen O'Brien for the first time, nor could he remember when he had first identified the voice as O'Brien's. But at any rate ... [i]t was O'Brien who had spoken to him out of the dark.
>
> (Orwell 1984: 26)

The structure of this dream is typical of medieval dream texts, in which the dreamer receives a message of prophetic importance in his/her sleep, altering the subsequent course of his/her actions. However, as Kathryn L. Lynch reminds us, such dreams typically heighten awareness of three aspects of the dreamer's consciousness: 'his existence before the vision, the vision itself, and his life afterward' (Lynch 1988: 47). That sequential insight is entirely lacking in Winston's case, making it impossible for him to dissociate cause from effect. Like Julia, O'Brien is a character to whom Winston is attracted initially because of the ambiguously motivated but unmistakeable notice he pays him. Both characters offer up the allure of alternative realities, although where Julia's proves utopian and unrealizable, O'Brien's proves dystopian and enforceable. Indeed, when O'Brien eventually initiates contact with Winston and they meet in an inner room of O'Brien's house,

Winston realizes he has simultaneously walked into his own dream, completing O'Brien's half-formed parting phrase: 'We shall meet again – if we do meet again' with the words that came to him then: 'In the place where there is no darkness?' O'Brien concurs, 'nodd[ing] without appearance of surprise. "In the place where there is no darkness," he said' (Orwell 19843: 157). Sadly, what Winston here hopes will prove an entry into dreamland, later reveals itself as a portal into horror.

The second presiding dream attaches itself to Winston's guilty memories of his mother and younger sister. These follow a gothic framework, as he imagines them both 'down in some subterranean place – the bottom of a well, for instance, or a very deep grave – but it was a place which, already far below him, was itself moving downwards' (Orwell 1984: 30). In part, this dream pre-dates his consciousness of the party as he recounts a childhood memory of the atomic bombing of Colchester and his family 'hurr[ying] down, down, down into some place deep in the earth, round and round a spiral staircase which rang under his feet … Finally they had emerged into a noisy, crowded place which he had realized to be a Tube station' (Orwell 1984: 33). Increasingly, however, Winston's experience of political oppression becomes a life-in-death existence in which images of the grave, his mother's and his own, predominate. So, again after the meeting with O'Brien, Winston 'had the sensation of stepping into the dampness of a grave' (Orwell 1984: 141) and, later on, he awakens in a torture chamber with the sense of 'swimming up into this room from some quite different world, a sort of underwater world far beneath it' (Orwell 1984: 207). Later still, O'Brien encourages Winston to look in the mirror, wherein he perceives 'a bowed, grey-coloured, skeleton-like thing', a kind of living corpse (Orwell 1984: 233). It is when Winston finally describes Room 101, however, as being 'many metres underground, as deep down as it was possible to go', that we recognize this political arena to be the crypt-like destination towards which both his childhood memories and adult dreams have been leading him, all along (Orwell 1984: 244).

The passage of time can alter our reading of fantasy as well as of politics. In the 1980s, as an undergraduate student, I was given the opening sentence of *Nineteen Eighty-Four* as the basis for a seminar discussion: 'It was a bright cold day in April, and the clocks were striking thirteen' (Orwell 1984: 7). In those days, the very mention of 'thirteen', an hour that does not exist on a clock face, sufficed to tell us that Orwell's novel was fantasy and that the society he was depicting was anti-realist. When I shared that same narrative opening with my own students, thirty years on, they passed over it without comment, simply interpreting it as meaning 'one in the afternoon'. Though clocks still do not chime out thirteen, the twenty-four-hour clock is now in as familiar everyday usage as decimalization (another of Orwell's futurist visions). This anecdotal example underscores an interesting aspect of political fantasy, which is that it typically operates as much through *defamiliarization* as invention. Orwell does not *invent* the twenty-four hour clock: its origins are believed to lie in Ancient Egypt and it starts to enter into specialized usage in the West around the turn of the twentieth century, first being adopted as 'military time' in Britain at the end of World War I (Anon 2019b). Nevertheless, it seems reasonable to suggest that, domestically, analogue clock time predominated in the lives of ordinary people for most of the twentieth century, only really coming into everyday usage when personal computer technology became commonplace.

The guilt that plagues Winston Smith, especially linked to his mother, returns in George Saunders's twenty-first-century political story 'Escape from Spiderhead' (2010). Jeff, a convicted murderer, has been transferred from prison to a scientific research laboratory, in which he becomes a human 'lab-rat', injected with a variety of chemicals to provoke emotional and sexual responses to a partner similarly engineered for scientific purposes. On the face of it, this might be a text one would expect to belong in Chapter 6 of this book, except that the lust experienced by the characters is so obviously chemically induced that it does not translate into eroticism for the reader at all. Instead, the sexual content manifests itself as a *political* rather than sensual intervention, inflicted upon a set of characters whose liberty has been removed and, as such, 'Escape from Spiderhead' resonates much more closely with *Nineteen Eighty-Four* than, for example, J.G. Ballard's *Crash*, which will be discussed in detail in Chapter 6.

Several interesting echoes and reverse echoes of *Nineteen Eight-Four* resonate through 'Escape from Spiderhead'. Where Orwell's Oceania attempts to reduce the diversity of the English language to its absolute minimum ('We're destroying words – scores of them, hundreds of them, every day. We're cutting the language down to the bone'; Orwell 1984: 48), part of the chemical cocktail introduced into Jeff's bloodstream looks to enrich his linguistic abilities to the optimum. In a kind of scientific simulacrum of the Genesis myth, we first encounter Jeff in an 'Interior Garden'. It is the Garden which is first used to test his linguistic sensors, as his description of this virtual/imaginary space shifts from 'Garden looks nice ... Super-clear', to 'It was as if I could suddenly discern, in this contemporary vignette, the ancient corollary through which Plato and some of his contemporaries might have strolled; to wit, I was sensing the eternal in the ephemeral' (Saunders 2013: 45–46).

In *Nineteen Eight-Four*, we recall that one of Winston Smith's key acts of resistance is to start keeping a diary, the sensual materiality of it being almost as important as the act of writing itself. It is a 'thick, quarto-sized blank book with a red back and a marbled cover', in which he writes using a fountain pen (Orwell 1984: 10). In that sense, his relationship with Julia emerges directly as a kind of extension of literary and linguistic pleasure. One might argue that something similar occurs in 'Escape from Spiderhead', in which a satisfactory rhetorical response to the garden leads directly to an erotic experiment in which Jeff is required to interact romantically and sexually with two different women, Heather and Rachel. In each case, the sensory response between Jeff and Heather/Rachel moves from 'about average, i.e., no big attraction or revulsion either way', to a chemically induced perception that 'we had known each other forever, were soul mates, had met and loved in numerous preceding lifetimes, and would meet and love in many subsequent lifetimes, always with the same transcendently stupefying results' (Saunders 2013: 47–48). At its height, the eroticism is detailed and intense: 'the sensations her vagina was producing along the length of my thrusting penis were precisely those I had always hungered for, though I had never, before this instant, realized that I so ardently hungered for them'; there again, so is the linguistic pleasure: 'I dare say we had become poets ... Everything seemed moist, permeable, *sayable*' (Saunders 2013: 49, 50). What Orwell and Saunders therefore reveal, despite writing fifty-five years apart, is that overlooking the importance of language's role in our politics will have an attendant detrimental impact on our human subjectivity. Language is as innately sensual, enticing, slippery and 'moist' (to use Saunders's word) as sexual play and as intrinsic to our self-expression and political self-worth as democracy.

However, for Jeff, sexual play is only half of the experiment. In phase two, he has to choose whether it should be Heather or Rachel who will receive 'Darkenfloxx{TM}', a chemical designed to propel the recipient into a morass of misery and depression (Saunders 2013: 55). The rationale for requiring Jeff to choose is to see if, once the previous erogenous chemical mixture is removed, he is left with any residue of romantic feeling for either woman. Displaying none, the chemical is randomly administered to Heather, who begins to display alarming and physically violent behaviour towards the furniture and herself until she eventually collapses, lifeless. The intertwined elements of sex and death that we will see inform so much erotic fantasy take on an overtly political slant here. Just as Winston is tortured into betraying Julia, tormented by his self-centred sacrificing of his mother and sister and brain-washed into an artificially induced love of Big Brother, so Jeff cannot continue to inhabit a world in which people become subordinate to the chemical replacement and thus regulation of love, romance and erotic desire. At the end of the story Jeff commits suicide, despite knowing his actions will bring unbearable torment to his mother. As he contemplates this final thought, just as the story begins in a Garden, with all its biblical connotations, so he ends with another allusion to biblical paradise: 'I hoped someday, in some better place, I'd get a chance to explain it to [Mom], and maybe she'd be proud of me, one last time, after all these years' (Saunders 2013: 80–81).

POLITICAL DYSTOPIAS II: *THE HANDMAID'S TALE* AND *ORYX AND CRAKE*

One year after the fictional setting for Orwell's *Nineteen Eighty-Four*, Margaret Atwood published *The Handmaid's Tale* (1985), a novel which plays, similarly, on society's anxieties about surveillance. As David Lyon puts it,

> Suddenly, you realize that someone – or something – is watching. You are enjoying a quiet drink in the bar, when you see the small camera, unobtrusively observing the scene. Why is the camera watching you? ... It is hard to find a place, or an activity, that is shielded or secure from some purposeful tracking, tagging, listening, watching, recording or verification device.
>
> (Lyon 2001: 1)

Atwood sets her novel in Gilead, a society which, like Oceania, has turned in on itself, becoming self-enclosed and ensnaring its citizens within an oppressive regime. Instead of Orwell's Thought Police, Atwood gives us The Eyes, another secret but faceless organization established to create fear and compliance. The two human attributes to which these political organizations refer, thought and sight, combine to demonstrate how political coercion functions. Independent thought is a basic principle of Western democracy and is connected intrinsically with intellectual freedom, thought and speech, while sight is becoming associated increasingly with the curtailment of that freedom. From Jeremy Bentham's eighteenth-century invention of the panopticon onwards (a prison architecture designed to ensure prisoners could be placed under continual scrutiny, but by unseen guards), the asymmetrical power relationship between the unseen watcher and the one who is seen and identified is one of the key ways in which inequality is established and, in the twenty-first century, growing. In *Nineteen Eighty-Four,* even the countryside is monitored, and when Winston and Julia arrange to meet there, Julia's nervousness about the possible presence of a microphone seems especially Benthamite in its manifestation: 'I don't suppose there is, but there could be' (Orwell 1984: 106). Thought Police or not, power is most successfully imposed in society by self-policing.

When a twenty-first-century reader situates *Nineteen-Eighty-Four* alongside *The Handmaid's Tale*, what emerges is the realization that certain cultural shifts which would be less politicized at the time of writing have become far more so now, paramount among these being the habit of smoking. In *Nineteen Eighty-Four*, in line with post-World War II reality, almost everybody smokes and so ubiquitous is the habit that Orwell makes little observation about it, except to bemoan the fact that cigarettes are rationed in Oceania and the quality of the tobacco is poor.[3] Winston's body is ulcerated, stiff and impaired, even at the start of the book, but none of that deterioration is attributed to his smoking. By the time Atwood writes *The Handmaid's Tale*, the dangers smoking poses to unborn babies is much more fully accepted by society and, in her novel, cigarettes are forbidden to the handmaids on health grounds. Nevertheless, smoking retains its illicit appeal here, much more so than it would in twenty-first-century writing. Thus is smoking enabled to become one of several means via which the Commander's Wife, Serena Joy, affirms the power inequality between herself and Offred, enjoying contraband cigarettes in front of her while Offred looks on 'with longing' (Atwood 1987: 24). When, later, Serena Joy suggests to Offred she might have a clandestine affair with Nick the chauffeur, thus increasing her chances of conceiving, she 'takes the cigarette she's been fiddling with and, a little awkwardly, presses it into [Offred's] hand', simultaneously endowing the cigarette with the allure of a guilty pleasure and suggesting it as a clichéd post-coital prop (Atwood 1987: 216).

Rather like the changing attitudes towards race discussed above, such changes alter the twenty-first-century reader's understanding of political freedom, a concept interrogated explicitly in both novels. In *Nineteen Eighty-Four*, the Party issues the slogan 'FREEDOM IS SLAVERY' (Orwell 1984: 239), one which acquires ironic truth in the characters' freedom to enslave themselves to a deadly nicotine addiction. In *The Handmaid's Tale,* the 'Aunts' who train the Handmaids remind them that 'There is more than one type of freedom … Freedom to and freedom from. In the days of anarchy, it was freedom to. Now you are being given freedom from. Don't underrate it' (Atwood 1987: 34). Here we encounter a different type of guilty pleasure: scopophilia, or the pleasures of looking. The 'freedom from' to which Aunt Lydia refers is the handmaids' newly acquired freedom (at least politically) from institutionalized objectification by the masculine gaze. In actuality, even in Gilead, individual encounters lead to covertly exchanged glances, such as when Offred's pass is checked by a guard and he bends to obtain a clearer view of her face: 'he blushes ... He is the one who turns away' (Atwood 1987: 31). Here, Offred is able to wrest power from this situation only because she recognizes the guards' social impotence to act: 'As we walk away I know they're watching ... and I move my hips a little ... I enjoy the power ... I hope they get hard at the sight of us and have to rub themselves against the painted barriers, surreptitiously' (Atwood 1987: 32).

That policing of space and transitional movement between spaces, also applies inside, even to the extent that the Commander is required to knock before entering the sitting room, 'supposed to be Serena Joy's territory' and Offred waits for the morning bell before descending the stairs each day (Atwood 1987: 97). Much like Winston, Offred takes greatest consolation from small (seemingly) private spaces and, in the cupboard of her room, delightedly discovers a covert message, inscribed in Latin on the wall: '*Nolite te bastardes carborundorum*' / 'Don't let the bastards grind you down' (Atwood 1987: 62). It is when inside the Commander's room, playing Scrabble, however, that the greatest spatial and political breach occurs and, as with the earlier transgression of boundaries with the young security guard, that breach becomes sensual. A former librarian, Offred is as clear about the pleasure-based possibilities of language as is Jeff in 'Escape from Spiderhead', comparing the Scrabble tiles to 'candies, made of peppermint' and imagining 'put[ting] them into [her] mouth' (Atwood 1987: 149).

In Atwood's later dystopia, *Oryx and Crake* (2003), books and reading have become a thing of the past, but so has eroticism. When the protagonist, formerly named Jimmy and now self-named Snowman, enters a deserted house and encounters 'The lady of the house ... in the bedroom, tucked under the king-sized pink and gold duvet', he recognizes, more quickly than the reader, that she is dead (Atwood 2003: 230). Thinking of himself as a castaway, Snowman realizes that such a character needs a narrative for existence and 'he'll have no future reader, because the Crakers can't read' (Atwood 2003: 41). Like Offred, he has flashbacks in which he savours 'words of precision and suggestiveness ... *wheelwright, lodestone, saturnine, adamant'* and, while Offred finds words sensual, he associates them with a 'strangely tender feeling ... as if they were children abandoned in the woods and it was his duty to rescue them' (Atwood 2003: 195). Nevertheless, his fairy-tale allusion seems implicitly to connect words with oral pleasure, as we recall that one of the most influential stories about abandoned children in the woods is 'Hansel and Gretel', itself a story in which oral delights (a house of sweets) cloak powerful and potentially fatal villainy (the cannibalistic witch).

The political impetus of *Oryx and Crake* is environmentalist. A post-apocalyptic novel, almost all of humanity has disappeared and we follow Jimmy/Snowman in his quest for survival along a coastal strip devoid of utilities, supplies, technology or medicines. While Orwell's room above Mr Charrington's shop features an 'old-fashioned clock with [a] twelve-hour face ... ticking away on the mantelpiece' (Orwell 1984: 122) and the hallway in Atwood's Commander's house features a 'grandfather clock ... dol[ing] out time' (Atwood 1987: 18), in *Oryx and Crake* clock time has disappeared. Though Snowman still wears his watch, it now constitutes 'a blank face' and tidal time now predominates, as 'wave after wave slosh[es] over the various barricades, wish-wash, wish-wash, the rhythm of heartbeat'. Snowman's accusation, 'You did this!', hurled at the ocean, implies that a tsunami might at least have been partially responsible for the desolate landscape, but as with our own fears of climate change, it is humanity, above all, that is shown to have been culpable (Atwood 2003: 3, 12).

Science research on animals is blamed, above all, for the wholesale environmental destruction in *Oryx and Crake.* Irrespective of whether it is for medical advancement or cosmetic enhancement, the challenge to animal species integrity is held accountable for this dystopia. There are two main fictional chronotopes in Atwood's novel: Jimmy's pre-apocalyptic childhood past and Snowman's post-apocalyptic present. Though Atwood sets her novel in the future, seemingly reassuring the reader that what has happened in *Oryx and Crake* can be prevented from happening in our own society, Jimmy's childhood memories are commensurate with our own present and thus raise the contrary possibility that such an apocalypse is already in train. Hence, as Snowman recalls the fictional incineration of diseased animal carcasses on a huge bonfire when he was a child, the reader recalls the factual pyres of cattle in Britain following the foot and mouth outbreak in of 2001. Similarly, when Snowman thinks back to the 'pigoon' project, in which 'an assortment of foolproof human tissue organs' is developed within 'a transgenic knockout pig host' for medical purposes, we remember that xenotransplantation, or the process whereby the organs of one species are transplanted into another, is already happening in our society (Atwood 2003: 22). As Andrew Griffin observes, 'There are several medical procedures [already] using pig tissues such as heart valves in cardiac surgery, insulin producing pancreatic cells to correct diabetes in man [sic] and corneal transplants which have been used safely … for many years' (Griffin 2017). Atwood's novel extends the process a stage further, the medical research laboratory (OrganInc Farms) utilizing the pig as a repository: 'A rapid-maturity gene was spliced in so the pigoon kidneys and livers and hearts would be ready sooner … Such a host animal could be reaped of its extra kidneys; then, rather than being destroyed, it could keep on living and grow more organs (Atwood 2003: 22–23). When Snowman recalls the café at the research institution serving increasing amounts of pork products on the menu, people suspecting they were being fed part-human tissue, the British reader also recalls the bovine spongiform encephalopathy (BSE or 'mad cow disease') scandal of the 1980s and 1990s, partly caused by cattle being fed contaminated animal products.

In Chapter 4, we saw the role Ovid's *Metamorphoses* has played, throughout literary and cultural history, in inspiring the creation of successive generations of hybrid monsters that feature in epic and popular fantasy narratives, the human hero battling the evil monster in the name of good versus evil. In *Oryx and Crake*, Atwood changes the terms of that struggle and, in the process, renders the political inequalities already implicit in such epic tales explicit; humanity has already lost and Snowman is certainly no hero. Consequently, where Ovid's bestial monsters can operate as metaphors for nationalistic or class struggles,

Atwood's animals *remain* animals, albeit predatory fantasy hybrids: pigoons, snats, wolvogs, spoat/giders, kanga-lambs and rakunks. As Snowman remembers, when not used for organ transplants, the pigoons 'were being used to develop skin-related biotechnologies … replacing the older epidermis with a fresh one … wrinkle- and blemish-free' (Atwood 2003: 55). Created in laboratories for the sole purpose of extending human life and youth, it seems the pigoons have had the last laugh.

In all four of the dystopian novels discussed in this chapter, an underlying narrative of mother (and sometimes child) loss presides. Irrespective of the type of politics that informs the narrative, the personal is persistently shown to be political. Offred and Snowman both have mothers who are deemed to be dissidents by the totalitarian regimes in power and both protagonists are forced to watch film footage of those women in custody or labour camps. Shown an image of an otherwise unrecognizable woman, her utterance proves her identity beyond doubt to Jimmy/Snowman: 'Goodbye. Remember Killer. I love you. Don't let me down' (Atwood 2003: 258). As only Jimmy/Snowman knows, Killer was Jimmy's pet rakunk, taken by his mother when she abandoned the family to engage in sustained and direct political action. At the time Jimmy mourned the loss of his pet as much as the loss of her, perceiving in her actions a gratuitous attempt to cause him pain. Only on witnessing the camera footage does Jimmy realize that taking Killer was the only way his mother could have foreseen being able to corroborate her identity to him, in a situation in which political punishment might render her unrecognizable, physically.

THE FEMINIST UTOPIA

Despite the gender politics that inform so much of Atwood's writing, and despite the interest that feminist literary critics have taken consistently in Atwood's work, she has persistently resisted self-definition as a feminist writer. For Atwood, the version of feminism portrayed in much literature of the Second Wave (circa 1968–1990) idealizes women's sisterhood in a manner she finds politically suspect. Certainly the feminist utopian impulse of the

1970s and 1980s reveals a very different relationship between women and the environment than we find in Atwood's work. In 1978, Susan Griffin wrote a work of feminist philosophy which situates woman at the centre of (or *as*) land and man as its conqueror: 'Sea. Mountain. River. Plain. Forest. Gorge. Field. Meadow. Rock. Plateau. Desert. Mountain. Valley. Sea. He is the first ... Only the mark of his shoes effaces the soil. Pine. Otter. Canyon. Musk ox. She gives up her secrets' (Griffin 1994: 47). Here we find man's foray across new territory written in his footprints, once again emphasizing the importance of inscription to the construction of a fantasy landscape. Everything beyond him is both 'Other' and feminized. A similarly essentializing environmental approach to gender politics is mapped out in Sally Miller Gearhart's 1979 utopian novel *The Wanderground: Stories of the Hill Women,* which might almost be read as a fictional version of Griffin's political treatise and in which the narrative voices interweave from woman to woman, collectively offering up a storytelling sisterhood.

As a seemingly *natural* extension of those politics, Gearhart's women are able to commune telepathically, for which a range of different terms exist: 'shortstretch', 'mind-touch', 'Mindstretch', 'softsens[e]', 'mindreach' (Gearhart 1985: 5, 19, 35, 114, 142). This form of communication is extended to animals and, unlike the children's animal fantasy narratives discussed in Chapter 3, in which a hierarchy of speaking and non-speaking animals is established, in *The Wanderground*, female human characters interact with *all* animals, be they birds or mountain lions. That equality of ontology requires an adjustment on the part of the reader who, particularly in the early chapters, sometimes presumes an animal character to be human, simply because of the way the female character addresses it. At other times it is difficult to ascertain if an animal is actually there or imagined. As the child character Clana digs with her hands at a hole in the ground, the soil gradually falls away and she starts to wonder if it is a home for snakes. Momentarily wary, she conjures up in her mind a variety of species of snake, which are then brought into material existence and, as they squirm and intertwine around her, a drumbeat is emitted which causes her 'to move in sometimes clumsy, sometimes graceful steps with the serpent dance … She added her own keening voice to the hissing, sighing, purring, pounding, screeching, slickly swishing, rattling, cacophony that surrounded her' (Gearhart 1985: 32–33).

The elemental bonding that evolves from the perceived connection between women and nature in *The Wanderground* sometimes manifests itself as 'windriding'. Unlike in J.K. Rowling's *Harry Potter* novels, in which a broomstick is required to provide the magic means of flight, windriding requires no magical accessories at all and is described in a manner quite close to swimming: 'She dared to float and breathe … As she hovered and breathed … she began to push her arms gently to her sides; then up again, above her head … Again she stroked and again … face up and stretched full length' (Gearhart 1985: 114–115). Though clearly anti-scientific, one might argue that such narratives are no more outlandish than children's fantasy narratives such as J.M. Barrie's *Peter Pan*. The key difference is that, here, flight is both a means of political empowerment and a pragmatic mode of long-distance transport for a community lacking automated vehicles. As a by-product, however, it becomes a means of achieving atmospheric harmony with nature. As in Clana's encounter with the snakes, windriding is also accompanied by incantation, written here in the typical 'greeting's card' metre of first, second and fourth lines in iambic trimeter and third line in iambic tetrameter: 'The wind she lifts my laughter / the wind she lifts my cares, / and bearing both my pain and joy / she thus my body bears' (Gearhart 1985: 113).

However, that trite metrical rhythm sits perfectly with what I find to be the general political awkwardness of these women losing collective touch with material reality. Despite being a long-established and enthusiastic reader of fantasy and despite being an equally long-established and enthusiastic feminist, I do not warm to this type of utopianism, which seems to me neither to serve women nor the environment well. For example, when the character Bessie tells Clana how the otherwise unspecified apocalypse occurred and led to the inevitable segregation of men and women, she simply explains: 'The earth finally said "no". There was no storm, no earthquake, no tidal wave or volcanic eruption ... It only became apparent that it had happened, and that it had happened everywhere' (Gearhart 1985: 172). Part of the problem is that environmentalist politics have changed radically since the 1970s. Reading *The Wanderground* in the wake of Atwood's *Oryx and Crake* and at a point in time when it is clear that humanity-instilled climate change might very well result in the earth saying 'no' to us all, genuine environmental politics makes it equally clear that it will be *precisely* through storms, earthquakes, tidal waves and volcanic eruptions that such a message will be conveyed.

Gearhart's depiction of windriding is genuinely interesting, but its ideological foundation compares less favourably with the work of Mary Russo who, in *The Female Grotesque* (1994), also makes a case for politically informed flight as liberating for women, but does so, ironically, in a much more 'grounded' manner. Beginning with an analysis of the early pilot, Amelia Earhart (1897–1937), Russo identifies in Earhart's pioneering flights and stunt work a form of 'thrilling and emancipatory' political 'tightrope walking' which literalizes the 'high-flying' woman and introduces 'a principle of turbulence' into the patriarchal status quo (Russo 1994: 25, 24, 19 and 29). Starting with cultural history, Russo is able to introduce a political utopianism while retaining its material contact with gender politics. Angela Carter, similarly, delights us with her fictional portrayal of Fevvers, the *fin-de-siècle* 'winged aerieliste' in her 1984 novel *Nights at the Circus.* Like Gearhart's women, Fevvers compares learning to fly with learning to swim, but again in a more persuasive manner: 'I kicked up my heels and then ... brought the longest and most flexible of my wing-tip feathers together over my head; then, with long, increasingly confident strokes, I parted them and brought them back together' (Carter 1984: 35). Fevvers's appeal remains partly utopian, but it is also fleshly. The closest Gearhart comes to emulating that more persuasive political impulse is when Clana visits 'the Kochlias', a set of caves of pseudo-magical significance to the women, falls asleep and starts dreaming of 'women who skated only a few centimetres above the floor; women who carved stones with their minds or lifted huge burdens without ever touching them' (Gearhart 1985: 148). Those images work, politically, because they utilize elevation as a metaphor for longing. More generally in *The Wanderground*, there is an earnest literalness that takes itself *too* seriously, almost as if fearful that any levity will undermine its political effect.

Similar problems surround Gearhart's treatment of that aspect of magic which we associate traditionally with wise women and healers. Non-traditional medicine is certainly the norm in *The Wanderground*, but the possible associations with witchcraft is something Gearhart appears to resist:

> Once some hunter found a whole homeopathic pharmacy – a cave full of herbs and potions. Then there were some tales of tribal gatherings of women, peyote circles, covens. And that's what did it. It was the re-emergence of that word, *witch*, that sent the men at the station up the wall.
>
> (Gearhart 1985: 164)

Surely, in the context of fantasy, there are far more utopian political connections to be made between women and witchcraft than Gearhart attempts, as even William Shakespeare's *Macbeth* (1623) demonstrates. Confronted by the three witches on the heath in act I, scene 3, Macbeth is seduced into their plot; later, when he addresses them as 'secret, black and midnight hags! / What is't you do?' (act IV, scene 1, ll. 48–49), he does so with an air of reluctant reverence, identifying in them a form of female-oriented power he neither understands nor can control. Lady Macbeth, similarly, is 'witchy' and seductive, embodying an ambition and single-mindedness far in excess of anything of which Macbeth is capable and openly inviting the 'Spirits/That tend on mortal thoughts [to] unsex me here' (act I, scene 5, ll. 40–41). The women in *Macbeth*, then, are *impressively* terrifying, forces to be reckoned with, awesome in the literal sense of provoking awe and Macbeth is clearly in thrall to them. In that sense the witchcraft of *Macbeth* is not simply superstitious, it is political. That is precisely the kind of transformative message for which Mary Daly argues in her radical feminist work *Gyn/Ecology* (1978), contemporaneous with Gearhart's: 'Our foresisters were the Great Hags whom the institutionally powerful but privately impotent patriarchs found too threatening for coexistence, and whom historians erase' (Daly 1979: 14). That erasure, Daly argues, is best countered through loudness, for 'There is nothing like the sound of women really laughing. The roaring laughter of women is like the roaring of the sea' (Daly 1979: 17). By contrast, we recall the earnest solemnity of Gearhart's *The Wanderground* and its silent and surely politically self-defeating celebration of telepathy.

Returning to my earlier observation that, in *Nineteen Eighty-Four,* where Julia's version of reality proves utopian and thus unrealizable, O'Brien's is dystopian and therefore enforceable, we recognize that pessimistic political fantasies are easier to assimilate than idealizing ones. Utopias, in fact, are very difficult to write, because they leave very little room for manoeuvre. The reader either has to glory in the totality of the sealed vision presented, or is left with nowhere to go, politically. Nevertheless, in the midst of his otherwise pessimistic futurist vision, we recall Winston's realization that it is the sexual drive, above all, that is most feared by the Party, both for the privacy of its expression and the power it wields over our every waking thought. In Chapter 6 we explore in more detail the complicated nature of the relationship between sex, fantasy and sexual fantasy as explored in fiction, poetry and illustration.

NOTES

1 The 26 counties now constituting the Republic of Ireland only gained full independence from Britain in 1937, the remaining six being partitioned off as Northern Ireland, which remains part of the UK.
2 According to Bob Dixon, 'in 1968, the year of [Blyton's] death, the Noddy books had sold more than eleven million copies' (Dixon 1978a: 56). By 1992, David Rudd tells us that 'Noddy books were reported to have sold over 100 million copies, with overseas sales of 46 million' (Rudd 2000: 65).
3 In 2014, in a *Guardian* newspaper article, James Miekle uses figures from the Office for National Statistics to reveal that, in the 1940s, 'well over half' of the UK population smoked cigarettes, reducing slightly by 1974 to 45%. By 2013, however, levels had reduced dramatically to 18.4% (Miekle 2014).

6

FANTASY AND THE EROTIC

Ironically, and despite our shared love for smutty jokes, sexual swear words, not to mention sex itself, whenever critics write 'seriously' about sex and the erotic in fantasy, it is surprising how coy or full of obfuscation they become. As Ann Morris explains:

> In 'Sweeney Agonistes' T.S. Eliot reveals that birth, copulation, and death are 'all the facts when you come to brass tacks.' But most of us would rather not come to brass tacks, for birth, copulation, and death are experiences that can be both painful and frightening – experiences that, if mentioned, frequently produce shock, social embarrassment, and laughter.
>
> (Morris 1986: 77)

Despite the enticing title of Donald Palumbo's essay collection *Erotic Universe: Sexuality and Fantastic Literature* (1986), remarkably few of the essays in his collection actually discuss sex *as* sex. Instead, they gesture towards it, writing about gender equality, sexual orientation and, most commonly of all death, especially the perceived connection between Thanatos and Eros, or the sex and death drives. Geoffrey Gorer admits that 'There seem to be a number of parallels between the fantasies which titillate our curiosity about the mystery of sex, and those which titillate our curiosity about the mystery of death' (Gorer 1995: 21) and certainly death and its connection with the erotic will be discussed here, but not to the detriment of exploring fantasy as erotica.

In his introduction, Palumbo retraces fantasy to classical adventure narratives such as Homer's *The Odyssey*, identifying in it a journey to an 'unknown world', but one that 'leads one home'. It is this concept of entry into foreign but paradoxically familiar parts that forges the analogy Palumbo needs to connect fantasy with sex (Palumbo 1986: 4). His argument also reveals a common presumption shared by so many critics of erotica within and beyond fantasy: he views it wholly through a masculine lens, but presumes to speak for all. Colin Wilson is even more presumptuous in his essay 'Literature and Pornography', claiming mistakenly that 'women ... are seldom interested in sex in the abstract. For them, it means sex with a specific male, as part of a definite relationship, preferably involving love and protection' (Wilson 1982: 208). Nevertheless, Palumbo is right to argue that fantasy constitutes a kind of 'forbidden fruit' that renders it especially well-placed for the exploration of sexual desire (Palumbo 1986: 22). One might add that the distance fantasy establishes between worlds, as argued throughout this book, renders this exploration of the forbidden both 'safer' and, paradoxically, more immersive: we dream deeply, but ultimately re-surface unscathed.

FANTASY VERSUS SEXUAL FANTASY

Before going further, we must tease out the complicated relationship between fantasy in general and fantasy specifically applied to sex. Stephen Prickett claims that 'most pornography, except in the most pathological sense, does not fall into the realm of fantasy' (Prickett 2005: 103), an approach this Chapter sets out to challenge: after all, at least in common parlance, when one talks of fantasies it is often presumed that they contain at least some essence of the sensual. Other critics would agree; Peter Webb claims that 'Pornography *is* fantasy' (Webb 1982: 119; my emphasis) and Peter Green notes that erotic literature *relies* on fantasy for its existence, dealing 'not so much [in] sex *per se* as sexual fantasy and propaganda: sex in the head' (Green 1982: 19; his emphasis). Of course, it is not just 'sex in the head' which interests us, but sex on the page, more specifically a page which takes a distinctly utopian turn for, as Webb also observes, 'Jealousy and possessiveness have little part to play in this fantasy, for here, everything is for the best in the best of all possible worlds' (Webb 1982: 119).

Since the early 1970s, Nancy Friday has written books narrativizing women's sexual fantasies. While her work can be read for a variety of purposes, not least pure arousal, its key political importance is the legitimization she brings to the expression of women's sexual desires recounted on their own terms. We have already seen how commonly erotica is presumed to equate to phallocentrism and the necessity for Friday's project is never clearer than when reading books such as Alan Bold's edited volume, *The Sexual Dimension in Literature* (1982). All but one of Bold's ten contributors are male, and the voices in this collection routinely and collectively treat women simply as objects of erotic fascination. In his introduction, Bold belies his own stance on feminism when he tells us that 'the male chauvinist writer has much in common with the strident women's libber whose most dogmatic (and therefore suspect) desire is to deprive women of any sexual allure' (Bold 1982b: 11). It is against this backdrop of confusion and ignorance that Friday's work gains strategic significance. Often, the accounts she anthologizes are recounted through narrative realism and this raises one key difficulty for a book on fantasy. However, the relationship between fantasy and narrative realism is complicated by the erotic content.

Take the example of 'Isabel', one of Friday's contributors, who recounts her recurrent sexual fantasy about a male ice hockey team. To some extent, the verisimilitude of Isabel's fantasy is enhanced by the fact that she is a 'real life' supporter of ice hockey and knows some of the players. During sex with her husband, she imagines having intercourse with some team members, thus using fantasy to enhance her real pleasure. The enclosed nature of her fantasy is broken by the fact that, when really watching matches, she 'like[s] to imagine [the players] naked ... so by the time they enter into this fantasy, [she has] already thought up how they look' (Friday 1994: 233). What pertains, between

Isabel fantasizing about these men in her bedroom and imagining them naked while at the rink, is not just her relationship with the men, but with fantasy: she is immersed in her fantasy, but the men are not. Her fantasy therefore relies on a space differentiating between and connecting competing worlds, just like all the other fantasy works discussed in this volume.

Of course, it is not just women for whom erotic fantasy provides a short-cut to sexual control; Steven Marcus also emphasizes the importance to heterosexual men of being able to utilize fantasy to control otherwise taboo desires: 'in the pornographic fantasy, as in the comic cartoon, one can be destroyed or dismembered without being hurt' (Marcus 1970: 60). Wilson evokes comic heroes in this context, claiming that the appeal of pornography is similar to the appeal of 'Batman or Superman. But unlike Batman and Superman – which make no attempt to disguise their unreality – pornography pretends … that sexual intercourse is [our] highest happiness' (Wilson 1982: 214). The appeal of sexual fantasy is that it allows us to flirt with danger in a manner that tames and safely choreographs it: unlike actual sex, it places the author of the fantasy in total control. To some extent like George MacDonald, Hans Christian Andersen or J.M. Barrie's treatment of the shadow, discussed in detail in Chapter 4, sexual fantasy is an outward projection of the ego. Better still, and unlike those authors' treatments of the shadow, it teases us that what might seem impossible could become possible. To clarify: it might be improbable or unwise for an ice hockey team to play a match naked, but it would not be impossible to do so; one's shadow separating itself from one's feet and entering a house alone *is* impossible.

VICTORIAN EROTIC FANTASY

Webb uses a similarly sporting metaphor when he claims that 'The Victorian pornographic novel represents the fantasy of the Victorian male: all men are sexual athletes, all women flow with the juices of love'. Nothing Webb says here seems specifically Victorian, but it acquires greater resonance because of the superficially prudish reputation we have retrospectively attached to that period. In fact, Webb insists that 'The strict code of morality that lay behind this [Victorian] world of literature was in real life being breached continually … and if the brothels provided the opportunities, the pornography catered for the fantasies' (Webb 1982: 119, 92). Play, indeed, seems to form a connecting point between respectable and salacious worlds in the nineteenth century and, at times, children's fantasy writing provided a seemingly safe surface for an undercurrent of adult-oriented suggestiveness. For Prickett, one cannot ignore the key role of the major Victorian illustrators in this respect, many of whom 'elaborated' upon or 'made more explicit' the suppressed eroticism inherent in narrative fantasy (Prickett 2005: 99). Among those, Prickett gives special mention to the children's illustrator Richard Doyle (1824–1883), to whose illustration of 'a tiny girl (perhaps a fairy?) being menaced by a gigantic stag beetle' he attributes C.S. Lewis's published claim that, having witnessed it as a child, it 'gave him nightmares' (Prickett 2005: 99). 'The Fairy Queen's Messenger' (c.1875 Fig. 2) might be the image to which Prickett is alluding, though it is unlikely to be the one to which Lewis refers.

Figure 6.1 Richard Doyle, 'The Fairy Queen's Messenger' (*c.*1875), Florilegius/ Alamy Stock Photo

Lewis does not, in fact, identify Doyle as the illustrator in question, simply referring vaguely to 'a certain detestable picture in one of my nursery books' and, to an extent, whether it is this or another image does not matter for our purposes. What does matter is that Lewis is speaking in the specific context of having developed a childhood phobia of insects, a category he seems to extend to spiders, which meant that he 'would rather meet a ghost than a tarantula' (Lewis 2012: 8, 7). Hence the 'menace', which might otherwise seem misplaced in 'The Fairy Queen's Messenger', in which the beetle is simply a means of transport akin to a horse or, here, stag. The larger point is that Doyle's insect illustrations, a series of which were produced in the 1870s, are unsettling on sexual grounds, not least the fact that the naked child fairy, ambiguously gendered though possibly male, is surely riding side-saddle partly to conceal his/her genitalia and partly to avoid the more explicit erotic connotations of 'straddling' the beast. Others of Doyle's illustrations are disturbing by inference, such as 'Saying Bo to a Beetle', in which a malevolent-looking boy sprite or pixie faces down a ladybird; though 'Saying Bo' suggests a sweet game, there is nothing 'sweet' about the look on the pixie's face. In similar vein is 'Teasing a Butterfly', in which a group of six children, three of whom are uncannily similar to John Tenniel's illustrations of Alice, are depicted tormenting the creature with sly or 'knowing' facial expressions. These are not 'innocent' illustrations, and the connection between faerie, teasing (of a variety of kinds), children and narrative mischief is clearly suggested. One who wishes to do so might well claim that a child who teases in one way is a tease in another. It is in this context that I find Doyle's illustration 'A Rehearsal in Fairyland' (*c.*1870) particularly sinister. Here, a naked girl fairy holds court, sitting with knees drawn up and ankles crossed to conceal her genitalia from the onlooker, ringed by a choir of forty birds, some of which are depicted calling full-throatedly into the air. On one level a simple choral assembly, on another it seems to me that the mood of this image could very easily switch to one of rapacious assault on the part of such a large group. After all, while the noun 'rehearsal' refers to a concert, it can as easily apply to an orchestrated sex act.

The point is that one person's pleasure constitutes another's fear and one person's innocent play is another's seductive tease. According to James R. Kincaid, 'Different people in different places at different times feel wildly different things about quite specific children' (Kincaid 1992: 10) and Doyle's illustrations provide clear evidence of such differentials. Certainly, the Victorians could be amusingly ingenious in their sexual play. Marcus tells us that flagellation was the erotic perversion *par excellence* for the Victorians and, in 1828, a prostitute called Theresa Berkeley invented 'a machine "to flog gentlemen upon"', a contraption which Marcus wryly describes as 'perversity's contribution to the Industrial Revolution'. Competing with this contraption was the commonly held fantasy of the existence of 'a female whipping club' in which groups of like-minded (lesbian) women gathered 'for the mutual application of the birch'. However, another, more modern aspect of these fantasies of flagellation also attracts comment from Marcus. He notes that the sexual identity of both flogger and recipient during these practices often became irrelevant, enabling 'anybody ... [to] become anybody else' and 'the differences between the sexes [to become] blurred and confused' (Marcus 1970: 67, 61, 257). Here we have an early approximation to what Angela Carter calls, a century later, the 'moral pornographer ... [one] who uses pornographic material as part of the acceptance of the logic of a world of absolute sexual licence for all the genders, and projects a model of the way such a world might work' (Carter 1979: 19).

While flagellation cannot be found in Christina Rossetti's fantasy poem 'Goblin Market' (1862), there is plenty of rough sexual play: 'Scratch[ing] ... pinch[ing] ... / Kick[ing] and knock[ing] ... / Maul[ing] and mock[ing]' (ll. 427–429). Here, the forbidden fruits of sexual desire take a decidedly adventurous turn for two nice Victorian ladies, Laura and Lizzie. Rossetti's poem begins as a traditionally folkloric vision of goblin mischief, written in a kind of travelling street-seller's patter: 'Come buy, come buy, / Apples and quinces, / Lemons and oranges, / Plump unpecked cherries ...' (ll. 4–7), but once Laura and Lizzie appear, we instantly recognize, by Laura's 'bowed' head and Lizzie's 'veiled ... blushes' (ll. 34–35), that something more saucy is on offer. The goblins themselves can be interpreted in a variety of ways: as examples of the Fair Folk, as disreputable men, as unsuitable but alluring men (there is an implied class bias in the costermonger identity). Whatever their nature, that both young women are genuinely tempted by them is clear in their shared insistence that they 'must not look', nor 'buy their fruits', for 'Who knows upon what soil they fed / Their hungry thirsty roots?' (ll. 42–45). The obviously phallic connotations of 'roots' here raises the issue of sexual appetites, and the missing comma between 'hungry' and 'thirsty' suggests the goblins' gobbling might take manifold forms.

Accosting Laura and finding her penniless, the goblins persuade her to surrender a lock of hair, in return for which they provide her with fruit on which 'She sucked and sucked and sucked the more / … She sucked until her lips were sore' (ll. 134–136). Not only is this orally driven engorgement a kind of fruity fellatio, its travelling supply chain means Laura really does not know where it has been. As Terence Holt observes, there is a kind of second-handedness to what these goblin men offer: 'The honey [the women] gather is tainted: it has already appeared in the poem, literally in a goblin's mouth. "In tones as smooth as honey" (l. 108)' (Holt 1996: 134). Read in this way, the 'honey' also become suggestive of semen, ingested in an orgiastic frenzy in which the gorging is also a phallic satiation by mouth: a sucking dry and a sucking full, depending on whether we read Laura as subject or object, for both are possible under Rossetti's fluid vision of longing.

The labial and oral suggestiveness of this gorging on the fruit of goblin men may seem surprising from a nineteenth-century woman poet who also wrote hymns such as 'In the Bleak Midwinter' and 'Love Came Down at Christmas'. That readers have been keen to salvage a more spiritual reading from 'Goblin Market' is made clear by Jerome J. McGann, who notes that it was also read as 'a Christian allegory … [about] the story of the fall in Eden' (McGann 1996: 104). For once, it seems that the spiritual reading requires a more active imagination than the erotic one. That is not to say that the sexual fantasy reading is purely hedonistic; Laura falls prey to a kind of sexual contagion in which she can no longer hear or see the goblins and her health and sense of self-esteem dwindles away. Fearing the worst, Lizzie goes searching for the goblins once more, hoping to buy more fruit for her sister. Buying their wares, but oblivious to their charms, the goblin men grow nasty: 'They trod and hustled her, / Elbowed and jostled her, / Clawed with their nails, / Barking, mewing, hissing, mocking, / Tore her gown and soiled her stocking …' (ll. 399–403). The message is clear: women who play men at their own game risk being punished, but steadfast Lizzie sticks to her own rules and hence returns home bruised but (morally) intact. Just at the point at which we might expect the poem to provide a resolution, it takes a momentarily unpredictable turn. Reunited with Laura, Lizzie's own oral desires are aroused, and she implores her sister to 'Come and kiss me, / Never mind my bruises, / Hug me, kiss me, suck my juices / Squeezed from goblin fruits for you' (ll. 466–469). Lizzie's kisses, however, though initially revitalizing, cannot compete with those of the goblins and this fluid exchange turns bitter in Laura's mouth.

The final section of the poem (ll. 543–567) offers a rapid reversal of everything that has gone before, as Rossetti is careful to add a major dose of cautionary moralizing, depicting Laura and Lizzie as safely married mothers of children who will learn from them not to dally with 'wicked, quaint fruit-merchant men' (l. 553). Such retractions are common in the work of Victorian women writers, fearful of recriminations from a society that largely resented women publishing at all, let alone writing erotic poetry, and, as such, the apparent retreat into modesty should not be permitted to overwrite the pervasive insistence on the pleasures of sucking a lover's juice, be that lover male, female, or 'other' (goblin). Here we have, indeed, Carter's moral pornographer a century ahead of time, offering up 'absolute sexual licence for all the genders', wrapped in the cloak of a nursery world. In part, it is the very fact that Rossetti dresses up this poem as a child's nursery tale that enables her to smuggle in the sexual content, for it encourages in the adult reader an uncomfortable sense of guilt that perhaps s/he is the one reading sexual meanings into an innocent poem. The supposedly prudish Victorians, then, were reading between the lines while simultaneously keeping within the lines. Prickett, indeed, explains 'the revived popularity of fairy stories in Victorian times' on the grounds that 'they were one of the few accepted ways in which stories about sexual fantasies could be told' (Prickett 2005: 98).

TWENTIETH-CENTURY PORNOTOPIAS OF DEATH

We have seen how Doyle's insect illustrations open up a space of fantasy in which nursery tales lead to more adult fantasy content, but the presumed point of view in all of his images of insects lies solidly with the child/fairies in them; the insect, whether friend or foe, is 'othered' consistently. In Patrick McGrath's short story 'The E(rot)ic Potato' (1988), on the other hand, narrative point of view lies with the insect, more specifically Gilbert the fly and his beloved Ariadne, a dragonfly. As soon as one endows an animal character with a name, one assumes it to belong to the type of children's fantasy narrative we discussed in Chapter 3, but McGrath's story remains wholly adult-oriented, as Gilbert and Ariadne feast, voluptuously and sensually, on death in what might be termed a utopia of decomposition. For Marcus, 'The literary genre that pornographic fantasies … tend most to resemble is the utopian fantasy' (Marcus 1970: 268) and he goes on to coin the term 'pornotopia' for such texts. Accordingly, he continues, a 'pornotopia is a pornocopia as well', in its belief in 'the richness and inexhaustibility of life in this imaginary world' (Marcus 1970: 273) and this is perhaps never more true than in 'The E(rot)ic Potato'.

As in 'Goblin Market', sexuality is driven orally in McGrath's story and the eponymously misnamed 'potato' (which turns out to be a human corpse) is not the first delicacy on offer. Discovering a poisoned rat, dying at the edge of a pond, the insects gather excitedly: 'Several flies and some ants had already mounted the body and were sampling tissue … There was more than enough for all, but naturally we wanted to lay open the belly first and get at the inner organs' (McGrath 1989: 167). It is here that Gilbert first catches sight of the teasing Ariadne:

> I felt a tremor run through her as my proboscis glanced against her articulated thorax, and then something rather wonderful happened.

> Ariadne fluttered aloft and, hovering close, delicately displayed the milkwhite tip of her ovipositor to me. I was flooded by an irresistible genetic impulse to penetrate and fertilize her, but the trembling organ was withdrawn and the flashing blue-green dragonfly fluttered away.
>
> (McGrath 1989: 168)

McGrath's achievement in this story is to convey the eroticism of the encounter while retaining Ariadne's essential 'insect-ness'. As Gilbert follows her to the potting shed, he glories in 'inhaling drunkenly the subtle wisplets of insect love juice she was secreting' and it is only as McGrath describes a momentary encounter between first Ariadne and then himself with the amusingly named Roger, a wasp employed as a 'bouncer' at the open window to the shed, that anthropomorphism intrudes, momentarily replacing sensuality with parody, as she 'rub[s] her gossamer wings one against the other and fill[s] the air with a silky rustle', which Gilbert notes, 'excited me beyond words', a phrase, obviously, that only has meaning if one can speak words to start with (McGrath 1989: 169).

I began this chapter by arguing that it is wrong-headed for critics of fantasy to take an evasive approach to sex by conflating it with death, and yet in 'The E(rot)ic Potato' McGrath genuinely does make death sexy, despite the scene he is depicting being one that we would ordinarily find repulsive: 'a dead man lying on his back under a table … And [his] eyes and ears and mouth and belly were alive with insects!' Because the sight instantly propels Gilbert and Ariadne into an orgiastic frenzy resulting in ecstatic copulation and because Gilbert describes his climax in a manner to which the human reader can relate, the reader's eroticism is undiminished: 'I quivered to the very quick of my being; I surrendered, fragmented, melted in the molten intolerable pleasure of it and dissolved to pure nonbeing, wrapped in shattering slithering Ariadne' (McGrath 1989: 170–171). That same drive towards sexual fulfilment through bodily annihilation can be identified in J.G. Ballard's extreme sexual narrative *Crash* (1973), in which Ballard explores the erotic possibilities inherent in violent car accidents, mainly focused upon the erogenous point of impact between human body parts and their penetration by metal and plastic automotive parts. The question is whether the same eroticism pertains here.

Ballard's first-person narrator, also named James Ballard, is locked into a homoerotic duel with Robert Vaughan, a former television scientist, and Ballard's fixation with Vaughan's engorged penis drives their connection: 'He knew that as long as he provoked me with his own sex … I would never leave him' (Ballard 2014: 2). At the same time, both men primarily identify as heterosexual and women are repeatedly objectified by death and near-death experiences at both men's hands. Beyond the world of Ballard's novel, sex tends to operate through repetition in combination with innovation: sexual advance initiates and is welcomed or rebuffed; when welcomed it is repeated and augmented, on the same occasion and/or subsequently. Narratologically, *Crash* works in an identical manner, except through the mechanism of what we might call 'bad sex'. Ruth Charnock associates bad sex in literature with predictable figures of speech: 'clunky metaphors' and 'inevitable, but awful genital euphemisms' (Charnock 2019). This pattern is not quite what we find in *Crash*, because implicit in Charnock's summary is the concept of cliché, the well-worn route to arousal, rendered mechanical on the page. Instead, Ballard presents us with arousal *by* the mechanical, imprinted on the page: thus engineering becomes the prosthetic and automated supplanter of the sex toy, forging a violent cybernetic fusion with the body, its known orifices and those new ones created through literal impalement. Instead of genital euphemism, one finds genital augmentation:

> sitting beside her physiotherapy instructor in her new invalid car, [Gabrielle] held the chromium treadles in her strong fingers as if they were extensions of her clitoris … The crushed body of the sports car had turned her into a creature of free and perverse sexuality, releasing within its twisted bulkheads and leaking engine coolant all the deviant possibilities of her sex. Her crippled thighs and wasted calf muscles … The posture of her hands on the steering wheel and accelerator treadle, the unhealthy fingers pointing back towards her breasts, were elements in some stylized masturbatory rite.
>
> (Ballard 2014: 79)

In her study of disability and its relationship with subjectivity and sexuality, Margrit Sheldrick identifies two typically uncomprehending approaches to the theme: 'a normative imperative to devalue or silence' the sexuality of differently embodied people and 'a highly evident strand of voyeurism … that spills over into a fetishistic focus on disabled bodies' (Sheldrick 2009: 96). Ballard's book represents the second. When Ballard first sees Helen Remington, whose husband has just died in a collision caused by him, he instantly notices 'the unusual junction of her thighs, opened towards me in [a] deformed way'. It is never made clear whether Helen's unusual gait is caused by the accident or birth, but Ballard fastens on it as a repeated point of reference: 'It was not the sexuality of the posture that stayed in my mind, but … the extremes of pain and violence ritualized in this gesture of her legs, like the exaggerated pirouette of a mentally defective girl I had once seen performing in a Christmas play at an institution'. Clear and persistently reductive labelling of disability recurs in *Crash*, most notably perhaps in relation to Gabrielle, whom Ballard introduces as 'crippled' (Ballard 2014: 14, 76). While some disability theorists have reclaimed the term 'crip' as a positive affirmation of identity politics (Kafer 2013), no such reclamation is at work here. In Ballard's eyes, as the aforementioned passage shows, Gabrielle is simultaneously dehumanized (a 'creature') and reduced to parts ('crippled thighs and wasted calf muscles').

Ballard tells us that his first erotic collision resulted from an in-car sexual liaison, when he and his wife Catherine were disturbed by a police patrol. Hastily reversing, Ballard drives into a tree, at which point Catherine vomits. Ballard continues:

> This pool of vomit with its clots of blood like liquid rubies … still contains for me the essence of the erotic delirium of the car-crash, more exciting than her own rectal and vaginal mucus, as refined as the excrement of a fairy queen … In this magic pool … I saw my own reflection, a mirror of blood, semen and vomit, distilled from a mouth whose contours only a few minutes before had drawn steadily against my penis.
>
> (Ballard 2014: 8–9)

As in 'Goblin Market', in *Crash* fluid exchange is the form by which perverse sexual fantasy finds its apotheosis, and certainly their sexual play continues along these lines, as Catherine paints her nipples 'liberally' with lipstick, against which Ballard 'press[es] … [his] face, arms and chest, secretly imagining the imprints to be wounds' (Ballard 2014: 22). Scopophilia equally features here. It is as Ballard looks into 'this magic pool' that his existence as originator of the scenario, both as driver and possessor of the penis, secures his significance to it. Like Rossetti's Laura, Catherine may have initiated the oral connection between them, but her act of regurgitation, otherwise read as rejection or denial, here seals rather than dissolves Ballard's potency, simply because it allows Ballard's output to become (im)printed and thus affirmed by his literally self-regarding narration. Gradually it becomes clear that, despite often being fixed centre-stage, it is never actually the woman who constitutes the desired other in *Crash*; she simply provides multiple orifices into which the engorged penis may be thrust, the ultimate aim being for semen to be spilled, spurted, dripped and drizzled over car parts, simultaneously endowing both with quasi-spiritual status.

This concept of 'woman as prop' culminates in Vaughan's fetishized longing to victimize screen actresses, women who are already constructed as a shadow layer of celluloid desire separated from and yet connected to the human original from which the screen image deviates. Supreme among them is Elizabeth Taylor and, when Seagrave, the production company's stuntman, commits suicide in a multi-vehicle collision dressed as her, complete with wig, Ballard later realizes he did it to avenge Vaughan, 'pre-empt[ing] that real death which Vaughan had reserved for himself' (Ballard 2014: 154). In her introduction to the 2014 edition of the novel, Zadie Smith claims Ballard also possesses the kind of social conscience we have seen Carter define as a moral pornographer:

> [Ballard's] fictional Elizabeth Taylor – written twenty-five years before the death of Princess Diana – is as prescient as anything in Ballard's science fiction. How did he get it so right? How did he know that the price we would demand, in return for our worship of the famous and

> beautiful ... would be nothing less than the bloody sacrifice of the worshipped themselves?
>
> (Smith 2014: vii)

Smith's purportedly moralizing view can be tested in an embedded piece of hallucinatory fantasy within the main text. When Vaughan successfully slips Ballard some lysergic acid diethylamide (LSD), his resulting 'trip' takes the form of a celestial vision, in which 'An armada of angelic creatures, each surrounded by an immense corona of light, was landing on the motorway', and Vaughan metamorphoses into an 'ugly golden creature, made beautiful by its scars and wounds' (Ballard 2014: 164–165). This King Midas-like vision, in which all Ballard beholds 'glisters', but lacks any of the morality one might conventionally associate with angels, reminds us that *Crash* is a product of advanced capitalism and so we might claim Ballard's approach to be one in which his violent fetishization of dismembered body parts forms an analogy for a socio-political deconstruction. Building on the perceived connection between sex and death in the specific context of advanced capitalism, Gorer argues that in developed societies, in which so-called 'natural' death is unusual in younger people, untimely violent death looms large in fantasy and 'the diffusion of the automobile, with its constant and unnoticed toll of fatal accidents, may well have been most influential in bringing the possibility of violent death into the expectations of law-abiding people in time of peace' (Gorer 1995: 21). Notwithstanding such possibilities, it seems to me that the erotic morass Ballard depicts in *Crash* remains destructive and misogynistic. Although male characters die, become disfigured, hospitalized and scarred *too*, only the female characters become fetishized through their disfigurements: this is bad sex indeed.

WOMAN-CENTRED DESIRE

When Marcus poses the rhetorical question 'What time is it in pornotopia?' answering his own riddle with the word 'bedtime' (Marcus 1970: 269), we realize that in novels such as *Crash* very little of the sexual activity actually takes place in bed and, when it does, Ballard compares Catherine pejoratively to 'a sexual exercise doll fitted with a neoprene vagina' (Ballard 2014: 38). In *Crash*, then, bedtime tends to mean hospital time, as characters recuperate from a series of self-inflicted or deliberately inflicted injuries. In Charlotte Roche's novel *Wetlands* (2008), however, bedtime is simultaneously hospital time *and* autoerotic time. Here we meet Helen, a hospital patient recuperating from an operation to remove embedded haemorrhoids from her rectum. The entire novel is scatological in orientation, as the multiple newspaper 'blurbs' emblazoned across the front cover of my copy attest: 'Got a strong stomach?' (*London Lite*); 'Profoundly unsettling' (*Daily Mail*); 'Haemorrhoids, hairy armpits and halitosis, mixed together into an erotic pot pourri' (*Irish Independent*). Of these publications, only the *Irish Independent* seems to have noticed that *Wetlands* is an erotic novel, and that the eroticism in question is feminized, 'hairy armpits' being worthy of note only when attached to women. In fact, Helen is inventively sexual, even cultivating avocado stones in glasses of water to allow her to insert them into her vagina, and substituting artificial perfumes with her own secretions: 'I dip my finger into my pussy and dab a little slime behind my earlobes' (Roche 2009: 14).

That inventiveness, however, does not in and of itself make *Wetlands* a fantasy novel: in fact, on the whole it is an interesting example of 'larger than life' woman-centred erotic realism, except when Helen dreams or daydreams, or struggles with her memories, for, as she notes herself, 'I often blur the distinctions between reality, lies and dreams'. Likewise, she indulges in allusions to fairy tales such as 'Hansel and Gretel', as she inserts the handle of a razor into her vagina and compares it to 'the finger of a fourteen-year-old. Like Hansel's finger of bone'; or to *The One Thousand and One Nights*, as the cleaner pushes her around on her bed, which Helen compares to 'being on a magic carpet', before realizing the cleaner means her harm, when Helen imagines retaliating, 'push[ing] her around like Aladdin' until she screams (Roche 2009: 57, 52, 162). At these moments we slip into a competing world in which children's fantasy narratives are revealed to be already underwritten with erotic or violent bodily content.

Helen is proactively heterosexual, but her major source of erotic pleasure is masturbation and it is here we realize that when heterosexual women fantasize about men, the men, too, become simple props in a dynamic rooted in woman-centred self-pleasure. In the controversy surrounding *Wetlands*, we identify a more pervasive socio-cultural hostility towards all kinds of female pleasure when that pleasure is not centred upon the aggrandizement of men. Take, for instance, the 'urban legend' Helen recounts in which two young women order a pizza delivery and complain when it does not arrive. Eventually it does, but then it 'looks a little funny and tastes odd' and, as the father of one of the young women is a food inspector, they take it to him for testing. Now they learn that 'there are five different people's sperm' on it. Helen offers the following interpretation of this (tall) tale: 'Since the complaints are made by girls, the delivery guys have rape fantasies … and all whip out their cocks to jerk off on [their] pizza' before finally delivering it. Two main observations are worth making here. First, although Helen claims this story pre-exists, we receive it from her and therefore, for us, she becomes its originator. Second, rather than expressing disgust, Helen uses it as inspiration for more sexual fantasy, reversing its original power relations: 'It would be like having sex with five strange men at the same time … like having five strange men blow their loads in my mouth' (Roche 2009: 67, 68–69).

Only one aspect of Helen's auto-eroticism is troubling politically, and that is the manner in which she seems to focus upon her body's pleasure to compensate for the horror of what she experiences as parental abandonment, another aspect of the novel evoking 'Hansel and Gretel'. Although both her parents and her brother visit her in hospital, she perceives herself persistently to be neglected. Two memories from childhood apply here: her parents' broken marriage, and her mother's failed attempt to commit suicide and kill Helen's brother by gassing them both in the kitchen; it is Helen who finds them and calls the emergency services. These memories and her parents' absence Helen describes as 'A gaping abyss', a phrase that obviously recalls her many forays into and descriptions of the various parts of her vaginal opening, especially as she widens it to its fullest extent through a variety of artificial means (Roche 2009: 190). What becomes troubling, therefore, is the fact that it is possible to read *Wetlands* as a narrative in which a woman immerses herself into a transgressive, inventive and elaborate series of autoerotic rituals and fantasies simply to offset an emotional and psychological void. As it is so difficult to find genuinely erotic narratives in which heterosexual women feature as subjects rather than objects, this aspect of Roche's novel is disappointing, especially as the ending sees Helen leaving the hospital with Robin, her male nurse, determined to return as a volunteer supporting patients, in effect transforming the narrative into an X-rated Mills and Boon romance.

One aspect of *Wetlands* that refuses any possible political negation is the manner in which Roche constructs a landscape of vulvic pleasure: 'Just don't wash too much. For one thing because of the all-important flora of the pussy. But also because of the taste and scent of the pussy, which is so important during sex.' Like every landscape it has a topography and Helen personalizes hers, rather in the way Tolkien personalizes Middle Earth, perhaps, endowing its features with imaginative names: 'the inner labia … I call the dewlaps – and the outer labia … I call the ladyfingers … my clit … I call my snail tail' (Roche 2009: 12, 16). The female anatomy is similarly rendered topographical in Marcus's study: 'It is usually seen at eye-level … On the horizon swell two immense snowy white hillocks; these are capped by great, pink, and as it were prehensile peaks or tips – as if the rosy-fingered dawn itself were playing just behind them' (Marcus 1970: 271). Marcus makes his way down the female form until he reaches the vagina or 'chasm', at which point his description both slows and adopts a closer focus:

> From its top there depends a large, pink stalactite, which changes shape, size, and color in accord with the movement of the tides below and within. Within the chasm … there are caverns measureless to man, grottoes, hermits' caves, underground streams – a whole internal and subterranean landscape. The climate is warm but wet. Thunderstorms are frequent in this region, as are tremors and quakings of the earth … This is the center of the earth and the home of man.
>
> (Marcus 1970: 271–272)

In Marcus's vulvic cartography, geology combines with folkloric references ('grottoes, hermits' caves') and the lexicon of adventure fantasy narratives such as Jules Verne's *Journey to the Centre of the Earth,* in a very similar manner to the multi-layered landscape of female erotic desire we find in Monique Wittig's *The Lesbian Body* (1973).

What Sally Miller Gearhart attempts politically in *The Wanderground* (discussed in Chapter 5), Wittig attempts erotically in *The Lesbian Body*: the production of a woman-centred utopia segregated from phallocentrism, here as an island culture. Less a novel than a piece of erotic prose poetry, *The Lesbian Body* adopts an epic tone and reaches back to mythology for its depiction of Amazonian, island-dwelling women, Wittig's narrative being closest in form to the kind of high Modernist writing we find in James Joyce's *Ulysses* (1922). Homer's mythic hero is indeed evoked by Wittig, as the narrator imagines 'Ulyssea … return[ing] from a long voyage' and the women prepare themselves with unguents and a heady mix of 'sandalwood … amber … benzoin … musk … [and] opoponax' (Wittig 1986: 23). Like *The Odyssey, The Lesbian Body* is written as a kind of journey narrative, but one which adopts a circular and sometimes subterranean route, again treating the woman's body as simultaneously a space of desire and a topographical map to be traced out by the lesbian lover. As part of that subterranean exploration, Wittig also re-visits Ovid's 'Orpheus and Eurydice'. As we will recall from our discussions in Chapter 2, in Ovid's tale, despite Eurydice being dead and underground, her appearance when retrieved by Orpheus is remarkably unscathed. By contrast, Wittig emphasizes the more credible appearance of Eurydice's reinvigorated corpse: 'The stink of m/y bowels surrounds us at m/y every movement. You seem not to notice it, you walk on steadily calling m/e in a loud voice all the love names you were used to call me.' Reversing the subject/object relationship of Ovid's story also transforms the power of the gaze, restoring its potency to Eurydice. While Ovid's tale focuses on the negated gaze (Orpheus must not look back), the teller fails to consider that Eurydice, following behind, can ogle Orpheus undisturbed: '*I* see your strong and powerful legs … the hair that reaches your shoulders whose chestnut colour *I* find so beautiful to look at that a pain rises in m/y breast' (Wittig 1986: 19).

We equally recall that Ovid's original text deals primarily in metamorphoses and in Wittig's *The Lesbian Body*, as in any island setting, the elemental aspects take on especial significance in relation to fantasy. Suddenly, on the beach, the narrator finds her beloved seized and transformed before her eyes. It begins as 'A great wind takes hold of us, we are flung down' and then 'I see you dragged along the shingle of the beach by a violent blast'. Now the wind has become a monster: 'I struggle with something an enormous flapping wing with invisible claws a kind of thing of immeasurable strength engaged in dragging you away'. As in any monster narrative, the antagonist is both a literal monster within the parameters of the text and a metaphor for the way in which we make monsters of those who would lure away our beloved. The impotent frenzy with which the speaker responds replicates perfectly our sense of panicked yet pointless struggle in situations of jealous rivalry: 'I beat the air, I seize you round the waist … you fly off raised from the ground … the thing seeks to reach your cheeks, I fight it without finding it … I am filled with hatred, I clasp you with all m/y might' (Wittig 1986: 43–44). Inevitably, the more the speaker strives to win her back, the more everything falls apart:

> you becomes disarticulated, your bones in collision your muscles breaking off ... one of your legs falls torn off from the pelvis ... *I* try to envelop you ... *I* cry your name ... *I* try to reach your chest and wait with m/y hands, the second leg falls off thigh torn and separated from the tibia and fibula.
>
> (Wittig 1986: 44)

Ultimately the beloved is *at one* with the monster as its irresistible power proves too compelling to resist:

> Despite your gigantic size the length of your flagella and the speed of their propulsion you touch m/e with great gentleness ... Nowhere within you is there a neural circuit ... You move your mass away from the point I touch when m/y fingers brush against you.
>
> (Wittig 1986: 45)

What was once beloved now turns predator:

> you project yourself abruptly towards m/e, all at once your bulk surrounds m/e ... your mouth applied to m/y throat, it's then that my fine protozoan m/y green infusorium m/y violent vorticella that slowly drawn in by the suction of your mouth *I* faint away.
>
> (Wittig 1986: 45)

In Wittig's utilization of a feminist rewriting of the mythic monster narrative, there can be few better accounts than this of the process by which erotic desire consumes us and, when turned to jealousy, is in its turn consumed by another. Thus do we make monsters of those whom we love and those we hate and, in turn, are rendered monstrous by clamouring need.

In Jeanette Winterson's *Written on the Body* (1992), a similar utilization of jealous monstrosity occurs. As is typical of Winterson's writing, this narrative moves in and out of realism and, for much of *Written on the Body*, a realist code of romantic love dominates, but it is the undercurrent of a fantasy struggle that concerns us here. When Winterson's unnamed and non-specifically gendered narrator is informed by Elgin, her beloved Louise's husband, that Louise has cancer, realism can no longer accommodate the words needed to describe the narrator's traumatic response: 'Two hundred miles from the surface of the earth there is no gravity. The laws of motion are suspended. You could turn somersaults slowly slowly, weight into weightlessness, nowhere to fall' (Winterson 1992: 100). This vertical propulsion once more evokes Angela Carter's Fevvers and her own winged defeat of the laws of gravity: 'What made her remarkable as an *aerialiste*, however, was the speed – or, rather the lack of it – with which she performed even the climactic triple somersault … a contemplative and leisurely twenty-five [miles per hour]' (Carter 1984: 17), but then morphs into the type of horizontal bodily destruction we have seen Wittig apply to the effects of jealousy on her Amazonian women: 'As you lay on your back … you notice your feet had fled your head … your joints are slipping away from their usual places … You will break up bone by bone, fractured from who you are' (Winterson 1992: 100–101). In *Written on the Body*, jealous rivalry is first established specifically in the context of Louise's diagnosis, for Elgin, a cancer specialist, is now better placed than the narrator to fight off this particular monster. At this point the body itself becomes more than a canvas upon which one inscribes one's desire, it amounts to a topography replete in flesh and sinew. It is here that Winterson's writing most clearly emulates Wittig's.

In *The Lesbian Body*, Wittig punctuates her text with eight lists of body parts, written in unpunctuated block capitals. The first opens: 'THE LESBIAN BODY THE JUICE THE SPITTLE THE SALIVA THE SNOT' and the last one ends: 'THE SPINE THE FLANKS THE NAVEL THE PUBIS THE LESBIAN BODY' (Wittig 1986: 28, 153). These lists simultaneously sum up and evade the body, demonstrating the difficulty of achieving what erotic fantasy above all must provoke: a bodily response in the reader that erupts directly from words. According to Jane Cleveland:

> The visual presentation of [Wittig's] lists, set in bold type, in a much larger font than the rest of the text, commands the attention of the reader. Writing and reading are signified here as visual, and therefore physical practices which demand the interaction of both the intellectual and the material body.
>
> (Cleveland 2001: np)

They are also politicized presences in the sense that, as Cleveland also acknowledges, 'the medicalized language contained in the lists and its spatial placement within the text, recalls the ways in which the practices of medical discourse have historically invaded women's bodies.' Though Cleveland goes on to argue that such medicalized interventions into the woman's body are never more intrusive than in relation to 'sexuality and reproductive functions' (Cleveland 2001: np), Winterson utilizes her narrator's role as simultaneous storyteller and lover to plunge beneath, immerse herself intravenously, as it were, below Louise's skin, employing a very similar list of medicalized terms and putting them to similar use as Wittig: 'CELLS, TISSUES, SYSTEMS AND CAVITIES OF THE BODY; THE SKIN; THE SKELETON; THE SPECIAL SENSES' (Winterson 1992: 113, 121, 127, 133).

In both Wittig's and Winterson's work, it is not simply the surface skin and curves upon which erotic fantasy is inscribed but the body's interior workings. In *The Lesbian Body*, Wittig examines how skin becomes enlivened through the sensuality of erotic touch:

> M/y cells enlarge beneath your fingers ... from m/y skin there emerge bodies comparable for the most part to glass marbles ... bubbles form continually at the surface of m/y body touched by your fingers, *I* see them burst silently on m/y arms in long orange green spurts ... *I* am the site of a great hubbub ... you come and go in m/y widened pores in m/y alveoli in m/y cavities in m/y furrows in m/y trenches in m/y crevices, you mine m/e, m/y surface caves in ...
>
> (Wittig 1986: 154–155)

As the pace of the passage quickens to the lover's fingers, breathlessness emerges from the lack of punctuation. Along with Wittig's characteristic blurring of the boundaries between self and other (replacing 'my' and 'yours' and 'me' and 'you' with 'm/y'), the punning use of the word 'mine' (meaning both to delve and something belonging to me) simultaneously conveys how any clear sense of subjectivity dissolves as orgasm approaches. In Winterson's text, however, it is her lover's cancerous body which becomes engorged from within and the space between self and other dissolves in a different way, as the fear of death overlays the words of a distraught lover with those of medical discourse: 'THE MULTIPLICATION OF CELLS BY MITOSIS OCCURS THROUGHOUT THE LIFE OF THE INDIVIDUAL … NEW CELLS ARE FORMED TO REPLACE THOSE WHICH HAVE DIED. NERVE CELLS ARE A NOTABLE EXCEPTION. WHEN THEY DIE THEY ARE NOT REPLACED' (Winterson 1992: 115). Increasingly, Winterson's narrator cloaks herself in the guise of a hero whose quest is to dive into Louise's flesh and revivify her, just as Orpheus does Eurydice: 'Will you let me crawl inside you … Why can't I dam [the white T-cells'] blind tide that filthies your blood? … You are full to overflowing but the keeper is asleep and there's murder going on inside.' Like Ovid's Orpheus, Winterson's fails: 'I dropped into the mass of you and I cannot find my way out … Myself in your skin, myself lodged in your bones.' The final subterranean passage is that of the open grave: 'For the bereaved, the hole is a frightful place. A dizzy chasm of loss. This is the last time you'll be by the side of the one you love and you must leave her, must leave him, in a dark pit where the worms shall begin their duty' (Winterson 1992: 120, 177).

CARNIVOROUS SEXUAL FANTASY

Such consumption as we will all face in death pertains earlier in *The Lesbian Body*, as Wittig's narrator adopts the oral approach we have seen recur in this chapter: 'I set about eating you, m/y tongue moistens the helix of your ear … inserts itself in the auricle … m/y teeth seek the lobe, they begin to gnaw at it … I spit, I fill you with saliva.' The obvious inference of cunnilingus gathers around this description, but then mutates into a different type of appetite as she goes deeper: '*I* burst the tympanum, *I* feel the rounded hammerbone rolling between m/y lips, m/y teeth crush it, *I* find the anvil and the stirrup-bone, *I* crunch them, *I* forage with my fingers, *I* wrench away a bone' (Wittig 1986: 24). This roughness goes further than the fruit-based gorging we saw in 'Goblin Market', taking a clearly carnivorous turn in Wittig's hands. A few pages earlier, Wittig's narrator dallies over her animal attraction to her beloved:

> Your hair is all black and shining. In the space between your long jaws teeth exposed … Your tall ears move and quiver … I touch your firm breasts, I squeeze them in my hand. You stand upright on your paws one of them intermittently scratching the ground … I feel your hairs touching m/y buttocks at the height of your clitoris, you climb on m/e, you rip off m/y skin with the claws of your four paws …
>
> (Wittig 1986: 22)

Here, those fluid boundaries between self and other accrue around another area of sexual taboo, that involving humans and animals. It is perfectly possible to read this passage from *The Lesbian Body* metaphorically, its lupine content simply reflecting the type of sexual fantasy we have discussed above. Such a symbolic reading is less easily available in Marian Engel's novel *Bear* (1976), in which our point of view protagonist, Lou, develops an erotic relationship with the eponymous wild beast.

Bear begins as a novel balancing on the borderline between realism and fable. Lou is an archivist, sent on secondment to a remote island in North Ontario, to catalogue the correspondence of the recently deceased Colonel Cary. Although it is not clear initially that sensuality is the missing link in Lou's life, a negative equation is established between her occupation and her bodily wellbeing:

> Things persisted in turning grey. Although at first she had revelled in the erudite seclusion of her job ... she now felt that in some way it had aged her disproportionately, that she was as old as the yellowed papers she spent her days unfolding.
>
> (Engel 1976: 19)

When Lou first sees the bear, her description of it as 'a good size: up to her hip and long with it; a full-grown bear with a scruff like a widow's hump' leads us to expect little beyond the norm in the way of intimacy between them. As the passage continues, however, the scatological aspects of the bear become emphasized: 'As it turned to drink, she got a large whiff of shit and musk. It was indubitably male ... and its hindquarters were matted with dirt'. Gradually the behavioural differences between woman and animal break down as Lou, rising in the morning, 'raised her nose to the air', before going outside and urinating in the snow. Coming in from the cold later, she begins to fantasize about the bear: 'His bigness, or rather his ability to change the impression he gave of his size, excited her' (Engel 1976: 35–36, 45, 47).

The erotic adventure upon which Lou and the bear embark is certainly fleshly, but it is also bookish. The bear's presence leads her to ruminate on Lord Byron's relationship with his pet bear, which he kept with him in college rooms at Cambridge, but it is also while perusing the various volumes in the Colonel's house that slips of paper fall from them at separate intervals during the novel. The first note offers a Linnaean classification of the bear's genus before describing its various anatomical features: '*Carnivorous ... Senses acute ... able to rear up and dance. Tongue has a longitudinal groove ... Bone in penis. In the female, the vagina is longitudinally ridged. Clitoris resides in a deep cavity.*' By the time the second slip of paper is discovered in another book, the bear has already learned to make itself at home in front of the fire. Things have progressed so much by the time she finds the third slip of paper that it is dislodged when the bear, without preamble, comes up the stairs and, 'His tongue ben[ding] vertically ... put it up her cunt'. This note draws on Scandinavian folklore and offers a precedent for inter-species reproduction: '*The offspring of a woman and a bear is a hero, with the strength of a bear and the cleverness of a man – Old Finnish legend*' (Engel 1976: 44, 99; original italics).

The question of whether we read Lou's erotic liaison with the bear literally or metaphorically affects whether we read this novel as realism or fantasy. If realism, the bear remains solidly a bear: it never speaks, nor does anything else a real bear could not. At the same time, the nature of Lou's increasingly self-referential erotic and romantic yearnings for the bear, coupled with the fact that it is sometimes expressed in the register of a daydream, renders it a fantasy bear, as discussed in Chapter 3. As in so many of the narratives cited by Friday (1994), masturbation features highly for Lou. When she masturbates while lying alongside the bear, not surprisingly the bear joins in: 'He put out his moley tongue ... The tongue that was muscular but also capable of lengthening itself like an eel ... And like no human being she had ever known it persevered in her pleasure' (Engel 1976: 93). Earlier, when discussing McGrath's 'The E(rot)ic Potato', I noted that when Gilbert the fly describes his own 'molten intolerable pleasure' in the face of Ariadne the dragonfly's 'shattering slithering' arousal, the eroticism of the encounter communicates itself directly to the reader, despite the distinction in genus between them and us. That word 'slither' appears in *Bear*, too, as Lou contemplates 'the horrifying slither of [Bear's] claws on the linoleum; his change of stature at the top of the stairs'. Simultaneously afraid and aroused, 'She had quailed, literally quailed: sunk back into the window nook' before reflecting on their similarity of species, rather than its differentiation: 'He was shorter than she was, not much over five feet tall, but immensely dense, deep in the chest, large-limbed. His outstretched arm was twice the girth of a man's'. Finally we come to the body part that will prove her undoing: 'Non-retractable claws, he has: she stared at the bear with respect and a residue of fear' (Engel 1976: 60). What we have, here, is an evaluation of the nature of sexual fantasy itself as the bear slips ('slithers', to use the term in the passage) backwards and forwards between 'otherness' and familiarity, human and animal.

At this point we return to the questions of anthropomorphism discussed in Chapter 3. As the novel continues, Lou becomes increasingly controlling of the bear, issuing commands of the kind one might make to a pet, but requiring a lover's response: 'Bear, I cannot command you to love me, but I think you love me.' At one point she realizes that 'she always expected it to be someone else' and considers 'if he [the bear], like herself, visualized transformations, waking every morning expecting to be a prince, disappointed still to be a bear. She doubted that.' Self-evidently, this is Lou's 'handsome prince' fantasy, not the bear's, and it leads to her commanding the bear to dance with her, despite her realization that 'it hurt or confused him to stand long on his hind legs, that his muscles did not obey him easily in that position' (Engel 1976: 89, 113). If nowhere else in the book, the reader becomes uncomfortable here, conscious of the abusive treatment of dancing bears at fairgrounds. Moreover, we recognize that the bear/fantasy object is there purely to reflect on the point of view protagonist/speaker. We may delight in, or be horrified by Lou having an erotic relationship with a bear, but either way we make judgements about Lou, not about the bear.

Engel therefore provides a narrative which is much more complex than a simple erotic day-dream for the reader, and in which we are required, continually, to step back and question Lou's credibility. In fact, far less convincing than Lou's relationship with the bear or her autoeroticism, are the claims she makes for having had past sexual relationships with men. Recollecting 'a time when, in a fit of lonely desperation, she had picked up a man in the street' and remembers 'he had turned out not to be a good man', or when she unexpectedly reveals that her boss at work 'fucked her weekly on her desk', neither of these claims seems in keeping with her otherwise mousy disposition (Engel 1976: 64, 92). Worse, as these memories become harder-edged they remain difficult to believe, provoking an ethical dilemma in the reader, who is unwilling to doubt such confessions of abuse, but still unable to give them full credence as Lou remembers 'as a half child in a school gym, being held to a man's body for the first time, flushed, confused, and guilty' or confides in her reader about a former relationship in which her partner 'made Lou have an abortion' before leaving her for another, in response to which Lou 'carved anagrams of her rival's names on her arm' (Engel 1976: 114, 118). When she tells us about spending a year as a mistress, however, 'waiting for her exigent man to come home hungry not for her but for *steak au poivre*', we identify in this story the origins of her sexual interest in the bear: here we find another carnivorous lover, but this time she is both his desired and his delicacy. Up until this point in the text, Lou has been disturbed by her inability to rouse the bear's penis to tumescence, despite the generous attention it pays to her own pleasure. What Lou has forgotten is that animals, unlike humans, only come into season periodically and, when it does so, Lou is no match for his appetite: 'She took her sweater off and went down on all fours in front of him, in the animal posture. He reached out one great paw and ripped the skin on her back' (Engel 1976: 121, 131). This is no playful scratching of the kind we encountered in 'Goblin Market', but a gash that pours with blood and which instantly brings Lou to her senses, banishing him from the house with a flaming stick from the fire. Lou has crossed the line between sexual fantasy and bestial reality, and learnt, just as harshly as Rossetti's Laura and Lizzie, that transforming fantasy into reality can be deadly. As Friday observes, reflecting on her own work: 'I relish the totally unacceptable in my fantasies', but 'I live in the real world' and 'love my life the way it is' (Friday 1994: 253).

CONCLUSION

The concept of 'living in the real world', with which Chapter 6 leaves us, resonates across this entire volume. Fantasy, in its establishment of competing worlds, its immersion into child's play and nonsense, its journeys into strange and extraordinary landscapes, its utopian and dystopian visions and its erotic daydreams requires an active engagement of its readers, viewers and audiences, leading to a re-examination of the unthinking 'givens' of reality. When, in C.S. Lewis's *The Lion, the Witch and the Wardrobe*, Peter observes of Narnia 'I suppose this whole country is in the wardrobe' (Lewis 1972: 54), he unwittingly reveals, not simply the parameters of Narnia, but of all fantasy: fantasy elongates the human scale of distance, time and the body, rendering visible that yearning long*ing* by which we are driven.

Hence my sustained belief that the best model for fantasy is that of competing worlds. Irrespective of whether that elongation extends into impossible cartographic terrain, as in J.R.R. Tolkien's *The Lord of the Rings* trilogy, the body, as in Lewis Carroll's *Alice in Wonderland*, or the political future, as in George Orwell's *Nineteen Eighty-Four*, the parameters of realism, of today, of known geographical space resonate around it by way of implied comparison. As Stephen Prickett reminds us, the etymology of the word 'fantasy' returns us to the Ancient Greek '*phantasia* – which meant, literally, "a making visible"' (Prickett 2005: 5), a point that implies fantasy's pre-existence. On the one hand, that rendering visible works to give presence to the traditional unseen species of fantasy: fairies, demons, Gods, or mythical creatures. At the same time, it gives imaginative presence to previously un-thought philosophical, political, unconscious desires and fears, be they utopian, dystopian or erotic.

Also from the Ancient Greek comes the coinage 'phantasmagoria' which, as Marina Warner informs us, can be understood as an 'assembly of phantasms' (Warner 2006b: 147). 'Fantasmagorie' was the name the eighteenth-century Belgian scientist, Etienne-Gaspard Robertson, gave to his pioneering 'moving picture show' in Paris, in 1798. According to Warner, the vibrancy of the spectacle Robertson created was due in part to technological ingenuity ('He ... mounted his newfangled magic lantern on rollers, so that when, concealed behind [a] screen, he pulled back from the audience, the image swelled and appeared to lunge forward into their ranks'; Warner 2006b: 147) and in part his appetite for sensationalism. Feeding on the mood of public excitation evoked by the French Revolution (1789–1799), Robertson sought active opportunities to elicit similarly excitable 'screams and squeals' from his audience (Warner 2006b: 147). Certainly, Robertson can be identified as one of the antecedents of early film-making, and one hundred years after Robertson, similar connections between sight and sensation are identifiable in films such as *L'arrivée d'un train á La Ciotat/The Arrival of a train at La Ciotat* (dir. Auguste and Louis Lumière, 1895), in which a train is filmed travelling obliquely towards the audience. As James Walters observes, '*L'arrivée d'un train* attract[ed] further notoriety due to reports from the time of audience members flinching at and even attempting to flee from the image' (Walters 2011: 33). Visibility, however, only takes us so far and it is important to remember that, just as Robertson looked to encourage shrieks from his audience, so it is often music that manipulates most successfully a spectator's mood in cinema.

Halfway through George MacDonald's *Phantastes*, Anodos, who has made his way to the fairy palace, suddenly realizes he has heard no music there. His realization undermines his whole relationship to his fantasy environment: 'I was convinced there must be music in it, but that my sense was as yet too gross to receive the influence of those mysterious motions that beget sound' (MacDonald 2005: 114). Indeed, Anodos's initial suspicions are well founded: he needs to become fully acclimatized to the fairy palace before he can find in himself the ability to hear and thus interpret the meaning of its music. Again, that knowledge returns us to questions of elongation and longing. For Anodos, the process begins in his own body, provoking in him an urge to sing and, as he does so, he surprises himself with the quality of his voice. Losing all sense of the physical boundaries of his own flesh, increasingly he comes to view himself as a *conduit* for sound, rather than its originator ('Entrancing verses arose within me as of their own accord, chanting themselves to their own melodies, and requiring no addition of music to satisfy the inward sense'; MacDonald 2005: 115). One bodily response evokes another and, as Anodos attunes himself to his new role, music becomes inseparable from movement, as he becomes aware of 'something like the distant sound of multitudes of dancers, and felt as if it was the unheard music, moving their rhythmic motion, that within me blossomed in verse and song' (MacDonald 2005: 116). When, eventually, he is able to perceive the dancers visually, but unawares, he finds the room 'full of the most exquisite moving forms' (MacDonald 2005: 119). Their animation is temporary, however, as they return to statues once they realize they are discerned. Precisely like the fairies of traditional folklore, human intervention into the fantasy realm of the unseen is not always depicted as welcome.

As well as engaging with the unseen, however, fantasy has a key role to play in embracing those whom society itself might consider unwelcome. Edward Lear's nonsense poetry and tales are read commonly as an inverted manifestation of a deep and recurrent depressive illness which he self-diagnosed as the 'morbids' and which Vivien Noakes believes to have emerged from the fact that, 'Already short-sighted and suffering from asthma and bronchitis, at the age of five or six [Lear] developed epilepsy' (Noakes 2001: xix). Certainly, an apparent sense of physical isolation is identifiable in Lear's nonsense work, which he illustrates typically through line drawings, sometimes in the form of a type of grotesque self-caricature, as if trying to exorcize his low self-esteem through playfully parodic humour. As Noakes also observes, fantasy provided Lear with an essential strategy for coping with his all-pervasive sense of 'Otherness':

> You may sense that you are strange and different, there may be things that set you apart, but in an imaginary world where people have unlikely noses and legs and the strangest modes of expression, where they seek out oddities which [sic] whom they can identify, and where they yet find kindness and spontaneity, you are never likely to feel alone.
>
> (Noakes 2004: 193)

That sense of belonging is also, perhaps, what appeals to child readers of fantasy in general, who come to love characters that are more unusual in shape or size than they are and who find surprising and unusual creatures alongside each other. Lewis's *The Lion, the Witch and the Wardrobe* is exemplary in this respect, as he incorporates, alongside the more conventional dryads, centaurs and minotaurs, largely unfamiliar species such as the 'ettin' (from the Old English word *eoten*, meaning 'giant'), and the 'efreet' (a type of genie) and in which Father Christmas rubs shoulders with fauns and talking beavers.

We began this volume by connecting fantasy to guilty pleasures, but also to versatility. As this book has shown, just as fantasy is inclusive in its character types, so does it manifest itself across the full spectrum of the arts, from literature to cinema, from theatre to visual art and from classical music to video games. One of the aims of *Fantasy* is to demonstrate that the seemingly 'timeless' appeal of fantasy is actually rooted in a long history from classical antiquity to the present day and that it transcends value judgements about high and low culture by educating as it entertains. Thus, at a time when fewer and fewer schools offer teaching in the classics, animated films such as

Disney's *Hercules* (dir. Ron Clements and John Musker, 1997) or *Atlantis: The Lost Empire* (dir. Gary Trousdale and Kirk Wise, 2001) become increasingly important in helping to familiarize a child viewer with at least some of the basic narratives of the Ancient world. Conversely, comic books play a similarly important role in offering up newer renditions of archetypal moral heroes in Batman, Superman, Wonder Woman and Captain America. As Les Daniels observes, 'Free from the burden of respectability, comic books have provided, for creator and consumer alike, an opportunity to explore the wild dreams and desires which seem to have no place in our predominantly rationalistic and materialistic society' (Daniels 1971: 180). Thus is imagination proven to be counter-cultural.

The only attribute sometimes associated with fantasy which I have deliberately avoided in this book is the unhelpful and inaccurate charge of 'escapism'. A retreat from reality is something we can ill afford at a time when a global environmental crisis calls for an ever more serious engagement with international politics, behavioural change and land reform and it is essential to emphasize that fantasy, in its utilization of a competing worlds model, always requires a re-thinking, never an evasion of the real. With this final point in mind, it seems timely to reiterate David Butler's astute observation that fantasy pertains every time we ask the open question 'What if?' (Butler 2009: 4). In asking that question, we recognize that all progress, all difference, all reform relies on the impetus, embedded *only* in fantasy, to imagine what has never been seen, thought, heard or felt, and utilize what seems impossible, and make it known.

GLOSSARY

Anthropomorphism The concept whereby something which is not human is endowed with human characteristics for the purpose of rhetorical play or storytelling. One example might be 'Brum', the eponymous car from the children's television series (Ragdoll Productions, 1991–2002). In this volume, the term is most commonly applied to animal fantasy, in which characters such as Mrs Tiggy-Winkle or Toad of Toad Hall are endowed with the powers of speech, clothed in human costume and/or given character names and act in a manner more typical of humans. Usually encountered in children's books, films, television or cartoons, anthropomorphism can enable the child reader to empathize more fully with a non-human character or characters.

Cartography Literally the study of map-making. In fantasy writing maps are used typically as a visual aid to facilitate the reader following the journey of characters when the terrain to be covered is both wholly imagined and of epic scale. Often such maps are incorporated into the fly-leaf of an edition. The most famous of such maps are those produced by J.R.R. Tolkien in collaboration with his son Christopher, to map out Middle Earth in *The Lord of the Rings* trilogy. According to Nick Baron, 'By using graph paper [Tolkien] was able to calculate the time needed for [his protagonists] to arrive at their positions and to arrange the story accordingly' (Baron 2016: 202).

Chronotope A concept most fully developed by Mikhail Bakhtin in *The Dialogic Imagination* (1981), it refers to a slice of space and time and, by extension, establishes the presumed existence of alternative worlds/slices. Innately comparative, chronotopes can either operate diachronically (across time), so that one place can be compared with the same place at another point in history; or synchronically, whereby different spaces can be compared within the same time-frame. Fantasy, which I have argued operates via competing worlds, is particularly well placed to facilitate the exploration of competing chronotopes.

Dystopia The opposite of a utopia (see below), this type of narrative posits a nightmare futurist vision, usually based on political change. As with all fantasy, the defamiliarized vision comments, by inference, on our present day reality. Dystopian narratives have become increasingly popular in the late twentieth and early twenty-first centuries as our concerns about global politics, the environment and political extremism have become more acute and widespread.

Eucatastrophe — The phrase J.R.R. Tolkien gives, in his essay 'On Fairy-Stories' (1938–1939), to the consolationist happy ending of a fairy tale. Where some might argue such a resolution to impoverish the creative originality of these tales, Tolkien embraced it as their rightful conclusion and an important provider of joy in the reader.

Fairy-lore — This is the term used for traditional beliefs linked to fairies, their rituals and characteristics. Particularly well developed in Celtic and rural cultures, an established tradition of stories and superstitions has accrued historically around fairies in these cultures, most of which warn of human punishment at their hands. Unlike the sanitized nursery versions handed down to us from Victorian times, traditional fairy-lore warns that humans must avoid all deliberate contact with fairies or risk blinding, abduction (of them or their children), sickness in cattle or the despoiling of food.

Fairy story — A story, usually written for a child reader, following a generically enclosed formula comprising the opening phrase 'Once upon a time' and the closing phrase 'And they all lived happily ever after'. These stories almost never contain fairies as characters and tend to follow the formula of hero/heroine faced with challenges/villains to be overcome. As the aforementioned closing phrase suggests, they always end happily.

Fantastic, the (Todorov) This is a broader concept than fantasy as outlined in this book. Tzvetan Todorov's concept of the fantastic, as explored in his book *The Fantastic: A Structural Approach to a Literary Genre* (1975), defines it as an impulse or urge in all literature to breach realism unexpectedly in a manner that requires a response of hesitancy on the part of the reader. That unresolved hesitancy manifests itself over questions of whether the disruption in the narrative derives from psychological or supernatural origins. In a genuine example of Todorov's literary fantastic that hesitancy will be remain irresolvable, even at the end.

Folktale A traditional story of ordinary people, originating in oral culture and later handed down into print culture. Folktales such as 'Jack and the Giants' were written in chapbook form at the end of the eighteenth century as literacy started to spread to ordinary people who were looking for stories containing characters like themselves. Often there is an anti-establishment message, in which the poor hero outwits an ogre or wicked or foolish monarch.

Marvellous, the Todorov's name, as outlined in his book *The Fantastic: A Structural Approach to a Literary Genre* (1975) for the type of writing one finds in fairy tales or the *One Thousand and One Nights*, in which objects such as flying carpets or talking

	animals appear without provoking any surprise in the reader. For ease of reference, Todorov's term 'marvellous' equates to what this book terms 'fantasy'.
Medieval dream vision	This is a type of dream narrative commonly found in ancient/biblical and medieval literature. A form of prophecy, the dream manifests itself to the dreamer as a cautionary or moral message, sometimes believed to have divine origins, altering directly the course of action or route of a journey to be undertaken by the dreamer, usually to avoid otherwise unsuspected danger.
Myth	An ancient story which has been handed down across history to modern times as an explanatory narrative linked to shared cultural origins. Myth continues to inform modern storytelling and adaptations of its ancient stories continue to be produced in literary, televisual and cinematic form.
Pornotopia	A coinage by Steven Marcus, in his book *The Other Victorians* (1970), for the typical narrative structure of an erotic fantasy. Because we construct such fantasies purely around wish-fulfilment and establish ourselves as the centrepiece and controller of their content, Marcus argues they are closest to utopias in form and structure, although one must remember they lack the utopia's typical socio-political content.
Portal fantasy	The type of fantasy in which one world is accessed from another by means of a physical entry point such as a rabbit-hole, a wardrobe, or a tunnel. Often the

fantasy world exists on the other side of the portal and the protagonist stumbles upon it inadvertently. The portal usually enables two-way travel and the world of realism is returned to via the same aperture at the end of the text/film.

Nonsense
: A playful work of prose or poetry, frequently aimed at a child reader, in which logic and the conventional association of ideas is replaced by illogicality and the comedic substitution of the expected for the unexpected. Sometimes word coinages occur, as in Lewis Carroll's poem *Jabberwocky* (1871), and sometimes the aim is to undermine overly earnest approaches to the moral and educative instruction of children, as in Edward Lear's *Nonsense Botany* illustrations (1870) or his *Nonsense Cookery* recipes for Amblongus Pie, Crumbobblious Cutlets or Gosky Patties (1870).

Secondary World
: The name J.R.R. Tolkien gives, in his essay 'On Fairy Stories' (1938–1939), to the realm of fantasy in any narrative which differentiates itself, by inference, from the Primary World in which we all live. Within its own parameters, a set of internal rules and logic apply which need not be credible in reality, but must be inherently consistent within the terms of that Secondary World.

Trickster
: A figure typically, though not exclusively, linked to animal fantasy. This figure is an anti-establishment, carnivalesque character who typically introduces an element of competition and outwits his/her opponent, usually via humiliating or sometimes violent humour. This

	character is thought to have its origins in African folklore, but has developed strongly in North American stories and cartoon characters since the nineteenth century.
Utopia	Literally from the ancient Greek word *outopia*, meaning no place, the concept of utopia gradually took on the related association of *eu-topia*, meaning good place, and tends to operate via a very tightly controlled set of rules in keeping with one single, unswerving political viewpoint. In Chapter 5 of this book I argue that utopias are far more difficult to sustain than dystopias, because they allow for no divergence of opinion on the part of the reader from that established in the text by the author.

References

PRIMARY TEXTS

LITERATURE

Adams, Richard (1974) *Watership Down* (Harmondsworth: Penguin).

Andersen, Hans Christian (1847) 'The Shadow' http://hca.gilead.org.il/shadow.html (accessed 28 February 2019).

Atwood, Margaret (1987) *The Handmaid's Tale* (London: Virago).

Atwood, Margaret (2003) *Oryx and Crake* (London: Bloomsbury).

Ballard, J.G (2014) *Crash* (London: Fourth Estate).

Barker, Clive (1986) *The Hellbound Heart* (New York: HarperCollins).

Barrie, J.M. (1995) *Peter Pan and Other Plays* (Oxford: Oxford University Press).

Barrie, J.M. (1999) *Peter Pan in Kensington Gardens: Peter and Wendy* (Oxford: Oxford World Classics).

Blyton, Enid (1960) *Noddy Goes to the Fair* (London: Sampson Low, Marston and Co.).

Blyton, Enid (1996) *Mr Plod and Little Noddy* (London: HarperCollins).

Blyton, Enid (2002) *The Faraway Tree Stories: The Enchanted Wood, The Magic Faraway Tree, The Folk of the Faraway Tree* (London: Egmont).

de Brunhoff, Jean (2000) 'The Story of Barbar: The Little Elephant' in Jean de Brunhoff *Childhood Favourites: Ten Complete Picture Classics* (London: Dean): 79–126.

Carroll, Lewis (1929) *Alice's Adventures in Wonderland and Through the Looking Glass* (London: Dent and Sons).

Carter, Angela (1981) *The Magic Toyshop* (London: Virago).

Carter, Angela (1984) *Nights at the Circus* (London: Picador).

Chandler Harris, Joel (2015) *Uncle Remus* (Wolcott, NY: Scholar's Choice).

Coleridge, Samuel Taylor (2005) 'Kubla Khan' in Fergusonet al. (eds) *Norton Anthology of Poetry*: 809–810.

Coleridge, Samuel Taylor (2005) 'The Rime of the Ancient Mariner' in Ferguson et al. (eds) *Norton Anthology of Poetry*: 812–828.

Engel, Marian (1976) *Bear* (London: Pandora).

Gearhart, Sally Miller (1985) *The Wanderground: Stories of the Hill Women* (London: The Women's Press).

Grahame, Kenneth (1983) *The Wind in the Willows* (Oxford: Oxford University Press).

Kingsley, Charles (2016) *The Water Babies* (London: CreateSpace Independent Publishing Platform).

Lear, Edward (2001) 'The Story of the Four Children Who Went Round the World' in Edward Lear *The Complete Verse and Other Nonsense* ed. Vivien Noakes (Harmondsworth: Penguin): 220–232.

Lewis, C.S. (1972) *The Lion, the Witch and the Wardrobe* (Harmondsworth: Penguin).
MacDonald, George (2005) *Phantastes: A Faerie Romance* (New York: Dover Publications).
McGrath, Patrick (1989) 'The E(rot)ic Potato' in Patrick McGrath *Blood and Water and Other Tales* (Harmondsworth: Penguin): 166–171.
Milne, A.A. (2002) *A World of Winnie-the-Pooh* with illustrations by E.H. Shepard (London: Dean).
Orwell, George (1984) *Nineteen Eighty-Four* (Harmondsworth: Penguin).
Ovid (2002) *Metamorphoses* ed. Madeleine Forey (Harmondsworth: Penguin).
Peake, Mervyn (1999) *The Gormenghast Trilogy* (London: Vintage).
Potter, Beatrix (2002) *The Complete Tales* (London: Frederick Warne).
Pratchett, Terry (1985) *The Colour of Magic* (London: Corgi).
Riggs, Ransom (2013) *Miss Peregrine's Home for Peculiar Children* (Philadelphia, PA: Quirk Books).
Roche, Charlotte (2009) *Wetlands* trans. Tim Mohr (London: Fourth Estate).
Rossetti, Christina G. (1862) 'Goblin Market' in Leighton and Reynolds (eds) *Victorian Women Poets: An Anthology*: 378–390.
Rowling, J.K. (1997) *Harry Potter and the Philosopher's Stone* (London: Bloomsbury).
Rowling, J.K. (1998) *Harry Potter and the Chamber of Secrets* (London: Bloomsbury).
Rowling, J.K. (1999) *Harry Potter and the Prisoner of Azkaban* (London: Bloomsbury).
Rowling, J.K. (2000) *Harry Potter and the Goblet of Fire* (London: Bloomsbury).
Rowling, J.K. (2003) *Harry Potter and the Order of the Phoenix* (London: Bloomsbury).
Rowling, J.K. (2005) *Harry Potter and the Half-Blood Prince* (London: Bloomsbury).
Rowling, J.K. (2007) *Harry Potter and the Deathly Hallows* (London: Bloomsbury).
Saunders, George (2013) 'Escape from Spiderhead' in *Tenth of December Stories* (New York: Random House): 45–81.
Sewell, Anne (n.d.) *Black Beauty* (London: Presentation Library).
Shakespeare, William (1979) *A Midsummer Night's Dream*, ed. Harold F. Brooks (London: Methuen and Co.).
Shakespeare, William (1980) *Macbeth* ed. Kenneth Muir (London: Methuen and Co.).
Spenser, Edmund (1966) *The Faerie Queene Book 1* ed. P.C. Bayley (Oxford: Oxford University Press).
Titmarsh, M.A. (pseudonym of William Makepeace Thackeray) (1855) *The Ring and the Rose, Or, the History of Prince Giglio and Prince Bulbo: A Fire-Side Pantomime for Great and Small Children* (London: Smith, Elder, and Co.).
Tolkien, J.R.R. (1999a) *Lord of the Rings, Vol. I: The Fellowship of the Ring* (London: HarperCollins).
Tolkien, J.R.R. (1999b) *Lord of the Rings, Vol. II: The Two Towers* (London: HarperCollins).
Tolkien, J.R.R. (1999c) *Lord of the Rings, Vol. III: The Return of the King* (London: HarperCollins).
Verne, Jules (2018) *Twenty Thousand Leagues Under the Sea* (Harmondsworth: Penguin).
White, E.B. (2003) *Charlotte's Web* (London: Puffin).
Winterson, Jeanette (1992) *Written on the Body* (London: Bloomsbury).
Wittig, Monique (1986) *The Lesbian Body* trans. Peter Owen (Boston, MA: Beacon Press).

FILMS

Aladdin (1992) (dir. Ron Clements and John Musker).
Aladdin (2019) (dir. Guy Ritchie).
Aristocats, The (1970) (dir. Wolfgang Reitherman).
Arrival of a Train at La Ciotat, The (1895) (dir. Auguste and Louis Lumière).
Atlantis: The Lost Empire (2001) (dir. Gary Trousdale and Kirk Wise).
Babe (1995) (dir. Chris Noonan).
Bambi (1942) (dir. James Algar, Samuel Armstrong, David Hand, Graham Held, Bill Roberts, Paul Satterfield, Norman Wright, Arthur Davis and Clyde Geronimi).
Beast From 20,000 Fathoms, The (1953) (dir. Eugène Lourié).
Chitty Chitty Bang Bang (1968) (dir. Ken Hughes).
Cinderella (1950) (dir. Clyde Geronimi, Wilfred Jackson and Hamilton Luske).
Conquest of the Pole, The (1912) (dir. Georges Méliès).
Dumbo (1941) (dir. Samuel Armstrong, Norman Ferguson, Wilfred Jackson, Jack Kinney, Bill Roberts, Ben Sharpsteen and John Elliotte).
First Knight (1995) (dir. Jerry Zucker).
Hercules (1997) (Ron Clements and John Musker).
Indiana Jones and the Crystal Skull (2008) (dir. Steven Spielberg).
It Came From Beneath the Sea (1955) (dir. Robert Gordon).
Jungle Book, The (1967) (dir. Wolfgang Reitherman).
Jurassic Park (1993) (dir. Steven Spielberg).
Karnival Kid, The (1929) (dir. Walt Disney and Ub Iwerks).
King Kong (1933) (dir. Merian C. Cooper and Ernest B. Schoedsack).
King Kong (2005) (dir. Peter Jackson).
Lion King, The (1994) (dir. Rob Minkoff and Roger Allers).
Little Mermaid, The (1989) (dir. Ron Clements and John Musker).
Lord of the Rings, The: The Fellowship of the Ring (2001) (dir. Peter Jackson).
Lord of the Rings, The: The Two Towers (2002) (dir. Peter Jackson).
Lord of the Rings, The: The Return of the King (2003) (dir. Peter Jackson).
Mr Magorium's Wonder Emporium (2007) (dir. Zach Helm).
One Hundred and One Dalmations (1961) (dir. Clyde Geronimi, Hamilton S. Luske and Wolfgang Reitherman).
7th Voyage of Sinbad, The (1958) (dir. Nathan H. Juran).
Snow White and the Seven Dwarfs (1937) (dir. William Cottrill, David Hand, Wilfred Jackson, Larry Morey, Perce Pearce and Ben Sharpsteen).
Sorcerer's Apprentice, The from *Fantasia* (1940) (dir. James Algar).
Steamboat Willie (1928) (dir. Walt Disney and Ub Iwerks).
Sword in the Stone, The (1963) (dir. Wolfgang Reitherman).
Thief of Baghdad, The (1924) (dir. Raoul Walsh).
Toy Story (1995) (dir. John Lasseter).
Toy Story 2 (1999) (dir. John Lasseter).
Toy Story 3 (2010) (dir. Lee Unkrich).
Toy Story 4 (2019) (dir. Josh Cooley).
Trip to the Moon, A (1902) (dir. Georges Méliès).
Watership Down (1978) (dir. Michael Rosen).

TELEVISION

Big Brother (2000–present) Channel 4.
Brum (1991–2002) Ragdoll Productions.
Game of Thrones (2011–present) Home Box Office.
Herbs, The (1968–1972) FilmFair London.
Magic Roundabout, The (1965–1977) BBC Television.
Merlin (2008–2012) Shine/BBC Wales.
Mickey Mouse Clubhouse, The (2007–2016) Disney ABC Domestic Television.
Paddington (1976–1980) FilmFair London.
Pingu (1986–2006) The Pygos Group.
Robin Hood (2006–2009) Tiger Aspect.
Room 101(1994–present) BBC Television.
Tortoise Beats Hare, Bugs Bunny and Looney Tunes (1941) Warner Bros.
Wombles, The (1973–1975) FilmFair London.

OPERA AND THEATRE

Fairy Queen, The (2009) (Jonathan Kent, Glyndebourne Production).
Orpheus in the Underworld (1983) (Derek Bailey, BBC Shepperton Studios).
War Horse, (2007) (Nick Stafford, Royal National Theatre Production).

SECONDARY TEXTS

Abrahams, Roger (1980) 'Play' in Venetia J. Newall (ed.) *Folklore Studies in the Twentieth Century: Proceedings of the Folklore Society* (Woodbridge: D.S. Brewer): 119–122.
Aldiss, Brian (1995) *The Detached Retina: Aspects of SF and Fantasy* (Liverpool: Liverpool University Press).
Allen, Mike (ed.) (2019) 'Reality Television' *The Sage Encyclopedia of Communication Research Methods*https://methods.sagepub.com/Reference//the-sage-encyclopedia-of-communication-research-methods/i11909.xml (accessed 6 July 2019).
Allison, Anne (2006) *Millennial Monsters: Japanese Toys and the Global Imagination* (Berkeley: University of California Press).
Anon (1950) *A Complete List of Books: Enid Blyton* (Edinburgh: John Menzies).
Anon (2018) 'Myths about Pigs' www.minipiginfo.com/common-myths-about-pigs.html (accessed 5 July 2019).
Anon (2019a) 'Big Brother' www.cbs.com/shows/big_brother/about (accessed 6 July 2019).
Anon (2019b) 'Military Time Chart – 24 Hour Time Clock' www.militarytimechart.net/history-24-hour-clock (accessed 30 June 2019).
Anon (2019c) 'Room 101' www.bbc.co.uk/programmes/b01pqlvy (accessed 6 July 2019).
Armitt, Lucie (1996) *Theorising the Fantastic* (London: Arnold).
Armitt, Lucie (2005) *Fantasy Fiction: An Introduction* (New York: Continuum).
Armitt, Lucie (2012) 'The Magical Realism of the Contemporary Gothic' in David Punter (ed.) *A New Companion to the Gothic* (Oxford: Basil Blackwell): 510–522.

Aronstein, Susan (2001) 'The Return of the King: Medievalism and the Politics of Nostalgia in the Mythopoetic Men's Movement' in Simmons (ed.) *Medievalism and the Quest*: 144–159.

Ash, Russell with Michael Bond (1988) *The Life and Times of Paddington Bear* (London: Pavilion Books).

Balanchine, George and Francis Mason (1954) *Complete Stories of the Great Ballets* (New York: Doubleday).

Baron, Nick (2016) 'Movement: Mapping Mobility to Mobile Mapping' in Harper (ed.) *Maps and the 20th Century*: 189–239.

Barrow, Mandy (2019) 'The Legend of St George and the Dragon' http://projectbritain.com/stgeorge2.html (accessed 25 March 2019).

Baudrillard, Jean (1983) *Simulations* trans. Paul Foss, Paul Patton and Philip Beitchman (New York: Semiotexte).

Blum, Matt (2010) '15 Years Ago, *Toy Story* Changed Animated Films Forever' *Wired* 22 November.

Bold, Alan (ed.) (1982a) *The Sexual Dimension in Literature* (London: Vision Press).

Bold, Alan (ed.) (1982b) 'Introduction' in Bold *Sexual Dimension*: 7–18.

Butler, David (2009) *Fantasy Cinema: Impossible Worlds of Science* (New York: Columbia University Press).

Carroll, Shiloh (2015) 'Rewriting the Fantasy Archetype: George R.R. Martin, Neo-medievalist Fantasy, and the Quest for Realism' in Young (ed.) *Fantasy and Science Fiction*: 59–76.

Carter, Angela (1979) *The Sadeian Woman: An Exercise in Cultural History* (London: Virago).

Charnock, Ruth (2019) 'Bad Sex (Scenes): Past, Present Future' www.youtube.com/watch?v=cBJXZr70pFQ (accessed 18 May 2019).

Clarke, Kevin (2019) 'A New Monography on Offenbach's "Orpheus in the Underworld"' https://operetta-research-center.org/monograph-offenbachs-orpheus-underworld (accessed 1 March 2019).

Cleveland, Jane (2001) 'The Power of the Word: The (Unnameable) Lesbian Body' *Third Space: A Journal of Feminist Theory and Culture* 1(1) July.

Coates, Karen (2004) *Looking Glasses and Neverlands: Lacan, Desire and Subjectivity in Children's Literature in Children's Literature* (Iowa City, IA: University of Iowa Press).

Coleridge, Samuel Taylor (1978) 'From "Biographia Literaria"' in I.A. Richards (ed.) *The Portable Coleridge* (Harmondsworth: Penguin): 517–525.

Coren, Michael (2001) *J.R.R. Tolkien: The Man Who Created The Lord of the Rings* (Basingstoke: Boxtree).

Curran, Dylan (2018) 'Are Your Phone Camera and Microphone Spying on You?' *The Guardian* 6 April www.theguardian.com/commentisfree/2018/apr/06/phone-camera-microphone-spying (accessed 2 August 2019).

Daly, Mary (1979) *Gyn/Ecology: The Metaethics of Radical Feminism* (London: The Women's Press).

Daniel, Estelle (2000) *The Art of Gormenghast: The Making of a Television Fantasy* (London: HarperCollins).

Daniels, Les (1971) *Comix: A History of Comic Books in America* (New York: Outerbridge and Dienstfrey).
Davis, Madeleine and David Wallbridge (1990) *Boundary and Space: An Introduction to the Work of D.W. Winnicott* (New York: Routledge).
Deutermann, Allison Kay (2010) '"Dining on Two Dishes": Shakespeare, Adaptation, and Auditory Reception of Purcell's The Fairy-Queen' *The Upstart Crow* 29: 57–71.
Dixon, Bob (1978a) *Catching them Young 1: Sex, Race and Class in Children's Fiction* (London: Pluto Press).
Dixon, Bob (1978b) *Catching them Young 2: Political Ideas in Children's Fiction* (London: Pluto Press).
Douglas, Mary (1978) 'Introduction' in Frazer *The Illustrated Golden Bough*: 9–15.
Duffy, Maureen (1972) *The Erotic World of Faery* (London: Hodder and Stoughton).
Elliott, Andrew B.R. (2015) '"Our Minds are in the Gutter, But Some of us are Watching Starz": Sex Violence and Dirty Medievalism' in Young (ed.) *Fantasy and Science Fiction Medievalisms*: 97–116.
Ferguson, Margaret, Mary Jo *Salter and Jon Stallworthy* (eds) (2005) *The Norton Anthology of Poetry, Fifth Edition* (New York: W.W. Norton and Co.).
Forey, Madeleine (2002) 'Introduction' in Ovid *Metamorphoses*: xi–xxvi.
Franklin, H. Bruce (2009) 'What is Science Fiction – And How it Grew' in James Gunn, Marleen S. Barr and Matthew Candelaria (eds) *Reading Science Fiction* (Basingstoke: Palgrave Macmillan): 23–32.
Frazer, Sir James Gordon (1978) *The Illustrated Golden Bough* (London: Macmillan).
Freud, Sigmund (1990a) 'Creative Writers and Day-Dreaming' trans. I.F. Grant Duff in *Penguin Freud Library Vol. 14: Art and Literature* ed. Albert Dickson (Harmondsworth: Penguin): 129–141.
Freud, Sigmund (1990b) 'The Uncanny' in *Penguin Freud Library Vol. 14: Art and Literature* ed. Albert Dickson (Harmondsworth: Penguin): 335–376.
Friday, Nancy (1994) *Forbidden Flowers: Women's Secret Sexual Fantasies* (London: Arrow Books).
Gorer, Geoffrey (1995) 'The Pornography of Death' in Williamson and Shneldman (eds) *Death: Current Perspectives*: 18–22.
Gray, William (2008) *Death and Fantasy: Essays on Philip Pullman, C.S. Lewis, George MacDonald and R.L. Stevenson* (Cambridge: Cambridge Scholars).
Green, Peter (1982) 'Sex and Classical Literature' in Bold (ed.) *Sexual Dimension*: 19–48.
Griffin, Andrew (2017) 'Pig Organs Could Soon be Transplanted into Humans After Major "Xenotransplantation" Breakthrough' *The Independent*10 August.
Griffin, Susan (1994) *Woman and Nature: The Roaring Inside Her* (London: The Women's Press).
Griggs, E.L. (ed.) (1956–1971) *Samuel Taylor Coleridge: Collected Letters* 6 vols (Oxford: Clarendon).
Guinness World of Records (2016) 'Fastest Speed for a Race Horse' www.guinnessworldrecords.com/world-records/fastest-speed-for-a-race-horse (accessed 19 December 2016).

Haraway, Donna J. (1991) 'A Cyborg Manifesto: Science, Technology, and Socialist-Feminism in the Late Twentieth Century' in Donna J. Haraway *Simians, Cyborgs and Women: The Reinvention of Nature* (London: Free Association Books): 149–181.

Harper, Tom (ed.) (2016) *Maps and the 20th Century: Drawing the Line* (London: British Library)

Harris, John, Stephen Orgel and Roy Strong (1973) *The King's Arcadia: Inigo Jones and the Stuart Court* (London: Arts Council of Great Britain).

Hartland, Edwin Sidney (1891) *The Science of Fairy Tales* (London: Walter Scott).

Hassini, Tony (2018) 'What is Magic?' www.imsmagic.com/Founder/What_Is_Magic.php (accessed 15 September 2018).

Heaney, Seamus (1972) *Wintering Out* (London: Faber & Faber).

Holt, Terence (1996) '"Men Sell not Such in any Town": Exchange in Goblin Market' in Leighton and Reynolds (eds) *Victorian Women Poets: A Critical Reader*: 131–147.

Hume, Kathryn (1984) *Fantasy and Mimesis: Responses to Reality in Western Literature* (New York: Methuen).

Irwin, Robert (1994) *The Arabian Nights: A Companion* (London: Allen Lane).

Irwin, W.R. (1976) *The Game of the Impossible* (Urbana: University of Illinois Press).

Jackson, Rosemary (1988) *Fantasy: The Literature of Subversion* (London: Routledge).

Jeger, Lena (1966) 'In Large Print' *The Guardian* 24 May.

Judd, Catherine Nealy (2017) 'Charles Kingsley's *The Water-Babies*: Industrial England, the Irish Famine, and the American Civil War' *Victorian Literature and Culture* 45: 179–204.

Kafer, Alison (2013) *Feminist, Queer, Crip* (Bloomington: Indiana University Press).

Kaufman, Amy (2010) 'Medievalism Unmoored' *Studies in Medievalism* 19: 1–11.

Kincaid, James R. (1992) *Child-Loving: The Erotic Child and Victorian Culture* (New York: Routledge).

Kingsley, Frances Eliza Grenfell (ed.) (1894) *Charles Kingsley, His Letters and Memories of His Life, Edited by his Wife, vol. 2* (London: Macmillan).

Kohl, Herbert (1995) *Should We Burn Barbar?: Essays on Children's Literature and the Power of Stories* (New York: The New Press).

Kristeva, Julia (1989) *Black Sun: Depression and Melancholia* trans. Leon S. Roudiez (New York: Columbia University Press).

Laing, Jane (1995) *Cicely Mary Barker and Her Art* (London: Frederick Warne).

Legman, Gershon (1963) *Love and Death: A Study in Censorship* (New York: Hacker Art Books).

Leighton, Angela and Margaret Reynolds (eds) (1991) *Victorian Women Poets: An Anthology* (Oxford: Basil Blackwell).

Leighton, Angela and Margaret Reynolds (eds) (1996) *Victorian Women Poets: A Critical Reader* (Oxford: Basil Blackwell).

Lewis, C.S. (2012) *Surprised by Joy: The Shape of My Early Life* (London: William Collins).

Lockley, R.M. (1964) *The Private Life of the Rabbit* (London: Andre Deutsch).

Lockwood, R. (1985) 'Anthropomorphism is Not a Four-Letter Word' in M.W. Fox and L.D. Mickley (eds) *Advances in Animal Welfare Science* (Washington, DC: The Humane Society of the United States): 185–199.

Lynch, Kathryn L. (1988) *The High Medieval Dream Vision: Poetry, Philosophy, and Literary Form* (Stanford, CA: Stanford University Press).

Lyon, David (2001) *Surveillance Society: Monitoring Everyday Life* (Buckingham: Open University Press).

Marcus, Steven (1970) *The Other Victorians: A Study of Sexuality and Pornography in Mid-Nineteenth Century England* (London: Book Club Associates).

Matarosso, Pauline (1969) 'Introduction' in Anonymous *The Quest of the Holy Grail* (Harmondsworth: Penguin): 9–29.

Mathijs, Ernest and Murray Pomerance (eds) (2006) *From Hobbits to Hollywood: Essays on Peter Jackson's Lord of the Rings* (Amsterdam: Rodopi).

Matthews, Cindy (1984) 'Well, Golly Bejabbers! Three Letters on Racism and Golliwogs' *The Guardian* 12 May.

McCloud, Scott (1994) *Understanding Comics: The Invisible Art* (New York: HarperPerennial).

McGann, Jerome J. (1996) 'Christina Rossetti's Poems' in Leighton (ed.) *Victorian Women Poets*: 97–113.

Mendlesohn, Farah (2008) *Rhetorics of Fantasy* (Middletown, CT: Wesleyan University Press).

Miekle, James (2014) 'Smoking Falls to Lowest Level in UK Since Recording Started in 1940s' *The Guardian* 7 October.

Moi, Toril (ed.) (1986) *The Kristeva Reader* (Oxford: Basil Blackwell).

Morris, Ann (1986) 'The Dialectic of Sex and Death in Fantasy' in Palumbo (ed.) *Erotic Universe*: 77–86.

National Park Service (2018) 'Theodore Roosevelt Birthplace, "The Story of the Teddy Bear"' www.nps.gov/thrb/learn/historyculture/storyofteddybear.htm (accessed 18 August 2018).

Noakes, Vivien (2001) 'Introduction' in Edward Lear *The Complete Verse and Other Nonsense* (London: Penguin): xix–xxxiv.

Noakes, Vivien (2004) *Edward Lear: The Life of a Wanderer* (Stroud: Sutton Publishing).

Palumbo, Donald (ed.) (1986) *Erotic Universe: Sexuality and Fantastic Literature* (New York: Greenwood Press).

Polack, Gillian (2015) 'Grim and Grimdark' in Young (ed.) *Fantasy and Science Fiction Medievalisms*: 77–95.

Prickett, Stephen (2005) *Victorian Fantasy* (Waco, TX: Baylor University Press).

Rayment, Andrew (2014) *Fantasy, Politics, Postmodernity: Pratchett, Pullman, Miéville and Stories of the Eye* (Amsterdam: Rodopi).

Rayment-Pickard, Hugh (2004) *The Devil's Account: Philip Pullman and Christianity* (London: Darton, Longman and Todd).

Reaper, William (1987) *George MacDonald: Novelist and Victorian Visionary* (Tring: Lion Publishing).

Roth, Elizabeth Elam (1997) 'Aesthetics of the Balletic Uncanny in Hoffmann's "Nutcracker and Mouse King" and "The Sandman"' *Children's Literature Association Quarterly* 22(1) Spring: 39–42.

Rouse, Robert and Cory Rushton (2016) *The Medieval Quest for Arthur* (Stroud: The History Press).

Rudd, David (2000) *Enid Blyton and the Mystery of Children's Literature* (Basingstoke: Palgrave Macmillan).

Russo, Mary (1994) *The Female Grotesque: Risk, Excess and Modernity* (New York: Routledge).

Scheub, Harold (2012) *Trickster and Hero: Two Characters in the Oral and Written Traditions of the World* (Madison: University of Wisconsin Press).

Schwarm, Betsy (2017) 'Orpheus in the Underworld' www.britannica.com/topic/Orpheus-in-the-Underworld (accessed 5 August 2017).

Sheldrick, Margrit (2009) *Dangerous Discourses of Disability, Subjectivity and Sexuality* (Basingstoke: Palgrave).

Shippey, Tom (2001) *J.R.R. Tolkien, Author of the Century* (London: HarperCollins).

Simmons, Clare A. (2001) 'Introduction' in Clare A. Simmons (ed.) *Medievalism and the Quest for the 'Real' Middle Ages* (London: Frank Cass) 1–28.

Skura, Meredith Ann (1981) *The Literary Use of the Psychoanalytic Process* (New Haven, CT: Yale University Press).

Smith, Zadie (2014) 'Introduction' in Ballard *Crash*: v–xi.

Stewart, Susan (1993) *On Longing: Narratives of the Miniature, the Gigantic, the Souvenir, the Collection* (Durham, NC: Duke University Press).

Swank, Kris (2015) 'The Arabian Nights in 21st-Century Fantasy Fiction and Film' in Young (ed.) *Fantasy and Science Fiction Medievalisms*: 163–181.

Swinfen, Ann (1984) *In Defense of Fantasy: A Study of the Genre in English and American Literature Since 1945* (London: Routledge & Kegan Paul).

Taylor, Ronald (1963) *Hoffmann* (London: Bowes and Bowes).

Thompson, Kristen Moana (2006) 'Scale, Spectacle and Movement: Massive Software and Digital Special Effects in *The Lord of the Rings*' in Mathijs and Pomerance (eds) *From Hobbits to Hollywood*: 283–299.

Todorov, Tzvetan (1975) *The Fantastic: A Structural Approach to a Literary Genre*, trans Richard Howard (Ithaca, NY: Cornell University Press).

Tolkien, J.R.R. (1983) *The Monsters and the Critics and Other Essays* ed. Christopher Tolkien (London: George Allen and Unwin).

Tolkien, J.R.R. (2001) 'On Fairy Stories' in J.R.R. Tolkien *Tree and Leaf* (London: HarperCollins): 1–81.

Walters, James (2011) *Fantasy Film: A Critical Introduction* (New York: Berg).

Warner, Marina (2006a) 'Fancy's Images: Insubstantial Pageants' in Marina Warner *Phantasmagoria: Spirit Visions, Metaphors, and Media into the Twenty-First Century* (Oxford: Oxford University Press): 131–143.

Warner, Marina (2006b) 'Darkness Visible: The Phantasmagoria' in Warner *Phantasmagoria*: 146–156.

Webb, Peter (1982) 'Victorian Erotica' in Bold (ed.) *Sexual Dimension*: 90–121.

Williamson, John B. and Edwin S. Shneldman (eds) (1995) *Death: Current Perspectives* (London: Mayfield).

Willock, Colin (1964) 'Foreword' in R.M. Lockley *The Private Life of the Rabbit* (London: Andre Deutsch).

Wilson, Colin (1982) 'Literature and Pornography' in Bold (ed.) *Sexual Dimension*: 202–219.

Wolff, Robert Lee (1961) *The Golden Key: A Study of the Fiction of George MacDonald* (New Haven, CT: Yale University Press).

Wood, Dafydd (2008) 'Adaptation of the Orpheus Myth in Five Operas' *The McNeese Review* 46: 1–25.

World Wildlife Fund (2019) 'Marine Problems: Climate Change' https://wwf.panda.org/our_work/oceans/problems/climate_change (accessed 1 July 2019).

Wright, Elizabeth and Edmond Wright (eds) (1999) *The Žižek Reader* (Oxford: Basil Blackwell).

Young, Helen (ed.) (2015) *Fantasy and Science Fiction Medievalisms: From Isaac Asimov to A Game of Thrones* (Amherst, NY: Cambria Press).

Index